NATURALIST ON THE BIBBULMUN

A walking companion

LEIGH W. SIMMONS

UWA PUBLISHING

First published in 2021 by
UWA Publishing
Crawley, Western Australia 6009
www.uwap.uwa.edu.au
UWAP is an imprint of UWA Publishing,
a division of The University of Western Australia.

ISBN: 978-1-76080-203-5
Design by tendeersigh
Printed in China by Imago

For Freddy,

without whom this journey would never have happened

Leigh W. Simmons is Professor of Evolutionary Biology at the University of Western Australia. He studied at the University of Nottingham where he received his PhD in 1986. After holding a research fellowship at the University of Liverpool UK, he moved to Australia in 1995 to take up his current position in the School of Biological Sciences at the University of Western Australia. His research interests lie in the evolution of reproductive behaviour, physiology and morphology in both vertebrate and invertebrate animals. He has published more than 350 scientific articles and five academic books. He is currently Editor-in-Chief of *Behavioral Ecology*, and has been an Editor of *Advances in the Study of Behavior* since 2009. He held a prestigious Australian Research Council Federation Fellowship from 2005–2009, is a recipient of the Zoological Society of London's Scientific Medal, the Association for the Study of Animal Behaviour Medal, and was elected to the Australian Academy in 2009.

Ngaala kaaditj Nyoongar moort keyen
kaadat nidja boodja

We acknowledge the Noongar people
as the Traditional Owners of this land

CONTENTS

Preface   xi

A Sense of Place and Time   1
Kalamunda to Dwellingup   13
Dwellingup to Collie   71
Collie to Balingup   91
Balingup to Pemberton   107
Pemberton to Northcliffe   129
Northcliffe to Walpole   143
Walpole to Denmark   181
Denmark to Albany   213

Acknowledgements   241
Birds Seen on the Bibbulmun Track   245
Plants Seen on the Bibbulmun Track   249

PREFACE

I am not quite sure how I ended up as an evolutionary biologist. It certainly wasn't planned. Indeed, despite growing up a bus-ride away from Downe House, Darwin's home in Kent, I had never heard of the man until after I left school. Evolution was not on the curriculum at the all-boys Catholic secondary modern in which I was confined until I left at age 16, with little to show for my time there. I have always been a naturalist, however. My earliest memories are of weekends and summer holidays collecting butterflies and birds' eggs from the woodlands that adjoined my childhood home, and in capturing everything from sticklebacks to hedgehogs to keep as pets in the garden. I had field guides to insects, birds and mammals; was a member of the World Wide Fund for Nature, the cloth membership patch proudly sewn to the arm of my anorak; and was an avid consumer of David Attenborough natural history programs. Little did I know then that one day my own work on the life and loves of crickets and burrowing bees would feature in episodes of *Life on Earth* and *Life*.

On leaving school I had the notion that I wanted to work with animals, and so obviously thought I needed to become a veterinary surgeon in order to do so. This I never achieved, despite considerable efforts to gain a scientific education at Woolwich College, the local college of further education. Through some bizarre symmetry, this is an ambition that my son Freddy has achieved where I failed. Instead, I enrolled at the University of

Nottingham in 1980 to study zoology. During my second year, I attended a field course held in Woodchester Park, Gloucestershire, where I studied the transmission of birdsong through woodland habitats. It was on this field course that I rediscovered my passion for field biology.

I remained at the University of Nottingham after my undergraduate degree, having won a postgraduate scholarship to do research. During my undergraduate degree I had become interested in the process of sexual selection and how it drives the evolution of reproductive behaviour and morphology of animals, and so I spent three years dissecting the behaviour and evolutionary ecology of field crickets. With a freshly minted PhD under my arm and a research grant from the Science and Engineering Research Council, I moved in 1986 to the University of Liverpool in the hope of finding a niche in teaching and research. It was while there in 1988 that I was presented with an opportunity to travel to Australia.

As part of Australia's bicentennial celebrations, the Royal Society of London and the Australian Academy of Science offered exchange visits for researchers in the UK and Australia to develop collaborations. I travelled to Perth in the spring of 1988 to work in the Department of Zoology at the University of Western Australia. Arriving in Western Australia as a field biologist was mind-blowing. Everything was different. The plants, birds, mammals, insects, everything I looked at was different. The biodiversity of the south-west of Western Australia offered boundless opportunities to study the evolutionary and ecological processes by which new species arise and coexist.

On my first night, my host, now dear friend and colleague, Win Bailey, took me into Kings Park armed with a head-torch and a bat detector. The Mangles Kangaroo Paws were in flower, and they were covered in small stick-like bushcrickets, often also referred to as katydids, on which Win suggested I might work. The bat detector was necessary to locate the calling males, whose call is broadcast in the ultrasonic range. I was astonished to discover that the insect was new to science, still as yet undescribed, as were at least five other species of singing insect in the park. Newly discovered species, right there in the middle of a modern city! My work led to return visits each year, until finally I moved permanently in 1995 to take up an Australian Research Council fellowship, which ultimately led to my appointment as professor of evolutionary biology in 2000.

I first walked on the Bibbulmun Track through the tingle forests of the Walpole-Nornalup National Park in the early 1990s on one of my research visits to the University of Western Australia. I was working with colleagues, who were visiting from the United States, on a species of field cricket commonly found in pastures across the south of Australia. We were trying to establish the information content of male calls and aspects of those calls that females find most attractive. In the Walpole Visitor Centre, I picked up a copy of the recently published *A Guide to the Bibbulmun Track* and found several stretches that could be done as day hikes. I fell in love with the beauty of the Gondwanan forests the moment I entered them.

From those early days I have returned with my family at least once a year to holiday on Riverside Drive in the hamlet of Nornalup, spending most of our time walking through the forests, or along the clifftops between Peaceful Bay and Conspicuous Cliff. When Freddy was little, my wife Carol and I would sustain his enthusiasm by challenging him to find the next Waugal, the Rainbow Serpent illustrated on the markers along the track. Freddy would run on ahead, returning to us excitedly to lead us to his discovery high on the trunk of a tree. He would walk twice the distance we ever managed. At Christmas 2018 we were walking from Boxhall Road, north of Nornalup, north-west to Frankland River Hut, a frequently walked and much-loved day on the Bibbulmun. Freddy was in the last year of his veterinary degree, and announced that when he completed it the following November, he was going to walk the length of the track, from Kalamunda at the north-western end to Albany at the south-eastern.

'What a great idea. Will you go with your mates?' I said.

'No, I want you to come with me,' came his reply.

'Yeah, right,' thought I. 'He'll have a change of heart and want to go with his mates, surely! No harm in agreeing, I won't actually have to do it.' How wrong was I? As the months passed and Freddy's planning took shape, it slowly dawned on me that I might just have to do this. My credit card was taken, and thousands of dollars later we were kitted out with packs, sleeping mats, endless packs of dried food, and just two pairs of undies, one to be worn and one to be drying! I had never attempted anything like this in my life. Freddy was 24 but I was 58. Was I physically capable of doing this? And would I go stark staring mad denied access to my books and journals?

That winter I visited an old friend and colleague, John Alcock, in the United States. We went for a day walk on the Appalachian Trail. John is an extraordinary naturalist and has written many natural history books, several of which describe his adventures through the Australian bush when he has visited us here in Perth to work on native bees and hunt for orchids. While walking on the Appalachian and chatting with John about his latest project, which described the natural history of his family farm in West Virginia, it suddenly occurred to me that I could focus my attention while walking the Bibbulmun on its natural history and write a narrative of all we encountered along the way. I could use the Bibbulmun Track as a transect to document the flora and fauna of the south-western corner of Western Australia, and in so doing share my knowledge of the evolutionary ecology of the animals and plants that cling to existence in our rapidly changing corner of the world.

One thing that so struck me on first arriving in Australia more than 30 years ago was that so much of the flora and fauna were unknown. In the UK where I grew up, almost everything has a common name. But here, many species of animals and plants remain to be described, and many have only scientific names. Throughout the text I have used common names when they are available but always provide the scientific names as well, because common names can often refer to several different species and so to correctly identify the animals and plants we found on our journey the scientific names are essential. For example, tettigoniids are known as katydids in America, bushcrickets in Europe, and go by either common name in Australia. In the northern hemisphere, magpies are crows, a member of the corvid family, while in Australia the magpie is completely unrelated to crows, being a currawong, and in America a robin is a member of the thrush family! To know exactly what species we are talking about we need the scientific name.

Scientific names are always Latinised, often difficult to pronounce and do not make for easy reading. Therefore, for the many birds and plants we identified, I have confined the scientific names to the appendices, where they are listed alphabetically by the species' common name used in the text. In the case of the plants, I have also provided any images I took in order to help identify them. For the few amphibians, reptiles, mammals and insects that we encountered on our journey, I have provided the scientific names in the main text, at least when first mentioned.

In some cases where common names are unavailable, the scientific names provide the only form of identification with which the reader can discover more information about the species I describe, should they wish to do so. Importantly, I also provide Noongar names, because these should take precedence as common names, given that it was the Noongar who first recognised and named the various species of animals and plants in the south-west, long before Western naturalists arrived in Australia. For the birds, I have given priority to Noongar spellings recommended as essential for the Languages other than English program in Western Australian schools. But before we start our journey, let us first get a sense of the prehistory of this place, its geology, its early evolutionary history and our place in this ancient landscape.

A SENSE OF PLACE AND TIME

A SENSE OF PLACE AND TIME

1

In the early Palaeozoic, some 570 million years ago, the south-western corner of Western Australia lay inland within Eastern Gondwana, the southern hemisphere landmass of Pangaea. The granite hills and outcrops that characterise the landscape had been formed much earlier, around 2,500 million years ago in the Archaean period of Earth's history, long before any plants or animals had evolved. Located further south than it is now, the Australian climate in the Palaeozoic was cool and temperate, the environment dominated by rainforest.

The Earth's surface can be likened to a collection of large rafts of rock floating on its molten core. During the late Palaeozoic, around 250 million years ago, these rafts, referred to as continental plates, began to drift apart. During the Mesozoic, between 225 and 65 million years ago, a great rift occurred, breaking the Australian continent from India, leaving a scar evident to this day in the Darling Scarp that runs from East of Shark Bay in the north to Point D'Entrecasteaux in the south. The rift between India and Australia allowed the Tethys Ocean to flood inland into Gondwana in much the same way as the Indian Ocean now feeds the Red Sea, bringing marine sediments that would eventually become the Swan Coastal Plain. As India floated north towards the equator, Australia remained relatively stationary until it broke

free from the Antarctic continent in the Cenozoic, around 50 million years ago, and drifted northward to its present location.

As the Australian continent drifted north, it experienced major changes in its climate. Not only did it move from a latitude that is predominantly cool and temperate to one that is warm and dry, but around 6 million years ago there was also the onset of cycles of glaciation during which the Earth became cold and dry. These repeated cycles of warming and cooling not only had significant impacts on the survival of animals and plants that already inhabited Australia, but also on the evolution and distribution of new species. Western Australia's rainforest vegetation became largely extinct as the continent dried and large tranches of land turned to desert. Some temperate rainforest patches remain, notably along the south coast of Western Australia, where the climate remains cool and temperate and we can still find relict fragments of Gondwanan temperate rainforest, for example within the Walpole-Nornalup National Park. Further north, however, rainforest plants were driven to extinction by the drying climate and were replaced by an evolutionary expansion of sclerophyllous plants – those with small, tough leathery leaves that are able to tolerate periods of extreme dryness. And that evolutionary expansion has been extraordinary.

The south-western corner of Western Australia is recognised as one of the most floristically species-rich areas on Earth. In part this species diversity developed as a product of the climatic changes that have occurred over the last 15 million years, and in part because the region has been geologically stable since its last significant event in the late Mesozoic, when India and Australia separated. While India crashed into Eurasia 50 million years ago, causing the great upheaval of the Himalayas, and the Rocky Mountains were thrust upward as the Farallon plate pushed beneath the North American plate, Australia was simply drifting northward, geologically unchanged and geographically isolated.

Long periods of geological stability can allow species of animals and plants to persist in the landscape relatively unchanged. Zamia palms (jeeriji), for example, arose in the ancient forests of Gondwana some 250 million years ago, and their ancestors have persisted throughout the south-western corner of Western Australia to this day. Geologically ancient landscapes are typically impoverished in nutrients and minerals, because these have been leached from the soil over millions of years of weathering.

Combine this with cycles of cooling and warming, changing rainfall and fire frequency, and you have one of the major ingredients for evolutionary change: selection.

There is evidence that persistence of relict species in our ancient landscape, combined with speciation in regions subject to environmental change, has contributed to the extraordinary biodiversity of the south-west corner of Western Australia. Melbourne-based palaeoclimatologist Kale Sniderman and his colleagues examined the particularly well-preserved fossil flora of south-eastern Australia, finding evidence of high levels of species extinction that has resulted in low species diversity relative to that found in south-western Australia. These patterns in the fossil record suggest that species of plants in the south-western corner of Western Australia may have been impacted less by the cyclic changes in climate over the last 15 million years. Likewise, within the south-west corner of Western Australia, the climatically stable high rainfall area has lower species diversity than the arid Kwongan regions of the northern (Lesueur) and eastern (Fitzgerald River) corners of the region. Western Australian botanist Hans Lambers has also shown how nutrient-poor soils harbour richer species diversity than nutrient-rich soils. These contrasting patterns of species diversity in benign versus variable environments are expected because of the greater selection imposed on species to adapt and change in harsh environments. As is so often said, 'it is not the strongest of species that survive, nor the most intelligent, but the most responsive to change'.

The movement of the Earth's landmasses and the evolution of life are on a scale that is difficult to comprehend. In his book *Sense of Place*, George Seddon offers a wonderful analogy, asking us to imagine Earth's history on the scale of a single year. In the middle of March, molten granite bubbled up through pre-existing rocks before cooling and solidifying into the granite outcrops that litter the landscape of the Darling plateau. The first living organisms appeared in the sea around May, and the first plants and animals to occupy the land appeared in late November. In mid-December terrestrial dinosaurs roamed the ancient forests of Western Gondwana. Although few made it into south-eastern Gondwana, perhaps because it was too cool, plesiosaurs did swim through the seas that filled the rift valley between India and Australia. But they were all gone by Boxing Day, 26 December. The first primates appeared as dusk fell on New Year's Eve and the ice sheets from

the last great ice age began to melt. As we count down the seconds to New Year's Day, Rome ruled the world for five seconds of the minute before midnight, and Cook set sail for Australia less than one second before the clock strikes twelve.

The south-west corner of Western Australia is now home to around 8,000 species of plants of which nearly half are found nowhere else on Earth. British ecologist Norman Myers recognised this extraordinary biodiversity in 2000 when he named south-western Western Australia as one of the world's twenty-five biodiversity hotspots. That sounds great doesn't it, a biodiversity hotspot. But it is not. For the definition of a biodiversity hotspot is a region that is a significant reservoir of plant and animal species that is threatened with destruction. A criterion to be in the biodiversity hotspot club is that anthropogenic changes to the natural environment, through burning and clearing of land, and the warming and drying effects of human-induced climate change, have resulted in the loss of 70 per cent of the natural habitat. With that anthropogenic change comes the risk of losing those species of plants and animals that are unique to the region. Humankind has the potential to wipe out Earth's metaphorical 24 hour evolutionary history within the blink of an eye.

2

During the last glacial maximum, some 33,000 years ago, the Earth's water was bound up in ice sheets that covered its poles and much of North America and northern Europe. Sea levels were correspondingly low, so that the continent of Australia, Tasmania and New Guinea formed a single landmass we call Sahul. The Malay Peninsula and the Indonesian archipelago were likewise a continuous landmass now known as Sundaland. It was at this time that the ancestors of Aboriginal Australians first populated Australia, making the crossing from Sundaland to Sahul via the islands of Wallacea. In their book *Prehistory of Australia*, John Mulvaney and Johan Kamminga provide a forensic analysis of the archaeological evidence of the arrival and settlement of humans in Australia. They suggest that a trickle of individuals and small groups, maybe as few as fifty to 100 individuals over the span of many years, arrived on Sahul's north-western shores. This founding

population expanded and spread across the continent. At the end of the Pleistocene, 12,000 years ago, three populations of these early humans became geographically isolated when the ice sheets melted and the lowland plains flooded to form the modern-day continent of Australia, and the islands of New Guinea and Tasmania. There is much evidence of this long history of human occupation of Australia. According to Mulvaney and Kamminga, the oldest human remains, of a woman found at Lake Mungo in New South Wales, are estimated to be in the region of 15,000 years old. But human artefacts such as stone tools, hearths and artworks date back even further, to more than 30,000 years. In the south-west of Western Australia, for example, human occupation of Devil's Lair, a limestone cave in the Naturaliste region, has been dated back as far as 31,000 years, while other sites in the Helena Valley near Perth date back as far as 29,000 years. The ancestors of the south-western Aboriginal population, the Noongar, have occupied these lands for a very long time, and they have had a significant impact on the evolutionary history of the region.

Anthropologist Norman Tindale conducted an extensive survey in the 1920s and 1930s of Indigenous Australians, producing his famous 1940 map of Australia that depicts the boundaries of more than 400 language groups. These language groups were composed of matrilineal or patrilineal extended families that lived in harmony with each other and with their neighbours. Groups ranged in size from 100 to 2000 individuals, with the area of a group's exclusive homelands varying largely due to the availability of food and water; those groups living in harsh arid environments tended to have larger homelands than those where resources were more abundant. Tindale describes, in his 1974 book *Aboriginal Tribes of Australia*, the marriage system that operated within and among language groups, whereby patrilineal or matrilineal families would exchange sons or daughters, so that 86 per cent of marriages were within language groups, and marriages between members of adjoining language groups made up the remainder.

In his 2014 book *Dark Emu*, Indigenous writer Bruce Pascoe presents evidence, from the observations of early explorers, of the sophisticated economic and cultural systems that characterised the people of Australia. Indeed, their long evolutionary history with the ancient landscapes of Australia culminated in a sophisticated agricultural system, whereby they modified the landscape to optimise their ability to grow indigenous grain and root vegetables,

and to harvest animals and plants in a sustainable way. Pascoe provides compelling evidence that the Aboriginal people of Australia had developed agricultural systems long before they emerged in northern hemisphere populations of humans. And 'firestick' farming was an important element of these agricultural systems. Aboriginal farmers would set fire to the land to stimulate the growth of fresh grasses that would foster populations of kangaroo they then harvested for meat. Fires would also promote the flowering of indigenous grasses, from which seed was collected and ground for the baking of bread.

Contrary to popular belief, many of the language groups had extensive, permanent settlements associated with their agricultural lands, travelling only to gather seasonally abundant resources that grew elsewhere, to trade with neighbouring language groups or for cultural and political gatherings with people from other language groups. To this end, as Tindale describes, members of a given language group had traditional paths that typically traversed the boundaries between adjoining homelands, respecting the country of neighbouring language groups and only entering each other's homelands with permission. To keep these pathways clear, Aboriginal people set fire to heavily vegetated areas that would otherwise soon become impenetrable. But the burning of bushland was done in a highly controlled manner. Fires were set at specific times of the year so as to prevent them burning out of control. They were monitored to avoid burning neighbouring homelands, which would constitute a punishable offence. Controlled burns were thus managed in such a way as to preserve, and indeed enhance the growth of indigenous plants and so maintain the biodiversity upon which the Aboriginal people so relied. The Aboriginal peoples of Australia evolved over their 30,000 years of geographical isolation, and developed an intimate knowledge and understanding of their environment, and how it could be managed to provide subsistence. Western Australian ecologist Alison Lullfitz and her colleagues have recently drawn together evidence of how the cultural and land management practices of the Noongar of the south-west have played a significant role in the coevolution and distribution of plant species across the Southwest Australian Floristic Region. Aboriginal habitation of the south-west is intimately linked with its ecology and evolution.

In 1829 Captain Charles Howe Fremantle landed at Arthur Head in Fremantle and claimed Western Australia for the British.

The Swan River Colony was the third British colony in Australia, and the first to be populated by free men who began arriving that year. George Seddon points out that the sophisticated land use of the Noongar was immediately accessible to European immigrants. They were able to follow the network of pathways cleared by Noongar farmers, use their strategically placed wells to obtain fresh water along the way, and find already prepared agricultural areas where they could graze the sheep and grow the wheat they had brought with them from Britain. Seddon quotes the colony's Anglican priest John Wollaston, who remarked how 'good native country is good European country'. But the delicate, nutrient-poor soils of Australia could not cope with the exotic livestock and crops of European settlers. Where Aboriginal people nurtured indigenous perennial grasses with minimal disturbance of the delicate soils, Europeans planted their annual wheat crops that required the land to be ploughed each year. Sheep and cattle compacted the soft soils, reducing their permeability to water and generating aridification. As Mulvaney and Kamminga point out, Europeans failed to recognise the profound knowledge of Aboriginal Australians; a single generation of cattle farming turned the Birdsville Track region in South Australia into desert.

Western Australia: An Atlas of Human Endeavour, published by the Western Australian Government in 1979 to celebrate 150 years of European settlement, boasts how, between the years of 1919 and 1939, almost the entire south-western corner of Western Australia was turned over to European agricultural farming practice, predominantly for the growth of wheat, sheep and cattle. And this, of course, came at a cost to the Noongar, who were dispossessed of their homelands, and to the natural environment of south-western Australia, where the soils, unable to sustain intensive European agricultural systems, have turned to salt pans. The height of the timber industry between 1893 and 1902 saw average exports of timber between 20,000 and 130,000 loads per year on the newly constructed railway line, with unrestricted and wasteful clearing of forests in the south-west corner. Urban expansion has increased exponentially since the 1950s and is currently unprecedented, as we clear banksia woodlands to the north and south of metropolitan Perth to build housing estates for the city's expanding population.

Western Australian environmentalist Thomas Wilson provides a grim narrative of the wholesale anthropogenic destruction of

the south-west of Western Australia in his book *Stepping Off*, noting how the current loss of natural vegetation from the Swan coastal plain is proceeding at a rate of around one football oval per day. This broad-scale clearing of natural vegetation by European settlers is what has qualified the south-west of Western Australia as a biodiversity hotspot. I try to be optimistic, but it is difficult to see how now may not be our last chance to save what remains of the ancient wilderness of south-western Western Australia. But we need to embrace the Noongar's sense of connection to boodja (country) if we are to save these lands.

3

There are fourteen language groups in the south-west of Western Australia that collectively represent the Noongar. The northern groups, the Whadjuk, Balardong and Yued, refer to the southerners collectively as the Bibbulmun, although the true Bibelmen come from the southern Karri forests that surround Pemberton and Manjimup. The Waugal, or Rainbow Serpent, is the major spiritual body for the Noongar, and is central to their connection to boodja. Noongar Dreaming holds that during the Nyitting (the 'cold time', which in Western scientific terms was most likely the end of the last glacial maximum) the Waugal created the rivers and swamps that now provide fresh water. It arose from Mount Eliza at the eastern end of the Kings Park escarpment and formed the Derbarl Yerrigan (Swan) and Djarlgarro Beeliar (Canning) rivers. As the Waugal slithered across the landscape it created the sand dunes and river courses of the south-west corner of Western Australia, and it now lies along its length in the form of the Darling escarpment.

The Bibbulmun Track runs along the Darling escarpment from Kalamunda in the north to D'Entrecasteaux in the south, before heading east along the south coast to Albany, a distance of 1000 kilometres, guided by way markers depicting the Waugal. The Bibbulmun Track was opened in 1979 as part of the 150th anniversary celebrations of the arrival of European settlers to the shores of Western Australia. The track was the brainchild of Geoff Schafer, a member of the Perth Bushwalkers Club, who proposed the idea to the Minister for Forests in 1972 as a means by which Perth's growing urban population could be afforded the

opportunity to experience the natural wilderness of the south-west, either for day walks or for more extended periods.

At the start of the 1990s the track attracted a new champion, Jesse Brampton. Brampton walked the Appalachian Trail in the United States in the late 1980s and sometime later walked the length of the Bibbulmun. At that time the track largely followed gravel roads and offered no facilities. Brampton recognised that the Bibbulmun could, with some investment, rival the world-class Appalachian Trail and become a major destination for long-distance walkers internationally. And so began a period of lobbying for an upgrade of the Bibbulmun. In 1993, when the then Department of Conservation and Land Management agreed to a

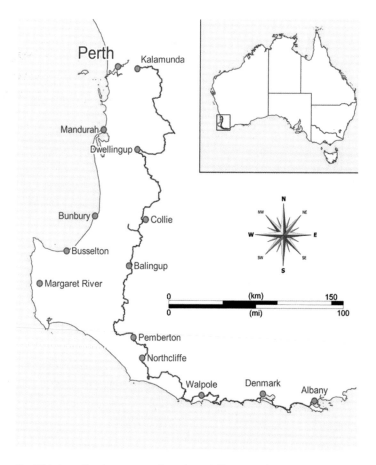

The Bibbulmun Track runs approximately 1000 kilometres through the south-west of Western Australia, between its northern terminus in Kalamunda and its southern terminus in Albany. Bibbulmun Track Foundation

complete revamp of the track, Brampton was assigned the role of project coordinator. With little to no funding, Brampton steered the project to produce the track we have today. Less than 20 per cent follows the original route. The Bibbulmun now traverses large areas of natural bushland, and huts are positioned along its length, offering accommodation and supplies of fresh water.

One remarkable thing about the Bibbulmun is that we owe its existence to convict labour. For in the absence of significant funding for its development, Brampton forged a unique collaboration with Bob Dixon, then manager of state Prison Industries and Denzil McCotter the director of Prison Operations, which saw the prefabrication of the track's huts within prison workshops, and their construction on site by minimum-security prisoners. These same prisoners were provided with work experience in the field, clearing the track along its length from Kalamunda to Albany. Not only did this see the opening of the new Bibbulmun Track in September 1998, but an enduring legacy that provides a host of community work projects delivered by minimum-security prisoners throughout the state. In his detailed history *The Bibbulmun Track: Its History, Its Beauty, Its Walkers,* Jim Baker estimates that staff and prisoners have contributed half a million hours of work to regional communities, to the benefit of all.

The Bibbulmun is a remarkable resource that is free for all to use. It is maintained largely by the Department of Biodiversity, Conservation and Attractions, with a huge input from thousands of volunteers who are members of the Bibbulmun Track Foundation. These individuals have spent time on the track and have developed that sense of boodja that is so desperately needed if we are to preserve the natural wilderness of Western Australia. My hope is that this narrative may in some small way arouse a sense of boodja and draw the reader into the small but growing mob who recognise the need to preserve the wilderness of this place, and of planet Earth more widely. We must all act to curb anthropogenic change now, or we will face certain extinction. In the words of David Attenborough, 'few people will help protect the natural world if they don't first love and understand it'.

KALAMUNDA TO DWELLINGUP

KALAMUNDA TO DWELLINGUP

1

We set off in mid-November, towards the end of kambarang, the Noongar season of birth. Stepping from the terminus onto the track, we were like greyhounds released from their traps. Eight months in the planning, with two months of training and the building anticipation – and yet daunting prospect – of walking more than 1,000 kilometres, and here we were at last. We could barely appreciate the beauty of the iron sculptures depicting the six language groups of the Noongar people of the south-west of Western Australia, through whose lands we would travel, or the inlaid iron Waugal that would be our trusted guide for the next eight weeks. Within 20 metres we were forced to pause for a lone Western Australian Magpie (koolbardi) that stood in our path, looking up at us and producing its soft melodious carolling call, the quintessential sound of the Australian bush: *hoohoo-oooHOOOorrrrrrrr urdle oodle oodle urdleee hoooooooooogh*. How fitting that this should be our first bird for the track list, and on that quiet morning the romantic in me could almost believe this individual was sending us on our way, wishing us well and reminding us to stop, appreciate and cherish the wonders of the Australian bush.

After passing through the long-disused golf course, we reached the head of Piesse Brook Valley and descended into Kalamunda National Park. Though it was late in the spring, the valley was

nonetheless ablaze with wildflowers, a snippet of the biodiversity we were expecting to document along our journey. The gully through which we descended had an overwhelming purple and grey–green hue, due to the dense stands of Large-fruited Thomasia, interspersed with flashes of scarlet from the One-sided Bottlebrush (kwowdjard), white from the Spider Flower, brilliant yellow from the Golden Spray and yellow-green-red from the Lemon-scented Darwinia. In science, all organisms are named following a system of binomial nomenclature, formalised by the father of taxonomy, the Swedish naturalist Carl Linnaeus. Organisms have both a genus and a species name; Lemon-scented Darwinia is called *Darwinia citriodora* because of its characteristic lemon *(citri-)* scent *(-odora)* and after Erasmus Darwin, a contemporary of Linnaeus and grandfather of the influential Victorian naturalist and father of evolutionary biology Charles Darwin. *Darwinia* is found only in Australia, and most species only in the south-west of Western Australia. Because of this limited distribution, they are said to be endemic.

Smaller plants flowering through this section of the track included several species of fringe lily (tjunguri), with their characteristic fringed mauve petals, yellow guinea flowers or hibbertia, and triggerplants. These three genera of flowering plant are each represented by considerable numbers of different species. There are around fifty different species of fringe lily currently recognised in Western Australia, nearly ninety species of guinea flower, and over 200 species of triggerplant. The extraordinary species diversity that typically characterises the plants of the south-west of Western Australia, coupled with the high rates of species endemism, are what make this region a biodiversity hotspot. Flowering along the track that day were the Branching Fringe Lily, a species whose leafless stems form a network that becomes entangled in taller vegetation as a scaffold to hold the plant erect, and the Many-flowered Fringe Lily, much more typical of a lily in its form, with long straight leaves and flowers surmounted on robust stems. Although we would see many different species of guinea flower and triggerplant in the days and weeks to come, this day we saw only one species of hibbertia, Yellow Buttercups, and two species of triggerplant, the Lovely Triggerplant, whose slender spikes of mauve flowers can grow as tall as 50 centimetres, and the Golden Triggerplant, a creeping prostrate species with white and red flowers.

It was Charles Darwin who described the natural biological processes that generate species diversity. Darwin was the ship's naturalist on board HMS *Beagle* during its voyage of South America under the command of Captain Robert FitzRoy. FitzRoy had been sent to South America to chart the coasts from Rio de Janeiro on the east coast, through Tierra del Fuego in the south and up to central Chile in the west, before heading home across the Pacific via Australia. The voyage was to last five years, from 1831 to 1836. Darwin left England a budding clergyman, but his observations of the natural history of the countries he visited on the voyage shook the very foundations of his belief in divine creation and led to the development of his theories on the origin of species. Darwin's account of his time on the *Beagle* published in 1839, *A Naturalist's Voyage Round the World*, was an immensely popular read in Victorian England, at a time when the wonders of the world's flora and fauna were first being revealed to Europe.

Naturalists travelling the world were sending home to England preserved specimens that were gathered together in the new cathedral to natural history, the Natural History Museum in South Kensington; living animals that would be housed and displayed at the Zoological Gardens in Regent's Park; and living plants and seeds that would be cultivated and grown in the Royal Botanic Gardens at Kew. It took Darwin twenty years before he published an abstract of his work on the origin of species in 1858. His hand was forced by an article written by another great Victorian naturalist, Alfred Russel Wallace, who had independently recognised the mechanisms responsible for organic evolution from his observations of the distribution of species across the Malay Archipelago. Darwin's full account, *On the Origin of Species*, followed shortly after, in 1859.

Darwin and Wallace recognised the ingredients for speciation (the evolution of new species) as variation, selection and time. For any species of organism you care to think of, the individuals belonging to that species will be distinguishable by slight differences in form. Some individuals will be larger than others, there will be differences in the depth of colouration, or, more cryptically, there will be differences in the physiological processes that sustain life, such as the digestion of nutrients and their transformation to energy. Given this variation, Darwin and Wallace realised that competition among individuals for limited resources – say, space to grow or food and water – would result in

only those individuals that grow quickest or are best able to extract food and water from their environment surviving to reproduce.

At the time, neither Darwin or Wallace were aware of the genetic basis of this individual variation, but they nevertheless recognised that if variation had a heritable basis then those individuals best suited to a particular environment would leave offspring bearing the same characteristics that made them successful, while those not well suited would leave few or no offspring. Given sufficient time, or more specifically after multiple generations of selection, the species would come to consist of only individuals bearing the traits that best allowed them to survive and reproduce. In this way, variation, selection and time generate changes in the form of organisms. The source of selection acting on a species comes from its natural environment, for example, temperature, soil depth or rainfall; from competition with other species for space and resources; or from competition among individuals of the same species. Selection arises from natural processes, hence Darwin's term, natural selection.

That selection can change the form of animals and plants became the focus of much of Darwin's lifework. For example, in his two volumes on *The Variation of Animals and Plants Under Domestication*, he documented how humans have artificially selected traits in animals and plants that are beneficial to us, such as milk or meat yield in cattle, egg-laying in chickens or wool quality in sheep. He also conducted his own experiments using artificial selection on, among other things, domestic pigeons. He, and pigeon-fanciers before and after him, generated any number of weird and wonderful feather colours and forms, and even behaviours, by artificial selection. Tumbler pigeons, for example, literally stall mid-flight, somersault and sometimes fall from the sky. Pigeon-fanciers were able to produce this bizarre behaviour in their domestic birds by selectively breeding from individual Rock Doves that exhibited this behavioural abnormality. Why they would want to do so is another question, but such experiments show us how animals and plants can change in form due to selection.

Returning to the fringe lilies that lined the track down to Piesse Brook, one could imagine that the Branching Fringe Lily might have arisen from an ancestral fringe lily whose form was more typical of lilies generally, like the Many-flowered Fringe Lily, because when growing among dense vegetation those individuals

that were taller were better able to present their flowers to insect pollinators – competition for air space, so to speak. But with increasing height comes the problem of remaining upright, so those individuals that had a branching form, which provided leverage on surrounding vegetation, might have succeeded in reaching the heights necessary to compete for pollinators, while those individuals that grew straight up might have collapsed before being able to reproduce. Whatever the selective pressures that drove the evolution of the fifty or more different species of fringe lily, their many different leaf and stem forms illustrate the phenomenon of divergent evolution, the accumulation of differences between populations that ultimately lead to the origin of new species. On the other hand, most species of fringe lily are readily identified because they all have the same mauve flowers with fringed petals. The relative uniformity of flower form found across closely related species of fringe lily is an example of what we call an evolutionarily conserved trait, a trait that has not been subject to divergent natural selection.

Our bird list accumulated species rapidly as we walked down the gully to Piesse Brook. The most common species that day, and as it turned out every day of our journey, was the Grey Fantail (kadjinak). This flycatcher is one of Australia's most common birds, found across the entire continent, and is conspicuous in the bushland due both to its noisy chatter, described perfectly by Michael Morcombe and David Stewart in their *eGuide to the Birds of Australia* as *twitch-twitchit, tsweeit-tseet, chit-twit, tswit-chat, tsweeit*, and its constant flitting from branch to branch in pursuit of the flies on which it feeds. Even when stationary, they fan their long tails and wave them from side to side, a highly conspicuous behaviour that flushes any flies that might be perched in the vegetation. A flock of Carnaby's Black Cockatoos (ngoolyak), with their loud wailing calls and slow funereal flight, contrasted with a flock of grey and pink Galahs (djakal-ngakal) flying frantically across the valley while producing their harsh, scolding screeches. Silvereyes (doolor) flitted through the thomasia and Red Wattlebirds (djangkang) fed from the One-sided Bottlebrush (kwowdjard).

As we reached the bottom of the gully a group of Splendid Fairy-wrens (djer-djer) hopped through a bottlebrush on our left, the male perched prominently on an outer branch, producing his high-pitched rhythmic trill – *trit-triiit-trit-tirreet-tirreet-trit-tirreet* – as his female companions passed through in the depths of the

undergrowth. For much of the year, male and female Splendid Fairy-wrens are barely distinguishable from each other, having a pale brown back, pale blue tail, and white chest and belly. During the breeding season, however, the male sheds his dull plumage and replaces it with feathers of vibrant blue, the chest a deep cobalt, cheeks and crown a light, almost iridescent sky blue, and a deep blue-black band through the eye, around the cheeks and across the chest. Splendid is an understatement. The difference in colour between males and females is an example of a second, equally important form of selection driving evolutionary divergence: sexual selection.

Darwin recognised that it was typical for the males of many animal species to be larger than the females, to have greater physical strength or to be endowed with traits such as horns or antlers, or bright colours like our male Splendid Fairy-wren. Often these exaggerated secondary sexual traits can render males highly conspicuous to predators, resulting in certain death. For this reason their evolution was difficult for Darwin to reconcile with the natural selection that acts so stringently on an organism's ability to survive. He is famously quoted as saying that the feathers in a peacock's train made him sick! Darwin came to recognise, however, that the currency of selection is offspring in subsequent generations, so that even if a trait reduces the lifespan of an individual, as long as that trait results in more offspring for its bearer, then it will be transmitted to future generations. Darwin thus defined sexual selection as distinct from natural selection in that it favours traits that contribute to an individual's ability to acquire mates when in competition with others of the same sex and species. In his volume *The Descent of Man, and Selection in Relation to Sex* published in 1871, Darwin recognised two forms of sexual selection: competition between males for access to females, typically favouring the evolution of weapons or physical strength necessary for males to win fights over access to females; and female choice, which favours ornamental feathers or courtship displays that serve to attract females and persuade them to mate.

Australian ornithologist Raoul Mulder has found that in the case of Superb Fairy-wrens, those males that develop their blue breeding colouration earlier in the spring are more likely to be chosen by females as breeding partners, generating sexual selection for increased male breeding colouration. Evolutionary biologists since Darwin have discovered how male sexual displays can convey

important information to females about male quality, such as their ability to offer food and protection for developing offspring, genes that will promote offspring health and survival, or genes that will make offspring attractive as mates and thereby increase the number of grand-offspring a female can produce. The benefits males can offer to females or their offspring help explain why females should choose among prospective males in the first place. One might ask then why male fairy-wrens don't stay blue all the time. But since being so conspicuous makes males vulnerable to predators, natural selection has favoured males that shed their bright plumage when it is not necessary for breeding.

After crossing Piesse Brook, we soon turned right and climbed steeply up through dry Wandoo woodland and out of Kalamunda National Park. From here the track entered mixed woodland of predominantly Marri and Jarrah with scattered stands of Western Sheoak (kondil), Parrot Bush (budjan) and Bull Banksia (mungitch). The genus *Banksia*, named after Sir Joseph Banks, naturalist on the *Endeavour* during Lieutenant James Cook's first voyage to Australia, has undergone an astonishing evolutionary divergence. With more than 170 species, the *Banksia* genus ranges in form from prostrate plants whose branches grow below ground and only the leaves and flowers appear above the soil surface, to tall trees that can reach 20 metres or more. The Bull Banksia is one of the most common in the Jarrah forests of Western Australia, and at the time we walked through on the track they were presenting impressive displays of their giant yellow flowers. The understorey of the forest was dominated by Grasstrees (balga) and Zamia Palms (jeeriji), and along the edges of the track were clumps of vibrant pink and white Rose-tipped Mulla Mulla, aptly named Pom-poms, and white-flowered Woodbridge Poison. Mulla mulla is another incredibly diverse genus, currently with 120 species, all of which are endemic to Australia and most of the diversity occurring in Western Australia. White Cottonheads, and the oddly named Pepper and Salt, with its pink flowers, were also in abundance. One often wonders about the derivation of some common names.

The change in habitat afforded by the Jarrah forest soon yielded a flush of new bird species. Red-capped (delyip) and Ringneck (doornart) parrots flew through the forest canopy, while Spotted Pardalote (widap-widap) gleaned insects from the leaves of the Marri and Jarrah. The loud *kling-kling-kling* of Grey Currawong

(djarbarn) was complemented by the soft, one has to say perfunctory, song of the Western Gerygone (waralyboodang), almost always ceasing as if the bird has forgotten the final phrase, or simply can't be bothered to finish its song because of something better to do. A Scarlet Robin (dermokalitj) turned suddenly on its perch exposing its vibrant-scarlet chest, a beacon in the gloomy understorey of the forest.

After crossing Glen Forrest Road, we entered an area of Beelu National Park that had been burnt eighteen months previously. The blackened trunks of the Jarrah, Marri and Grasstrees (balga) offered a striking contrast to the vibrant fresh green of their new leaf growth, and that of the Zamia Palms (jeeriji) that had flowered in profusion, stimulated to do so by the fire. The Zamia Palms and Grasstrees dominated the visual perspective of the forest, giving an almost prehistoric ambiance. I could almost imagine a brontosaurus or stegosaurus ambling through and feeding on the Zamia. Not surprising in some respects, as the Zamia are an ancient family of plants that have changed little since they first appeared on the Gondwanan continent. We don't generally think of plants as being male or female, but in fact many species do have separate sexes, the Zamia Palm among them. They are said to be dioecious. The male Zamias had long since shed their pollen and their flowers were brown and shrivelled, while the female's flowers were plump and swollen with developing seeds. Zamia seeds were an important food for the Noongar people, but they must be processed before consumption to remove toxins that induce severe vomiting, as the early European settlers in Western Australia discovered to their peril.

We soon arrived at Hewett's Hill Hut, just 10.2 kilometres from Kalamunda. The hut stands high on a slope overlooking the track, surrounded by large granite boulders and giving a view onto the tree canopy below. As we sat at the picnic bench soaking in the tranquillity of the forest, we watched Spotted Pardalotes (widap-widap) and Western Gerygones (waralyboodang) gleaning insects, and Black-faced Cuckoo-shrikes (noolarko) moving across the canopy. The soft repeated *whooo* of a Common Bronzewing Pigeon (nembing) was positively soporific. We expected to share the hut that night, being so close to Kalamunda, and indeed we saw below us on the track a lone figure walking towards the spur trail that led to the hut. We were soon to learn the important lesson of not judging a book by its cover.

Jens was carrying a lot of weight, and not in his backpack. It passed through my mind, 'Good on him for trying, but he's probably not going very far, maybe just an overnighter'. Jens asked us if this was our first time on the Bibbulmun, at which we explained how we had done day walks but never before overnighted. He then proceeded to tell us that he had walked end to end ten times, and that this year he was walking to Albany and back! Humble pie time. As it turned out, Jens was an inspiration for me in the days and weeks to come. On the steepest hills or the softest sand dunes when I thought I could go no further, I would think to myself, 'If Jens can do this, then so can I.' So thanks, Jens.

Shortly after Jens' arrival, a troop of twelve 14-year-old boys arrived with their responsible adults. 'Hi, I'm Amber,' one adult said as she looked over her shoulder at the boys swarming across the campground. 'The boys will camp but we will share the hut, sorry!' Five minutes later another two guys turned up: 'Hi, I'm Bill,' says Bill offering his hand. 'G'day, I'm Bill,' says his companion. I thought to myself, 'Well, that will be easy.' Then Bill one immediately started telling us a joke, while Bill two's eyes started to glaze over – no doubt he had heard them all before. I turned to Freddy and whispered in his ear, 'Think it's time for us to go and pitch our tent.'

Away from the hut in the furthest camping spot we could find, far from the hustle and bustle, tranquillity was restored once more, broken only by the raucous laughter of a pair of Kookaburras (kaa-kaa) as the sun set. And so we spent our first night on the Bibbulmun, under the stars.

2

The Kookaburras woke us at four-thirty, long before sunrise. They may as well have been in the tent with us they were so loud. Kookaburras typically broadcast their calls at dusk as they arrive at a communal roost within their territory, and again before dawn. Far from having fun, when Kookaburras 'laugh' they are engaged in serious business. Kookaburras are cooperative breeders, meaning that a dominant male and female breeding pair are typically helped by two or three other birds, often adult offspring from a previous breeding season. The group maintains a territory the size of which

TOP: A pair of Kaa-Kaa or kookaburra, *Dacelo novaeguineae*. These kingfishers are cooperative breeders, with subordinate males remaining in or joining a breeding group to help the dominant pair raise young. The coordinated laughs are a warning from the male to subordinate birds that they should not try to breed themselves and a call to attract additional females. On her part, the female laughs to warn other females that this male is taken. Leigh Simmons

MIDDLE: Kadjinak or Grey Fantail, *Rhipidura albiscapa*. By far the most common forest bird in south-western WA, this flycatcher makes short eratic flights from a home perch to capture insect prey on the wing. Leigh Simmons

BOTTOM: Dermokalitj or Scarlet Robins, *Petroica boodang*, glow like beacons in the dim understory of the Jarrah forest. They search for grubs and worms among the leaf litter on the forest floor. Leigh Simmons

depends largely on the number of individuals within the group. The more helpers there are, the larger the territory that can be defended, and the larger the territory, the more food it will provide for the group and its offspring. It is the dominant male and female who produce the laughing call in a duet.

While the call serves an aggressive signal to keep neighbouring birds out of the territory, it is also an aggressive suppression of helpers. All is not harmony and love among 'cooperative' breeders. The dominant male and female build the nest in a tree hollow where they will raise a clutch of two or three young. The dominant male provides the majority of parental care, bringing food to the chicks as they grow, typically lizards or the nestlings of other smaller forest birds. But the female and the helpers also bring food. Ornithologist Sarah Legge has found that the more helpers there are, the more likely the chicks are to successfully fledge.

Given helpers are feeding their siblings, they do achieve some reproductive success through what British evolutionary biologist William Hamilton termed kin selection. If an individual cannot raise its own young because of a lack of available breeding territory or mating partner, it can still leave genes in the next generation by helping to raise its siblings. Cooperative breeding can therefore evolve because of the reproductive benefits gained through relatives. But an individual will always leave more genes in the next generation if it produces its own offspring, so it should try to breed if it can. Thus helpers will try to assert themselves and take over the territory from the dominant birds.

Swiss evolutionary biologist Heinz-Ulrich Reyer found that if a helper produces a 'laugh' call, this will be immediately followed by a physical attack by the dominant bird, to suppress the youngster and so defend its breeding rights. Reyer also suggests that there is conflict between the dominant male and female. The male and female calls include sex-specific elements. The call consists of several different phrases. It starts with a 'kooaa' followed by a 'cackle', and then a 'rolling' phrase that precedes the 'laugh' proper. After the laugh the male utters a phrase called the 'gogo', while the female produces her own sex-specific phrase, the 'gurgle'. Reyer suggests that the male's call may serve not only to guard the female from rival males on neighbouring territories, but also to attract neighbouring females to join him on his territory. It is primarily the male that initiates the duet, with the female typically flying to him on hearing his introductory *kooaas* and joining him in the

full laughing duet. Reyer suggests that the female-specific phrases, could be telling neighbouring females, 'Keep out, he is feeding my offspring', and so the duet of male and female may not reflect their common interests but rather a manifestation of conflict between them over their individual reproductive interests. Regardless, the kookaburras' duet certainly served as an excellent early morning wake-up call.

By the time we had packed up our tent and walked over to the hut, it was deserted – no sign of the previous evening's frenzy. After filling our water bottles we set off on the 10.6-kilometre trek through Beelu National Park that would take us to Ball Creek Hut. The track follows an old forest road that runs along the edge of the Helena Valley with the river flowing far below. The slopes of the valley are forested, in some stretches with Wandoo, in others Jarrah and Marri. The forest frequently gives way to large areas of granite outcrop affording fine views across the valley. Many of the Grasstrees through this section sported fresh flower spikes, upon which insects were gorging on the abundant nectar. European Honeybees, of course – these feral bees are everywhere – but also an abundance of Painted Lady Butterflies (boornarr, *Vanessa kershawi*).

We stopped for second breakfast on an outcrop that offered fine views down the valley to Mundaring Weir and the reservoir beyond. Walking down from the track to the outcrop we passed through a broad band of Granite Featherflower, a species of *Verticordia* that grows prolifically around the edges of granite outcrops. Today they presented us with a spectacular display of purple. In winter these outcrops capture pools of water to which frogs come to breed. Shallower cracks and hollows provide home to beds of moss within which other plants find a foothold to grow. Plants such as insectivorous sundews and orchids abound in spring, and the Resurrection Plant, or Pincushion, is then bright green. But today the pools and moss beds had long since dried up, the Pincushion was bright orange and the moss brown and dormant. Nevertheless, Elbow Orchids were in full bloom.

In their *Orchids of South-West Australia*, Noel Hoffman and Andrew Brown report twenty-eight genera of orchid from Western Australia, with 394 named species in the south-west corner. Orchids are particularly abundant on and around granite outcrops, where the run-off from winter rains creates the moist soils in which they thrive. It is true to say that orchids offer one

of the best examples of the power of natural selection to generate often intricately detailed structures, or adaptations, that ensure an organism's survival and reproduction.

Orchids are unique among plants in their use of deception to achieve pollination. Not surprisingly, they hold a special fascination for evolutionary biologists generally, and Darwin used them to illustrate the power of natural selection in driving speciation. Shortly after publication of *On the Origin of Species*, Darwin published an entire volume on *The Various Contrivances by Which Orchids Are Fertilized by Insects*, in which he illustrated how different species of orchid were each adapted to their own, often unique, insect pollinator. A visitor to a granite outcrop could be forgiven for overlooking Elbow Orchids. If they are noticed at all, they appear at first glance like the dried stems of plants long since dead. Indeed, by the time they are in full bloom, their roots and single leaf have already died and shrivelled, the flower being nourished by food and moisture stored in the fleshy stem. The flowers themselves bear little resemblance to any conventional bloom. Flowers typically have sepals, the outermost part of the flower, and colourful petals that serve to attract pollinators. Flowers also generally offer nectar rewards to attract their pollinators, but not orchids. The sepals and petals of Elbow Orchids are highly modified in order to both deceive their pollinator, a single species of thynnine wasp, into grasping the flower so it can attach packages of pollen to the wasp for transportation to neighbouring plants. To understand this contrivance we need to know a little of the mating biology of the wasps.

My colleague John Alcock has described the breeding biology of several thynnines from eastern Australia, and the details of pollination of Elbow Orchids by a yet-to-be-named Western Australian wasp in the genus *Thynnoturneria*. Thynnine wasps are themselves unique in that the female is completely flightless, spending much of her time underground where she hunts for beetle larvae on which to deposit her eggs. Females must come above ground to mate, and when they do they emit a pheromone that is highly attractive to males. Male thynnines have territories they patrol, searching for females. When they detect the scent of a female, they fly immediately to her, grasp her and fly off with her lest another male also detect her.

The third petal or labellum of sexually deceptive orchids is highly modified to form a lure that serves to attract their insect

pollinators. The labellum of Elbow Orchids is shaped like the female wasp and is partly covered with fleshy deep-red glandular tissue that emits a pheromone that to the male wasp smells like the pheromone signal of a female. The column of the flower, the structure supporting the male (stamens) and female (style) organs, is equally highly modified. The tip of the column bears a pair of 'wings', large hook-like structures that lie either side of the column. Male thynnines are tricked into seizing the orchid's labellum by its irresistible sexual allure, and when they attempt to fly off with it, the hinged labellum flicks upward, pushing the wasp into the column, the hooks of which grasp its wings so that the wasp must struggle to release itself. In so doing it comes into contact with the sticky pollen bundle, which is attached to the wasp's back and carried off when he escapes. When the wasp is deceived by a second plant, the pollen from his back will be attached to the female part of the plant, the stigma, so resulting in pollination. Little wonder that Darwin thought the 'contrivances by which orchids are fertilised, are as varied and almost as perfect as any of the most beautiful adaptations in the animal kingdom'.

While the reproductive success of Elbow Orchids is assured by their duping of male thynnines, the costs of lost time and energy for the male wasps must take a toll on their own reproductive success. Not surprising to learn then, that natural selection has favoured adaptations in male wasps to avoid being duped. By cutting and moving Elbow Orchids to different locations within a male's territory, John Alcock found that male thynnines soon become wary of sources of pheromone that do not turn out to be female wasps. That is, they habituate to the deception of Elbow Orchids and cease to respond to their fake pheromone. The same is true of the European bee orchids in the *Ophrys* genus studied by Darwin. However, German ecologist Manfred Ayasse has found that in bee orchids a given plant will change the pheromone bouquet of successive flowers so that its bee pollinators are once again duped. Orchids and their pollinators, it would seem, are in an evolutionary arms race, each evolving counter-adaptations to maximise their own reproductive success.

On leaving the granite outcrop we continued along the forest road, eventually descending into Helena Valley. Walking across the weir wall we saw Pied Cormorants (midi) on Lake C. Y. O'Connor, and Australian Raven (waardong) flying across the valley. From the northern side of the weir the trail follows the Kalgoorlie pipeline,

TOP: Djiyaderbaat or Weebill, *Smicrornis brevirostris*. Australia's smallest bird, it is a common resident in Jarra and Marri woodlands. They are insectivorous, searching for insect prey on the leaves and trunks of trees. They travel in small groups communicating with high pitched notes *wheetiew whit, whit, WHEETiew*. Leigh Simmons

MIDDLE: Widap-widap or Spotted Pardalote, *Pardalotus punctatus*. Another common resident of the Jarra and Marri forests, these strikingly coloured birds travel in pairs or family groups competing with Weebills for their share of insects. Contact calls between group members are a musical whistle *weep-weeip* Leigh Simmons

BOTTOM: Doornart or Australian Ringneck Parrot, *Barnardius zonarius*. Four 'races' of this species are currently recognised across Australia. They may ultimately be described as different species once their DNA sequences are established. In the south-west of WA we have the Twenty-eight, named after its call. Here a male on the right is feeding a female. Courtship feeding is a common behaviour in birds; females may assess a male's ability to bring food to the nest before committing to breed with him. Leigh Simmons

past pumping station number one and up into Mundaring precinct. We passed the Mundaring Hotel just five minutes before noon, and there was but a millisecond's hesitation before we headed in for a beer. We vowed then and there that no café or pub would be passed unused on the weeks ahead; there would be precious few of them after all! We learnt to our shame that Jens had been in for a very early breakfast, so he must have left Hewett's Hill in the middle of the night. After lunch we continued through the Jarrah forests, along the north-eastern slopes of Helena Valley with fine views of the reservoir, finally arriving at Ball Creek in the early afternoon. We had the hut to ourselves that night, Jens having walked straight through.

3

We rose very early the next day, long before the Kookaburras began their cackle. We knew that the hut at Helena had been destroyed in a wildfire that had swept through the northern slopes of the Helena Valley in January 2018, and that the temperatures today were predicted to hit 38 degrees Celsius. Signs at Ball Creek Hut had warned us that there was no water at Helena, and we would have to walk the 19 kilometres to Waalegh. The topography indicated some pretty steep climbs. This was going to be a tough day. As we walked through the cool Jarrah forest, the sun rose above the ridge on our left, casting shafts of golden light through the Grasstrees (balga) and Zamia (jeeriji). The track ascended a small ridge before descending steeply into Manns Gully, through sections of Wandoo and granite outcrop. The Curved Mulla Mulla was abundant along the sandy trail that wound through the open granite sections, a low prostrate form with very little evidence of leaf but copious tiny fluffy balls of pink and white nestled close to the ground.

We sat briefly for second breakfast on a large granite boulder overlooking a small billabong before continuing through Manns Gully, eventually reaching the first of what would be many challenging climbs. The temperature was now rising as steeply as the forest road on which we walked. Heads down and bent double to take the weight of our packs like a pair of mules, we ascended out of Manns Gully and up to Allen Road. After a short distance the track left the shade of the forest and traversed a harvested pine plantation, now a barren stretch of sun-baked sandy gravel.

We would see little shade for the next 10 kilometres or so, the track passing steeply up and then along Driver Road as it traversed the burnt northern slopes of Helena Valley. Shortly after passing the turn-off to the now destroyed Helena Hut, Driver Road plummets almost 100 metres down into Chinaman Gully. Here the road was largely washed out, and the deep ruts and loose sand and gravel made the descent a hazardous one. After a brief stop in a small patch of shade afforded by some large granite boulders in the sandy bed of Chinaman Gully, we ascended the other side, just as steep and just as unstable underfoot. No respite from the sun because the trees had only just started to sprout new growth after losing their canopy in the fires of the previous summer. By the time we reached the top of the ridge, it was 38 degrees Celsius and we collapsed in the narrow band of shade cast by the trunk of a large blackened Marri. All around us the black and sooty trunks of the Jarrah and Marri were fringed with bright-green and rusty-red clumps of sprouting branches and leaves, and there was an abundance of post-fire regeneration on the dry sandy ground.

Fire has been a selective pressure on the flora and fauna of the Australian continent for more than 3 million years. Long dry summers with strong hot easterly winds make the south-west of Western Australia particularly fire-prone, and natural selection has favoured adaptations for fire tolerance among many evolutionary lineages of flowering plants. Indeed, many species actually require fire for their growth and reproduction. Plants can be broadly classified in terms of their response to fire as resprouters or obligate seeders. Jarrah, Marri and Sheoak, for example, have thick bark that, depending on the severity of fire, can protect the living tissue from being destroyed. After a fire has passed, fresh growth will sprout from buds that lie beneath the bark. Should the fire be severe enough to destroy the entire trunk, the tree can also resprout from tubers below ground. In addition to the eucalypts, resprouters with abundant fresh growth on the slopes of the Helena Valley included Grasstrees (balga), Zamia Palms (jeeriji), Yellow Buttercups and Basket Flower.

In contrast to resprouters, obligate seeders are generally killed by fire and regeneration occurs either from seeds stored in the canopy or in the topsoil. Slender Lobelia, Running Postman (wollung), Woodbridge Poison and Slender Podolepis were all flowering in abundance as we passed through and are examples of obligate seeders whose seeds lie dormant in the soil between fire events.

Germination following fire is stimulated by chemicals in smoke, known as karrikins, which penetrate into the topsoil and promote a rapid and prolific germination of the seed bank. Banksias are an example of species that have their seeds stored in the canopy, encased in follicles within their woody cones. Fire melts the resin that seals the follicles so that immediately after a fire has passed the follicles burst, shedding seed onto the cleared ground below.

Some 78 per cent of Banksia species only shed their seed in response to fire. Some, such as the Bull Banksia (mungitch), can both resprout and seed depending on whether they survive the heat of the fire. Couch Honeypot Banksia (bullgalla) was abundant along this section of the ridge, where they had clearly regenerated rapidly after the fire, most likely by resprouting given they were in flower. The Noongar would collect nectar (mangite) from the flowers of Couch Honeypot, and other banksias. Many species of plant respond to fire by increasing the amount of resources they put into flowering, as was evident that day from the Grasstrees (balga), Zamia (jeeriji) and Purple Flags. Flowering is induced by a number of fire-related stimuli, including temperature, ethylene and karrikins in smoke, nutrient input to soil from ash, and the increased soil moisture and light penetration that results from the forest canopy opening up.

It has been suggested that fire has been responsible, in part, for the considerable evolutionary divergence of flora in the south-west of Western Australia. For example, some areas of the landscape can be more or less fire-prone. Large expanses of relatively flat land covered in dense dry eucalyptus forest contrasts with elevated open granite outcrops or moist river gullies. Landscape variation affects the frequency and intensity of fire, so that some areas have favoured the evolution of fire-tolerant species while in other areas fire-susceptible species have persisted. Regions experiencing regular intense fires could thus represent barriers to gene flow across the landscape, resulting in divergence among separated populations of the same fire-susceptible species with resulting speciation.

The frequency and intensity of fires has also changed over evolutionary time, due to changing climate and, more recently, the arrival of humans on the Australian continent. Before humans, fires would have been relatively infrequent and random events, started naturally by lightning strikes during dry summer storms. Since human arrival, however, the frequency of fires has increased. Before European settlement the Noongar used fire to flush animals

when hunting, or to stimulate growth of edible fruits such as zamia nuts. Human-ignited fires would thus have become an increasing feature of the landscape after the arrival of the Noongar more than 30,000 years ago. But with the more recent arrival of Europeans, huge tracts of land have been cleared for farming, towns and cities have been built, and we have adopted the practice of prescribed burning, or 'hazard reduction', to protect our infrastructure. The Western Australian Department of Biodiversity Conservation and Attractions strives to maintain a mosaic of recently burned patches of landscape, with the aim of preventing wildfires that might otherwise sweep through vast areas with potentially devastating consequences for the human population and its infrastructure.

Many things influence the intensity of fire, but the amount of fuel on the forest floor is a significant component. Should a wildfire start, either naturally or, as in the case of the Helena Valley wildfire, purposefully, it will be slowed or stopped when it comes to an area in the landscape that has recently had a prescribed burn because of the resultant lack of fuel to maintain it. While we need to protect ourselves from fire, we must also recognise that we have fundamentally changed the fire ecology of the south-west, with potentially damaging consequences for its biodiversity. It has been estimated that 5 to 10 per cent of plant species in south-western Western Australia are short-lived species that germinate after a fire and live for just one to three years, shedding their seed into the seed bank and lying dormant until fire returns. Another 25 to 35 per cent are seeders that die following fire but regenerate from seed stored on the plant or in the soil seed bank. The remaining are resprouters.

The variation among species in their response to fire results in a changing composition of biodiversity following fire, with species abundance and richness at its peak immediately following fire, and a decline in diversity with time since fire as shorter-lived species senesce and die. Burning too regularly will result in the loss of those species that require long periods between fires in order to regenerate, flower and deposit seed in the seed bank. Before World War II, for example, Kings Park was regularly burned, leading to a loss of native plants and the establishment of invasive grasses and bulbous weeds such as gladioli and freesias. Conversely, if we prevent fire, then species of seeders may be lost from the landscape as the viability of the seed bank, both in the canopy and soil, can deteriorate with time. Ironically, the ravages of fire are essential

for the fragile, yet beautiful ecosystem of the south-west. If we are to conserve our biodiversity, we must strive to understand how fire affects the flora and fauna of this area, from individual species to communities, and in different regions of the landscape. Only with this knowledge can we protect our own interests while also protecting our environment. The Noongar appreciated this and managed the landscape effectively for more than 30,000 years. We have much to learn from them.

As we waited in the shade, the temperature rose to 40 degrees Celsius. Ordinarily, the risk of fire would have been a matter of concern, but there was no fuel left to burn on the slopes of the Helena Valley that day. The view south from the ridge on which we sat promised respite from the sun beating down through the open canopy and reflecting up from the bare sandy ground. So we set off, first descending the ridge steeply to the valley floor and the Helena River crossing. Beyond the river, we climbed steeply yet again, first skirting a pine plantation before turning left to climb through areas with large granite boulders and eventually into mature unburnt Wandoo woodlands, which provided welcome shade from the direct sunlight. Rainbow Bee-eaters (birin birin) and Dusky Woodswallows (kayibort) circled high in the sky, Western Thornbills (djobool-djobool) and Weebills (djiyaderbaat) gleaned insects from the leaves of the Wandoo, White-browed Scrub-wren (koorkal) flitted through the understorey, and a Rufous Whistler (bambon) called from high in the canopy *cheWIT-chWIT-chWIT-chWIT*. It was so wonderful to be away from the devastation of the fire.

After crossing Taylor Road, the track passed through alternating stretches of Jarrah/Sheoak forest and Wandoo, with sweeping views down the Helena Valley. The numerous granite outcrops through this section were home to large stands of Elbow Orchids, and were surrounded by dense beds of Yellow Starflower in full bloom. As beautiful as it was, this section of track was almost my nemesis. After descending, yet again, to cross a small creek, we made another steep ascent to Tableland Road, at which point I thought I could go no further. The combination of fatigue and heat, and just too many hills, had done for me. I was just not fit enough it seemed. Freddy sped on ahead to drop his pack and return to collect mine, but by the time he reached me it was only another 100 metres or so to Waalegh Hut, so I ploughed on.

Perched high on the ridge overlooking Helena Valley, Waalegh

offered a staggering view, and the trials of the day simply melted away. I realised then that this journey was going to be as much a psychological challenge as a physical one. I would need to find a way of fighting off the Dementors if I was to keep going. And I was encouraged to find that I was not alone. An hour or so later Tim arrived, just as hot, just as fatigued and just as unimpressed by the hills as I. Tim had walked from Hewett's Hill, passing through Ball Creek, and so had covered even more ground than us. After rehydrating and a lazy afternoon around camp, during which we flushed a Painted Button-quail (mooroolang) while taking in the views across the valley, we spent the evening discussing our respective plans.

Tim anticipated completing the track in forty days, and spoke enthusiastically of double- and triple-hutting – that is, staying at every second or third hut along the track. Just listening to his plans made me exhausted. I felt so fortunate that we had the time to spend walking the trail at a snail's pace. Our plan was to stay in every single hut we could, and so maximise our time on the track. Our entry into the logbook for expected duration was sixty-one days, and we were sticking to it. Tim soon acquired the track name of Sooty Tim. He had a liquid fuel burner that generated more soot than it did heat. After his supper, instant lasagna for four, he took on the appearance of a chimney sweep, leaving sooty residues on almost everything he touched.

4

The walk to Beraking Hut was a gentle 9-kilometre stroll through the cool shady forest. The first 3 kilometres or so of this section were built by hand in 1994 by inmates from Wooroloo Prison Farm, as was the original hut at Waalegh. The track then joins the long-disused Ruen Road, and travels through areas of Jarrah forest with dense stands of Bull Banksia (mungitch) and Parrot Bush, and patches of mature Wandoo woodland. It follows the edge of the Darkin River Valley with only minor dips and climbs, a great relief from the trials of the previous day. We covered the 9 kilometres in just three hours.

Along the way we came across several Western Brush Wallabies (kwoora; *Macropus irma*), a species found only in the south-west

TOP: Djakal-ngakal or Galah, *Cactua roseicapilla*. This pink and grey cockatoo is often seen in large flocks, flying fast and erratically through the sky, with screeching metalic cries *chirrink-chirink czink-czink-czink*. Leigh Simmons

MIDDLE: Waralyboordang or Western Gerygone, *Gerygone fusca*. This common warbler is often heard in the Jarra forests. Its song is not exactly melodious. It starts well and strong, and then the bird seemingly loses interest before ceasing abruptly as if in mid-sentence. Leigh Simmons

BOTTOM: Djangkang or Red Wattlebird, *Anthochaera carunculata*. One of Australia's largest honeyeaters, despite their name they also search among the leaves and branches of trees for insects which provide a source of protein to complement their carbohydrate diet. The loud *chock a lock* is a familiar sound of the Marri forests. Leigh Simmons

of Western Australia. Distinct white facial stripes, large round ears fringed with black, and black gloves readily distinguish this wallaby from the larger Western Grey Kangaroos (yonga; *Macropus fuliginosus*) that also bounded through the undergrowth along this section of the track. No doubt they were responsible for the huge population of ticks that we had to periodically flick off our trousers and shirtsleeves; I picked one off Freddy's face as it marched up his cheek. Kangaroos and wallabies have a singular antipredator response; they simply freeze and watch the perceived threat. It is remarkably effective, as one rarely notices them in the gloom of the forest until they bound off in the opposite direction. The brush wallabies watched us intently as we proceeded along the track. The one sure way to get them to move was to raise a camera and try to snatch a photo, which we failed to do on almost every occasion. Easier to photograph were the bright-scarlet flowers of Wilson's Grevillea, which was flowering in abundance in the Jarrah forest, and the tiny orange-flowered Pretty Sundews that were scattered on the forest floor where we stopped for second breakfast.

Sundews are a remarkable family of plants. Although found worldwide, they have their greatest species diversity in Australia, where more than 100 species have been recorded. Darwin was fascinated by these plants, as am I, because of their insectivorous habits. Sundews typically thrive in nutrient-impoverished soils, being most abundant in winter-wet swamps and in the moss beds of granite outcrops. Sundews compensate for the lack of nutrients in the soil by capturing and literally digesting insects. Darwin described the way sundews capture and consume their prey in his book *Insectivorous Plants*, published in 1875. The leaves of sundews are covered in long slender tentacles that secrete a sticky substance from their tip. When a small fly lands on the tentacles, attracted there by the sweet-smelling secretion, it becomes immediately stuck. Remarkably, its struggle to escape sends sensory impulses down the tentacles, triggering movement in the surrounding tentacles, which bend in towards the fly and make contact with it. The poor creature is soon dragged beneath a mass of tentacles that then begin to secrete digestive juices, dissolving the fly so that the leaves can absorb the nutritious juices. Stuff of nightmares! Darwin argued that this remarkable adaptation evolved via the modification of features found in the leaves of plants that obtain their nutrients by more conventional means, such as sticky hairs that defend leaves against herbivores. We were lucky to see the Pretty Sundews when

in full flower, as their growing season drew to a close with the increasing aridity of the forest floor.

Before arriving at Beraking we happened upon a common resident of the Jarrah forest, a Sleepy Lizard (yoorn; *Tiliqua rugosa*). While many bushwalkers will be familiar with these skinks, few will appreciate their unique natural history. South Australian behavioural ecologist Michael Bull followed a population of these lizards for almost thirty-five years, the entirety of his research career. Long-term studies such as Bull's offer unprecedented insight into the ecology and life history of our native flora and fauna, and importantly the impact environmental change can have on populations. Bull's work showed the Sleepy Lizards to be unlike any other lizard we know. The first astonishing feature is their longevity, some living up to fifty years. They are omnivorous, feeding on insects, birds' eggs and nestlings, carrion and a range of edible plants. Their home ranges can be as large as 9 hectares, or 90,000 square metres. Hard to imagine, given their rather slow and laborious movements.

Perhaps the most unexpected aspect of Sleepy Lizard biology is their reproductive behaviour, for like us, they form monogamous pair bonds that can last a lifetime. Despite this sexual fidelity, pairs spend much of their time apart, wandering through their expansive home ranges in search of food. But in late spring a male and female will start to spend increasing periods of time together, the male following his partner through their overlapping home ranges. When they become separated, they find each other again via scent trails left on the forest floor. These associations last for about eight weeks before mating finally occurs and then the pair separate again, going their own separate ways to live apart until the following year. Over the course of his studies, Bull made more than 53,000 captures of nearly 12,000 individual sleepy lizards, reporting 110 cases of monogamous pair bonds that lasted for ten years, thirty-one cases of more than fifteen years and one pair that had bred together for twenty-seven consecutive years when last seen together in 2012. He reports one case in which an individual closely attended its partner even after the partner had died. This behaviour is not what one would expect from a lizard. Bull did find some pairs that divorced, after two to three years. These were usually younger lizards. Just why they divorce remains unknown, though Bull suggests that it may follow reproductive failure, as occurs frequently in monogamous bird species.

Sleepy Lizards have many common names, including yoorn, the Noongar name, Shingleback, because of the heavy scaly plates that cover their back, Bobtail, due to their stubby stump-like tails, and Blue Tongue, because of their strikingly coloured tongues. But why would their tongues be blue? New South Wales herpetologist Martin Whiting and his colleagues have argued that the blue tongue is an adaptation to visually startle predators and so protect the lizards from becoming a meal.

The main predators of Sleepy Lizards are large birds of prey, for example, Wedge-tailed Eagles (waalitj) or the Little Eagles we had seen flying across the Darkin River Valley that morning. The tongue would be highly conspicuous to these birds of prey as birds perceive colour very differently from us. We have three types of light-sensitive cells in our eyes that detect red, green and blue light respectively. To us, the Sleepy Lizard's tongue appears dark blue–black at its tip and paler blue further back towards the lizard's throat. Birds, on the other hand, have a fourth colour-sensitive cell that detects light in the ultraviolet. To birds, the Sleepy Lizard's tongue would appear highly reflective bright blue–violet, much like a white shirt would appear to us under the black lights at the local nightclub.

When a Sleepy Lizard is disturbed it will generally remain still or slowly walk away. But if you touch one, it will puff up, throw open its mouth, stick out its tongue and hiss. This striking visual and auditory display, from what is otherwise a very cryptic and camouflaged lizard, would be sufficient to startle any predatory bird that might drop down on it from above, perhaps long enough to allow the lizard to disappear into the bushes. Our Sleepy Lizard obliged us with a magnificent antipredator display when we tried to delay its departure in order to snatch a photograph.

Beraking Hut is perched high on the rim of the valley, with densely wooded slopes offering views across the top of the canopy and down into the valley floor below. As we sat at the picnic bench having afternoon tea, a huge flock of Carnaby's Black Cockatoo (ngoolyak), some fifty head strong, flew by at eye height, their screeches echoing off the sides of the valley. Sooty Tim had, as planned,walked straight through, leaving only a residue of soot on the picnic bench, so we had the peace and tranquillity of Beraking to ourselves.

TOP: A yoorn or Sleepy Lizard, *Tiliqua rugosa*, found en route to Beraking. These lizards form monogamous pair-bonds that can last up to their 30-year lifespan. When disturbed, they will stick out their tongue which reflects ultraviolet, startling would-be predators. Freddy Simmons

MIDDLE: Kwoora or Western Brush Wallaby, *Macropus irma*. Kwoora are fairly common in the woodlands of the Perth hills, and on the track between Waalegh and Gringer Creek. Remarkably cryptic, this animal was adopting the classic freeze and stare antipredator response, bounding off only when we raised our camera to get a photograph. Leigh Simmons

BOTTOM: Ngoolyak or Carnaby's Black Cockatoo, *Calyptorhynchus latirostris*. Large flocks of these nomadic cockatoos can be seen travelling through the forests of the south-west. Their calls are long and wailing *ai-whileer-la* and their flight almost funereal in pace. They feed on the fruit of Marri and on banksia. Their numbers are declining rapidly due to ever increasing land clearing. Leigh Simmons

Alarmingly, we were awoken by gunshots close to the hut, and the sound of an approaching vehicle. I scrambled out of my sleeping bag and dressed hurriedly so as not to be caught off guard. Thankfully, the occupants of the vehicle, alerted by the gunman on the roof to our presence, reversed quickly back down the track that serviced the hut, and left. We guessed, optimistically, that they were out on a Saturday-morning feral pig hunt, though they could equally have been taking shots at the Western Brush Wallabies (kwoora) and Grey Kangaroos (yonga). No wonder the poor creatures are so skittish. Polish behavioural ecologist Adam Zbyryt and his colleagues have recently studied the levels of stress in natural populations of large ungulates in Polish forests. They quantified the levels of stress by analysing the levels of stress hormone metabolites in faecal samples collected from the forest floor. Remarkably, they found that red and roe deer were more stressed by human presence and hunting than by natural predators such as lynx and wolves. Our rude awakening had certainly got our stress hormones pumping.

The track south soon comes to Beraking pine plantation, which it skirts as it plunges down into the valley to cross the Little Darkin River. After a steep ascent we soon entered Dale Conservation Park, passing across granite outcrops with views to the north and east. That day we were to rendezvous with our track elf and her helpers. As we crossed an expansive granite outcrop, Carol and our dear friends Maxine and Ian emerged from the forest to the south, bearing fresh fruit and cheer for second breakfast. Carol had parked the car at Dale Road, to which we now headed to restock our packs. The track rises steadily as it travels through the Jarrah forests that shroud the eastern slopes of Mount Dale. Shortly before reaching Dale Road we passed through an open area with Western Sheoaks (kondil), Bull Banksias (mungitch) and Grasstrees (balga), and extensive areas of white sand. Here, flowering in profusion, we found stands of an extraordinary orchid, Brockman's Flying Duck.

There are currently twelve species of flying duck orchid described from south-western Western Australia, and a single species in eastern Australia. Flying ducks are so named because of their distinctive-looking flower. The labellum, like that of Elbow Orchids, is shaped like a female thynnine wasp, with the same dark-red glandular tissue covering its tip. The labellum is held out

from the rest of the flower on a spring-loaded lip stalk, while the column forms a rounded pouch below. The appearance is of a duck in flight, with the labellum the head of the duck, the lip stalk its neck and the column pouch its body. The sepals hang either side of the pouch like a duck's wings.

Though not closely related to Elbow Orchids, these two species have converged on the same contrivance by which they dupe male thynnine wasps into pollinating them. Thus, flying ducks emit a scent that resembles the pheromone of the female thynnine. The male is attracted to the scent and grabs the female-like labellum, upon which the spring-loaded lip stalk flicks down, carrying the unsuspecting wasp with it and trapping it inside the body of the duck. As the wasp struggles to free itself from the confines of the pouch, the pollen packages are attached to its back for it to carry away and deposit on the next flower that entraps the poor wasp as it searches for a genuine female with which to mate. The remarkable similarity between flying duck and Elbow Orchid labella, in terms of their form and chemical mimicry of the female wasp, is an example of convergent evolution. Both orchids have evolved the same means of attracting their pollinators, although the mechanisms by which they then entrap and attach their pollen to the male wasp are very different.

At the Dale Road picnic area, Carol, Maxine and Ian had a rare treat awaiting us. Lunch that day consisted of three courses with fine Western Australian wines. We dined in style as Wedge-tailed eagles (waalitj) circled above us. Good food, friends and the beauty of the Western Australian bush – what more could we ask for? The walk from Dale Road to Mount Dale Hut was only another 2.5 kilometres, which was just as well given the feast we had consumed.

Mount Dale Hut is wonderfully positioned in thick Jarrah and Marri forest. When we first arrived a male Golden Whistler (bidilmidang) was perched high in a mature Marri broadcasting its loud ringing song: *whit-whit-whit-whiet-wheet-quWHIT*. The male Golden Whistler is highly conspicuous, with a bright golden-yellow belly, black hood and breast band and bright white throat. In contrast the female is drab grey with an olive hue to her shoulders and rump. As for the fairy-wrens, these sexual differences in colour are due to sexual selection. Ornithologists Wouter van Dongen and Raoul Mulder have studied the breeding biology of Golden Whistlers in the Toolangi State Forest in Victoria.

The bright colouration of the male seems to be selected more in the context of male–male competition over breeding territories, with males assessing the competitive abilities of rivals based on the size of the white throat patch. Females, on the other hand, seem to care more about the rate at which males repeat their songs, paying particular attention to males that do so in quick succession.

As I watched the male broadcasting his song, a female arrived and hopped around the branches about a metre or so from the male. He became immediately interested in her, turning his back on her and fluttering his wings while repeating his song, I assume soliciting the female to copulate with him. She watched with interest as the male alternately faced her and sang, then turned away and fluttered his wings. Unimpressed, she soon flew off. Clearly his song rate was not to her taste. The male soon flew off himself, to start up his whistling again some distance from the hut.

Golden Whistlers are a widespread species, occurring throughout the southern regions of western and eastern Australia, and in the east their range extends into far northern Queensland. The population of whistlers in Western Australia has, however, recently been recognised as a separate species, the Western Whistler, because a series of genetic studies found that the sequence of base pairs – the building blocks of DNA – in their genome is distinct from that of eastern states birds. The Western Whistlers appear to be isolated from Golden Whistlers by the Nullarbor Plain, and this geographic separation of populations has resulted in them diverging genetically to form cryptic species, meaning their differences only become apparent when examining their DNA sequences.

Western and Golden Whistlers provide an example of a second mechanism that can generate new species: genetic drift. When DNA is replicated during the production of sperm and egg, random changes in the sequence of base pairs can arise simply by chance. If there is no gene flow between two populations of a species, the accumulation of random mutations can change the genetic make-up of each population. If they are isolated for long enough, such genetic drift can prevent those populations from interbreeding should they come into contact. Unlike adaptive radiation, whereby species arise because of selection acting on traits that make each more suited to its particular habitat, with genetic drift, speciation occurs simply because of the accumulation of random mutations during DNA replication and a lack of gene flow across a physical barrier to dispersal.

After setting up our beds for the night we opened the tin box on the picnic table that housed the registration book, to find a food package addressed to us! Our friend Heidi, herself an end-to-ender, was walking the section of track from Mount Dale to Randall Road and had stayed at Mount Dale the previous night. Seeing that we were on the track from Freddy's Facebook posts, she had left us fresh fruit and two-minute noodles. She was one of many track elves from whose kindness we would benefit on our journey south.

6

From Mount Dale it was a short 8 kilometre walk, mostly downhill, to Brookton. The path largely follows old vehicle tracks through patches of Jarrah/Marri and Wandoo woodlands that periodically open onto clearings where low shrubs dominate the shallow soils that cover the granite bedrock below. It was a chilly morning that took some time to warm up, but the cooler weather was both a welcome break and allowed us to linger in these open spots to marvel at the diversity of flowering plants. Common Smokebush flowered in profusion, as did Graceful Honeymyrtle (moorngan), while two species of pea, Heart-leaf Flame Pea and Handsome Wedge-pea, offered splashes of red and vibrant violet–blue respectively. A bright-red landing strip runs through the middle of the blue petals of the wedge-pea, guiding pollinating insects to the flower's nectaries. Plumed Featherflower offered a pale-purple contrast to the vibrant violet–blue of the wedge-pea, and the creamy-white hakea flowers infused the air with a sickly honey odour.

Two species of hakea were present in these clearings: the Harsh Hakea (berrung) with its spiky holly-like leaves; and Christmas Hakea (tanjinn) or Needle Tree, so called because of its sharp needle-like leaves. Stands of Milkwort lined the edges of the track, with their racemes of purple flowers. One particularly interesting species of grevillea was common through this area, the Fuchsia Grevillea, so called, I assume, because of the resemblance of the drooping heavy inflorescences to hanging fuchsia flowers. The abundant sticky nectar, which will splash onto your hand if you shake the flower gently, was providing a veritable feast for the Singing Honeyeaters (kool-boort).

We arrived at Brookton Hut just in time to shelter from a heavy thunderstorm that provided enough water from the overflowing gutters to wash both ourselves and our clothes. By mid-afternoon the storm had passed and the hot sun quickly dried the pools of water that had gathered around the hut. That evening we enjoyed a campfire, the only one we were to have on our journey, as we were days from the onset of the annual fire ban. But it was fun sitting around the fire in the cool evening watching the Tree Martins (kabi-kalangkoorong) hawking for insects in the fading light.

7

Next day we had a rendezvous with the track elves at Brookton Highway. The walk to the highway was just 2.5 kilometres, following the line of the pylons through a low-lying winter-wet swamp. An Australian Hobby (wowoo) flew low and fast across this open, now-dry swampland, no doubt in search of some small bird with which to feed its brood. It disappeared into the top of a tall Marri on the edge of the highway, probably nesting in an abandoned raven's nest high in its crown, as is their habit. After crossing the highway, we met up with Carol, this time accompanied by our old friends Jean and Peter, who were to walk with us to Abyssinia Rock. This was well-trodden ground for us, as we had done the return walk to the rock, which offers an ideal day hike within striking distance of Perth, many times.

After a quick restock in the parking area, we set off along the track, which climbs steadily to the top of a rocky ridge providing fine views to the south. The track then drops down the escarpment to the valley below and joins a vehicle track that leads to the base of Abyssinia Rock. Here we climbed to the summit and found a shady spot for an early lunch, which included treats of freshly brewed coffee from Jean and Peter's trusty thermos, fresh fruit and chocolate. After saying our farewells, we went our separate ways, the track elves back to their cars and us on to Canning Hut. The track passes through a beautiful area of low-lying swampland, with stretches of white sandy soil and stands of mature Swamp Banksia (pungura) and Swamp Paperbark (yowarl).

During the winter months this stretch of track would likely present opportunities for some serious wading, but it hadn't been

inundated for a long time when we walked through. As the track began to rise again, we passed through a grove of Western Sheoak (kondil) with the occasional Western Australian Christmas Tree (mooja), not yet revealing the spectacle that their flowering would offer in a few weeks' time. And so we arrived at Canning Hut, which is set 50 metres off the track, slightly elevated and surrounded by huge Marri.

Every hut it seemed would offer its own unique birding experience. Here at Canning we were treated to an afternoon spectacle of twenty or more Rainbow Bee-eaters (birin-birin) circling in the gaps in the Marri canopy, snatching bees that had come to feed on the Marri flowers. They gave the appearance of having immense fun, at first swooping high and then plummeting down at breakneck speed. These antics were accompanied by their cheery, shrill calls: *pirr-pirrrp-pirr-pirr-pirrr-pirr-pirrrp*. The flashes of bright-orange underwing, bright-green breast and turquoise belly were mesmerising. They must also have been taking insects from the ground, as periodically they would drop to the sand paths just metres from where we sat watching them. In his *Birds of Australia*, John Gould, the famous illustrator and publisher of works on birds in Victorian England, said that 'This bird has so many attractions that it will doubtless always be regarded as a general favourite with the Australians; the extreme beauty of its plumage, the elegance of its form, and the graceful manner of its flight all combining to render it especially worthy of their notice; besides which, many pleasing associations are connected with it, for its arrival is a certain harbinger of the return of spring.'

Gould was, of course, referring to the migratory habits of the Rainbow Bee-eater, which spends the winter in the islands of the Malay Archipelago, from Lombok in the west through to New Guinea in the east and Sulawesi in the north. The birds move south into Australia in the spring, arriving in September often at the same breeding ground that they used the previous year. They nest in small colonies on flat or gently sloping open ground, on which they excavate a burrow. The entrance is typically beneath a rock or tussock that serves to prevent the entrance from collapsing, and the tunnel travels about 1 metre underground to a nesting chamber where the eggs are laid and incubated.

Like the Kookaburra, Rainbow Bee-eaters are cooperative breeders. A breeding pair can be assisted by one to six helpers, usually unpaired males, with all birds assisting in tunnel

construction, incubation and the feeding of chicks once the eggs have hatched. Just why some bird species breed cooperatively has been a longstanding question among evolutionary biologists such as Andrew Cockburn and Ben Hatchwell. It is thought that strong philopatry – a lack of dispersal from the breeding sites – particularly by males, may play some role in the evolution of cooperative breeding. Sex-biased philopatry can lead to an accumulation in the environment of males that will be unable to obtain territories and mates. In such circumstances the only opportunity for a male to produce offspring would be via helping to raise younger siblings, a behaviour that would be favoured by kin selection.

The Rainbow Bee-eater might contradict this hypothesis, given that it is one of few migratory birds that breed cooperatively. However, the fact that it returns to the same breeding ground year after year will have the same effect as never leaving the breeding ground at all, especially if birds retain kin-structured social groupings during migration to the wintering grounds in the north. Evidence that the availability of mating partners is important for the manifestation of cooperative breeding comes from recent work on the European Nuthatch by James Cox and his colleagues, who showed that experimentally biasing the population towards an excess of either males or females can generate helping by the over-represented sex.

There is also evidence, from studies looking at the distribution of cooperatively breeding species across the world, that habitat quality might play a role in the evolution of cooperative breeding. Cooperative breeding is most commonly associated with environments that are highly unpredictable in terms of temperature, rainfall and food availability. Environmental unpredictability might explain why cooperative breeders tend to be more common in southern latitudes and in Australia, but exactly how this has evolved is unclear. It might be that environmental uncertainty favours the evolution of cooperation because groups of related birds are more successful at breeding during harsh years than are pairs, or it might be that cooperatively breeding birds are more resilient to environmental change, resulting in their persistence when environments become highly variable – a subtle but important difference between evolutionary cause and effect. There must have been a large colony of Rainbow Bee-eaters pretty close to Canning Hut, given the density of birds hunting among the Marri that afternoon.

Mid-afternoon, a fellow walker, soon to earn the track name of Action Man, arrived at the hut. Action Man pulled off his boots, prepared his lunch and began to tell us of all the new equipment that he had recently acquired, having worn his old kit out walking through Europe the previous August. While my eyes glazed over, Freddy gallantly engaged him in discussion on the various merits of inflatable versus solid mattresses, the weights and dimensions of various brands of tent, and how much weight each of us was carrying. Action Man seemed incredulous to discover that we had been walking now for just over a week. How on earth could we have taken so long to reach Canning? He had only decided on Saturday to walk the Bibbulmun, and he had caught up with us in just two days! Action Man replaced his boots and repacked his gear. Rather scathingly, he announced that he had 48 kilometres to walk today, lamented that after the first 20 kilometres or so the track was pretty much all the same, and marched off. I wonder if he even noticed the spectacle that revolved above his head.

8

We woke to another blissfully cool morning, with a predicted top of 25 degrees Celsius. We were being extremely fortunate with the weather for mid-November. The 16.5 kilometre walk to Monadnocks Hut would take us through some stunning changes of habitat. First back down into low wetland areas dominated by ancient Swamp Paperbarks (yowarl) and Coastal Tea-trees, and then steadily up into a stretch of old-growth Jarrah forest in the Monadnocks Conservation Park.

The Jarrah through here are magnificent, so tall and thickly girthed that you could almost believe them to be different species from the smaller trees that characterise the managed forests to the north. The understorey was also more diverse, no doubt due to the lack of repeated disturbance that characterises managed forests. Bull Banksia (mungitch) and Western Sheoak (kondil) were abundant, but larger and more mature than those in the forests to the north. There were clumps of False Blind Grass with their purple flowers; stands of Pincushion Hakea, not yet in flower; and two species of grasstree, the ubiquitous balga and the small Graceful Grasstree (mimidi).

There were also stands of Kingia. This species, closely related to the grasstrees, is found only in south-west Western Australia. Kingia can grow extremely tall in these old-growth forests, and live between 750 and 900 years. Two species of grevillea were in flower: the vibrant red Wilson's Grevillea and the sparse white-flowered Mangles Grevillea. There was also an abundance of very large Spreading Snottygobbles (kadgeegurr), with their dark trunks and fresh vibrant-green leaves, like bright-green beacons in the forest. Spreading Snottygobbles are a species of persoonia, and get their name from the slimy consistency of their fruits. Eaten by Emus (wetj) and Western Grey Kangaroos (yonga), the seeds are passed out in the animals' faeces, along with a ready dose of fertiliser for germination.

After passing through this section of old-growth Jarrah, the track descended slowly through a series of granite clearings to the Canning River. Shortly before arriving at the river crossing, we were stopped abruptly in our tracks by a large Gould's Goanna (kaarda; *Varanus gouldii*) warming itself in the early morning sun. Too cold to move, it simply ignored us as we passed by. Gould's Goanna is named after John Gould, the Victorian ornithologist who was so enamoured of Rainbow Bee-eaters. Goannas belong to a geographically widespread group of lizards known as varanids. They are carnivores, feeding on small mammals, other reptiles, frogs, and the eggs and nestlings of birds. Indeed, Gould's Goanna has been reported to be a predator of Rainbow Bee-eater nests, entering the breeding tunnels to access the eggs and chicks within. They are adept diggers and climbers, using their exceedingly long and sharp claws to crack open termite mounds, and to scamper up the trunks of trees. Remarkably, they will even feed on Tiger Snakes (moyop; *Notechis scutatus*), apparently immune to the venom that will kill a human. Thankfully, our largest species of goanna is the Perentie, found across northern Australia, for their close relative, the Komodo Dragon, reaches 3 metres, weighs up to 70 kilograms, and will kill and eat water buffalo and even humans if given half the chance. While Gould's Goanna is considerably smaller, at just 1.5 metres and up to 6 kilograms, it could nonetheless give a nasty bite, and its claws could do some serious damage, so it is always best to give one a wide berth.

Before crossing the Canning River bridge, we paused briefly for second breakfast, and watched a small flock of Black-faced Woodswallows (biwoyen) hawking for insects above the granite outcrop, New Holland Honeyeaters (bandiny) chattering and

TOP: Birin-birin or Rainbow Bee-eater, *Merops ornatus*, spend the winter in the islands of the Malay Archipelago, from Lombok in the west through to New Guinea in the east and Sulawesi in the north. The birds move south into Australia in the spring, arriving in September often at the same breeding ground that they used the previous year. Leigh Simmons

MIDDLE: Bidilmidang or Western Whistler, *Pachycephala occidentalis*. This species was recognised as distinct from the Eastern Australian Golden Whistlers in 2015, based on differences in the sequence of base-pairs in its DNA. The eastern and western populations diverged due to their reproductive isolation after the last glacial maximum. The vibrant yellow, white throat, and black band and hood, appear to serve as badges of status in aggressive interactions between males. Leigh Simmons

BOTTOM: Djida or Yellow-rumped Thornbill, *Acanthiza chrysorrhoa*. Common in woodlands, heath and farmlands these birds search for insects on the ground. They decorate their nests with moss, and the webs and egg sacs of spiders. Leigh Simmons

chasing each other from tree to tree, and a solitary Red-eared Firetail (djiri) that shot from one side of the outcrop to the other, olive green with a striking red tail. From the river came the sounds of Slender Tree Frogs (*Litoria adelaidensis)* and Clicking Froglets *(Crinia glauerti)*, the latter sounding like marbles in a jar being turned repeatedly on its ends. The water in the river was perfectly still, providing reflections of the Jarrah that lined its banks. After crossing the Canning, the track climbed steadily through old-growth forest until it finally reached Monadnocks Hut, perched high on a ridge at the start of the Monadnocks Range, with glimpses through the trees to Mount Cuthbert and Mount Vincent beyond. This is one of the most beautiful huts on the track. The Holly-leaved Mirbelia that grows all around it was covered in purple flowers. That afternoon we saw Striated Pardalotes (wida-wida) gleaning insects from the leaves of the surrounding Jarrah; and Variegated Fairy-wrens, with their silvery azure crown, black throat and bright-red shoulders. There is no Noongar name for the Variegated Fairy-wren, which is not distinguished from the Red-winged Fairy-wren, no doubt because the two species differ little in appearance, only in their geographical distribution, Variegated in the north and Red-winged in the south. But the birds that were to entertain us at Monadnocks Hut turned out to be a pair of Rufous Treecreepers (djini), which periodically came down to drink from the tap on the water butt, and to search the ground beneath the picnic table, and the sleeping shelves inside the hut, for any scraps that we might have left behind.

9

We were up and out by five-thirty next morning. The topology of the next 14 kilometres to Mount Cooke Hut had been playing on my mind for the last few days. Daunted by the prospect of ascending and descending not one but two mountains, we wanted to be at the summit of Mount Vincent by 10 am because the temperature was tipped to hit a high of 38 degrees Celsius by midday. Carrying 18 kilograms up a mountain in the heat was sure to bring out the Dementors. We were also going to meet up with Carol at the summit of Mount Vincent for second breakfast. The climb up Mount Cuthbert was spectacular. Steep in many places,

but we nonetheless made good time to the summit in the cool of the breaking day. The final stretch is up a very steep granite slope, but the view east from the summit was worth every step, across Jarrah forests as far as the eye can see.

On our ascent of the granite slope we sent many Ornate Dragons (yorndi; *Ctenophorus ornatus*), scuttling for cover under the exfoliating slabs of rock. Ornate Dragons are found exclusively on the granite outcrops of the south-west of Western Australia, and have many adaptations to life on these harsh, exposed landscapes. Their bodies are extremely flattened, appearing almost two-dimensional, which allows them to shelter within the narrowest of cracks in the granite, where they escape from extreme heat and predators. They are also remarkably cryptic, the markings on their bodies blending perfectly with the lichen-covered surface of the rocks on which they bask.

Both males and females are territorial, partitioning up the rock surface and defending large areas against intruders. Males typically have the larger territories, and not surprisingly they overlap the smaller territories of females so as to gain access to mating opportunities. During the breeding season males develop a black chest patch, which they display to other males via head-bobbing or push-up displays at their territory boundaries. One of my former students at the University of Western Australia, Natasha LeBas, found that males with larger chest patches command larger territories, providing them with access to a greater number of females. This suggests that chest patches act as badges of status, allowing males to assess the fighting prowess of their rivals without resorting to potentially damaging physical contests. Chest patches are thereby sexually selected through male competition for access to territories and mates. Females, on the other hand, appear uninterested in the size of a male's chest patch; a male's reproductive success ultimately depends more on his body size and, interestingly, the shape of his head! The extent to which female choice dictates the reproductive success of large males with thicker heads is yet to be established.

Granite outcrops are a common feature of the landscape throughout south-western Western Australia, and they vary considerably in both size and distance from each other. From an Ornate Dragon's perspective, outcrops are like islands in a sea of bushland that must be traversed if the lizards are to disperse. Once mated, females leave their granite outcrop and deposit their eggs

in chambers that they dig in the soil around the outcrop's periphery. On hatching, the young dragons will disperse from the nest, some returning to the granite outcrop on which they were conceived, others heading off through the forest towards a neighbouring outcrop. When a young dragon disperses to a nearby outcrop to grow up and subsequently breed, the result will be gene flow from one outcrop's population of dragons to another's. By examining the genomes of dragons across multiple outcrops, LeBas and her colleagues were able to show that populations of dragons are genetically isolated by the distance between adjacent outcrops; there are high levels of gene flow between outcrops in close proximity, such as Mount Cuthbert and Mount Vincent, which are separated by a short stretch of Jarrah forest that covers the saddle between them, but lower levels of gene flow to more distant outcrops, such as Abyssinia Rock or Mount Dale to the north.

Gene flow is healthy for populations, as it prevents the accumulation of genetic mutations that can be harmful. But for the most part there have been considerable changes to the landscape since European settlers came to Western Australia, with huge swathes of land cleared for growing wheat or raising livestock. Granite outcrops have largely been spared because they are unsuitable for agricultural purposes. All else being equal this might be thought as being good for outcrop specialists like Ornate Dragons. The clearing of native bushland between outcrops has, however, increased the barriers to dispersal for their inhabitants. Gene flow between populations of Ornate Dragons is much lower between outcrops in the wheat belt than between outcrops within natural areas of bushland, and the genetic isolation by distance in the wheat belt much more severe. In consequence, the relatedness among individuals on outcrops within the wheat belt is much higher. When relatives produce offspring together, harmful mutations are more likely to be expressed in their offspring, which will then fail to survive. The result can be further reductions in population size, which exacerbates the problem of mating with relatives, so that populations ultimately go extinct. Such findings illustrate the hazards of habitat fragmentation by human activities, and the importance of developing natural bushland corridors for animal and plant dispersal.

After descending Mount Cuthbert and traversing the saddle, we ascended Mount Vincent. The climb was extremely challenging but thankfully short, and we soon summited to find Carol waiting

with fresh oranges and good cheer. This section of the track was also well-trodden ground for us, the hike from Albany Highway across Sullivan Rock and up Mount Vincent being a frequent trip with visitors, especially in the spring when the slopes are rich with orchids. Encouraged to have Cuthbert and Vincent behind us, we descended through the Jarrah forest, past stunning clumps of vibrant-red Crinkle-leaf Poison, to the edge of Sullivan Rock. There we sheltered from the sun, had an early lunch and restocked our packs before heading off across the 6 kilometres of relatively flat exposed terrain to Mount Cooke Hut. The sandy track across these open plains was hot and dry, dotted with Coastal Tea-trees, Jarrah and Grasstrees (balga). Clumps of synapheas provided bursts of yellow along the narrow sandy track, which seemed endless in the rising heat of the day.

At midday we took shelter under the shade of a Western Australian Christmas Tree (mooja), something the Noongar would never do, for the mooja has great spiritual significance, as 'the tree of souls of the newly dead'. It is said that the spirits of the recently departed camp on the branches and flowers of the mooja on their journey to the land of ancestors. The anthropologist Daisy Bates wrote that 'No living Bibbulmun ever sheltered or rested beneath the shade of the tree of souls; no flower or bud or leaf of the tree was ever touched by child or adult; no game that took shelter beneath it was ever disturbed.' But we were in serious risk of becoming spirits ourselves in the now blistering sun. How good it was to finally arrive at Mount Cooke Hut that day.

In the late afternoon, as the sun began to set and the air began to cool, a chorus of ground crickets *(Bobilla bivittata)*, began calling from beneath the leaf litter around the hut. These crickets produce their calls using highly modified wings. Only male crickets call, and so only males have the wing modifications that allow them to generate sound. They do so to attract the females for mating. Female crickets typically show strong preferences for calls that convey information regarding the male's qualities as a potential mate, the acoustic equivalent of the male fairy-wren's brilliant-blue feathers. Within each of the male wings is a triangular area called a harp. The two harps act as resonators that are excited when a plectrum on the edge of the left-hand wing is rubbed along a toothed file that sits on the underside of the right wing, just below the harp. Thus the male sits with his wings raised above his body and rapidly opens and closes them, with one wing

closure producing a single pulse of sound from the harps set in resonance by the drawing of the plectrum across the comb. The faster the closing and opening of the wings, the faster the series of sound pulses.

The species of ground cricket at Mount Cooke Hut produces chirps that are a collection of fifty to sixty pulses within one second, and these chirps are repeated every two seconds. These crickets can also increase the volume of their calls by placing themselves between dry curled leaves so that the space between them and the leaf surface acts as an amplifier, increasing the distance over which females can hear their chirps, and so the chances of attracting a female. The better a male can do so, the more likely he is to mate and father offspring, so that sexual selection acts not just on the sound-producing apparatus, but also on how males use it. How sweet it was to fall asleep that night to the sound of singing crickets.

10

We rose early again the next day, with Mount Cooke looming ahead of us, the highest of the Monadnocks. Sooty Tim had commented in the logbook at Mount Cooke Hut, 'Mountains over. Yay.' Clearly he was not carrying a map, or he would have known that Mount Cooke is the tallest of the Monadnocks at 566 metres, and the morning's climb up its northern face would be a significant challenge. But the walk to Nerang Hut would be relatively short, just 13.4 kilometres, and the weather had cooled significantly, making it an enjoyable one. The biodiversity of plants on the slopes and summit of Mount Cooke is quite extraordinary. On the track to the summit were several species of grevillea, including Beautiful Grevillea and Fuchsia Grevillea; several species of hakea including Candle Hakea, Harsh Hakea (berrung), Wavy-leaved Hakea and Honeybush (djanda); and numerous species of acacia, including Winged Wattle and Net-leaved Wattle.

We reached the summit by 7.15 am, and so took our time to soak in the spectacular views north through the Monadnocks to Mounts Vincent, Cuthbert and Randall. A couple of Freddy's climbing buddies, Matt and Jess, met us at the top of Mount Cooke, bringing gifts of hot tea for second breakfast. The walk

across the ridge and then down the southern face of Mount Cooke was beautiful, scattered with giant granite boulders and vibrant-green stands of Pincushion Hakea, Albizia and Granite Net-bush. Like the Ornate Dragons (yorndi), Granite Net-bush is typically restricted to granite outcrops. Fire ecologist Neil Burrows studied the recovery of Granite Net-bush after the 2003 wildfire that consumed much of the vegetation on Mount Cooke. It regenerated rapidly from seed stored in its woody capsules and the population reached reproductive maturity in about seven years. Burrows estimated that recovery of the seed bank would take around fourteen years, illustrating how frequent fires in the forest matrix can lead to the extinction of fire-sensitive plants like Granite Net-bush, and restrict them to areas such as outcrops where fire is less frequent.

After descending Mount Cooke, the Bibbulmun follows vehicle tracks through Jarrah woodlands for most of the way, eventually entering Wandoo flats before reaching a creek, which is followed for some distance and then crossed to reach Nerang, Noongar for 'little house by water'. Just before crossing the creek, we walked through a large stand of Velvet Hemigenia that was swarming with native Blue-banded Bees (ngoowak; *Amegilla cingulata*). After dropping my pack, I hurried back to observe and photograph this spectacle.

We typically think of bees as social insects, nesting in large colonies led by a single reproductive queen that produces thousands of sterile female workers that care for and raise future reproductive males and females. In stark contrast, Blue-banded Bees are solitary insects. Females reproduce alone, though they do build their individual nests in close proximity to those of other females, often forming large aggregations in the banks of dried-up rivers and creeks. There must have been a large aggregation of nesting bees nearby because they do not travel far from the source of pollen and nectar that they use to provision their offspring.

Each female digs a tunnel into the ground that terminates in a brood cell. Once the cell is dug, she will line it with wax to protect it from moisture during the winter months when the creek is flowing. She will then make several trips to the host plant, in this case the Velvet Hemigenia, to collect pollen and nectar, which she will deposit in the brood cell before laying an egg, sealing the cell and then backfilling the nest. The egg will hatch in just a few weeks, and the grub will feed on the pollen and nectar soup

provided by its mother, growing quickly into a bee-sized grub that then enters a period of dormancy until the following summer, when it will emerge as an adult bee that digs its way out of the underground nursery. Male bees typically emerge first and search for females that emerge later, mating with them before they leave the aggregation to make their own way in the world.

While watching the Blue-banded Bees, I also saw Lesser Wanderer *(Danaus chrysippus)* butterflies passing down the creek bed, and managed to pick up two huge ticks that embedded themselves firmly into my thigh, and a smaller one that only made it as far as my knee before burrowing in. It took some pulling to persuade these parasites to relinquish their grip, and I was irked by the thought of yet more constantly itching welts to add to the growing collection. These parasites were an absolute scourge, as were the Horseflies that constantly landed and started drilling into my flesh as I tried to photograph the bees. Parasites come in all shapes and sizes, from ectoparasites such as ticks, to single-celled organisms that live inside the body, such as the parasite that causes malaria. Often these endoparasites are transmitted to their hosts by ectoparasites, as in tick-borne fever. Almost all species suffer attack from parasites of one form or another, and in fact they have been critical for the evolution of life on Earth. Indeed, parasites are thought to have played a role in the evolution of exaggerated ornaments of sexual selection that are the focus of female choice.

Imagine a jar of Bertie Bott's Every Flavour Beans. Some are a delicious fruit flavour while others taste of earwax. Imagine too that each time we take a fruit-flavoured bean, five new fruit-flavoured beans are added to the jar, and each time we take an earwax-flavoured bean, five new earwax-flavoured beans are added to the jar. Of course we all want the fruit-flavoured beans and will reject those tasting of earwax. If we can tell which is which by looking at the colour of the bean, say fruit-flavoured beans are red while earwax-flavoured beans are brown, we will soon learn to take the red beans and leave the brown ones. Over time, the number of red beans in the jar will increase relative to the number of brown beans because one red bean is replaced by another five, so that they multiply rapidly relative to brown beans, which are not taken. Before long, the probability of taking a fruit-flavoured bean from the jar is so high that it ceases to be necessary to look at the colour – no point in being choosy anymore because almost all the beans are fruit-flavoured. All else being equal, this thought

experiment is what should happen when females choose their mates based on genetic quality; if all females choose males with good genes and produce offspring with those good genes, then soon the population will consist of only males with good genes, making female choice redundant.

Evolutionary biologists William Hamilton and Marlene Zuk realised that parasites can be key in maintaining female choice of males with showy ornaments because parasites are the variable in the equation that make all things unequal. When parasites infest their hosts, some hosts will successfully rid themselves of their unwelcome guests, either behaviourally by pulling the little buggers off as I did, or by mounting an immunological attack that kills the parasite. Hosts bearing genes that enable them to resist infection from parasites will increase in frequency in the population because they will not suffer the negative consequences of becoming infected. However, parasites have genes too, and those that are better able to circumvent evolving host immunity will increase in frequency. In this way, parasites and hosts are locked in a never-ending cycle of adaptation and counter-adaptation for parasite virulence and host resistance. Hamilton and Zuk realised that because the ornaments of sexual selection are costly for males to produce and display, they would always be revealing of a male's underlying health and of his genetic quality in terms of his resistance to parasites. Genetic variance for this resistance will be maintained because of the constant coevolution with the third parties in the equation – parasites. When we look at the beauty of animals around us, we should appreciate the role that parasites have played in their evolution. But parasites can also be beautiful in their own right.

Many plants are parasitic. The Western Australian Christmas Tree (mooja) is a case in point, being a member of the mistletoe family. When young, the Christmas Tree's roots fuse with those of grasses and small shrubs, sucking water from their hosts to sustain their own growth. As they become larger, their roots travel further afield, grafting onto large shrubs and trees that serve as host to the mature trees. And how beautiful they are when flowering in late December. We saw two other parasitic plants that day: Broomrape was flowering on the summit of Mount Cooke, and Dodder was growing into the Grasstree (balga) fronds and Ramshorn Hakea growing in front of Nerang Hut. Broomrape has no chlorophyll of its own, and relies entirely on its host for nutrients and water,

TOP: Boyidjil or White-breasted Robin, *Eopsaltria georgiana*. Endemic to the south-west, this robin inhabits both Jarrah and Karri forests where it clings to the trunks of trees searching for insects, or drops to the ground from low perches to seize insects from the leaf litter. Leigh Simmons

MIDDLE: Bandiny or New Holland Honeyeater, *Phylidonyris novaehollandiae*. One of our most common honeyeaters throughout the south-west, in forests and coastal heaths, often travelling in large flocks constantly chattering among themselves, *tjik!* and *chwik!*. Leigh Simmons

BOTTOM: Kaarda or Gould's Goanna, *Varanus gouldii*. Our most widespread and abundant goanna. They are formidable predators of small mammals, frogs and birds. They are significant predators at Rainbow Bee-eater nests, digging into the birds' subterranean tunnels to access the eggs and chicks within. They will scale trees to reach the eggs and chicks of tree-nesting birds and will even eat tiger snakes, apparently immune to their highly toxic venom. Freddy Simmons

which it obtains by grafting its roots onto those of its host. Dodder is a remarkable plant in that it has no roots in the ground at all, but rather it grows into the vascular systems of its hosts above ground. Like ticks, Dodder is an ectoparasite, not of animals but of other plants, and can move through the undergrowth as it grows from host to host. Remarkably, Dodder uses airborne volatile compounds to sniff out its preferred hosts and grow towards them.

In addition to the parasites, we added several new birds to our list at Nerang: an Inland Thornbill (djoobi-djoolbang), a White-breasted Robin (boyidjil) and a pair of Grey Butcherbirds (wardawort) set the ambiance of the hut. In their *eGuide to the Birds of Australia*, Michael Morcombe and David Stewart describe the calls of the Grey Butcherbird as rich and varied, at times slow deep mellow songs, and at others vigorous piping notes that develop a strident quality. In the late afternoon, this pair contributed to the beauty and tranquillity of Nerang with their deep mellow songs, *quorrok-a-quokoo*, and bubbling *kworrok-a-chowk-chowk-chowk-chowk* as the shadows grew long and the sun cast its golden rays across the Wandoo woodland.

11

As we left Nerang the following morning, it was to a farewell from the resident Western Grey Shrike-thrush (koodilang). What this pale grey bird lacks in colour it makes up for with its haunting melodic calls – deep-throated, almost fluid whistles that echoed far across the woodlands: *wheit-wheit, WHIEET-chiew, wheit-wheit, WHIEET-chiew*. The call followed us for several hundred metres, fading gradually in the still morning as we walked south through the Wandoo-lined creek bed. From Nerang the 16.8 kilometre walk to Gringer Creek is reasonably flat, a blessed relief after the Monadnocks, and passes largely through Wandoo creek beds that feed the headwaters of the Canning and Serpentine rivers. No sign of water this time of year, but clearly these low-lying flood plains would be inundated in winter.

Along the route we spotted Western Yellow Robins (bamboon) dropping down into the creek bed to seize their insect prey; and Rufous Treecreepers (djini), with their shrill *peep-peep-peep*, gleaning insects from the bark of the Wandoo. At times it felt like

we were literally walking back into spring. Many of the flowers, long since finished further north, were still putting on a fine display: Purple Flags; Scented Banjine; Common Smokebush; carpets of mauve Swan River Daisy; Cunningham's Guinea Flower, with its distinctive stem-hugging leaves that are not too dissimilar in structure from those of Bookleaf Peas; and Star Guinea Flower, a prostrate species of hibbertia that thrives in winter-wet depressions and can have the yellow flowers typical of hibbertia or brilliant orange flowers that give it its other common name of Orange Stars. On one large, flat granite section stood tall stands of vivid pink Kunzea.

The last 4 kilometres of the track rises back into mixed Jarrah and Marri woodland. Fox Banksia (nugoo), with its perfectly spherical cones and pine-like foliage, were an abundant feature of the understorey through these woodlands. We arrived at Gringer Creek Hut in just over four and a half hours, and after setting up camp we took the 1 kilometre spur trail into North Bannister for a well-earned cold beer and a burger lunch, something that came highly recommend by Sooty Tim in the walkers' log.

12

Next morning we had a rendezvous with Carol and our supplies box on Wearne Road. This would be our last meeting for some time, as we were now too far from Perth to expect her to come out with supplies. So we stocked our packs to capacity, with the inevitable increase in pack weight. We also took the opportunity to dress our interminably itchy tick bites with lashings of hydrocortisone cream that she had brought with her.

Carol and Freddy went off in the car to North Bannister to purchase breakfast, while I stayed with the packs and did some early morning birding. As well as the usual suspects of the Jarrah forest, a new bird for the list was a Horsfield's Bronze Cuckoo (koodooban), which sat high in a tree broadcasting its sharp descending whistle: *tsieew, tsieew, tsieew*. These birds are social parasites, laying a single egg in the nest of another species. The primary hosts of Horsfield's Bronze Cuckoo are fairy-wrens, but they will lay their eggs in the nests of other species with red-brown speckled eggs, such as thornbills, robins and honeyeaters.

The resemblance of the cuckoo's egg to those of its host prevents the egg from being recognised and tossed from the nest by the unsuspecting foster parents. Once the cuckoo chick hatches, however, it will toss out the fairy-wren eggs before they have the opportunity to hatch.

Horsfield's Bronze Cuckoo chicks not only mimic the visual appearance of fairy-wren chicks but will also mimic their begging calls, to dupe the foster parents into keeping them and providing them with food. The resemblance between fairy-wren and cuckoo chicks is another example of a coevolutionary cycle between a parasite and its host. The cuckoo eggs and then chicks are selected over generations to resemble the host eggs and chicks because those that do not are rejected from the nest. Any change in fairy-wrens that results in cuckoo chicks being recognised and rejected will be countered by selection on cuckoos to better deceive the host parent. Australian behavioural ecologist Naomi Langmore, who has studied these birds in some detail, has reported that when cuckoos lay their eggs in the nests of alternative hosts, such as thornbills and robins, the chicks will quickly learn the begging calls of the novel host from feedback they get from the host parents. Such behavioural plasticity affords greater opportunity for cuckoo reproduction when fairy-wren nests are unavailable.

After breakfast, Carol walked with us for the first 5 kilometres along the boundary of farmland to the foot of Kimberling Hill. The highlight along this stretch of the track was a Christmas Beetle, a species of stag beetle (*Lamprima micardi*) that is a beautiful iridescent green with a golden head. These stag beetles are known as Christmas Beetles because of the time of year that the adults can be found, but they are not the same species as the beetle given that name in the eastern states. Therein lies the problem with common names, and the need for Linnaeus' binomial nomenclature. The Western Australian Christmas Beetle breeds in summer, the females laying their eggs in rotting logs on the forest floor. When they hatch, the larvae burrow through the log, feeding on the rotten wood and emerging as adults the following summer. The males have modified mandibles, enlarged by sexual selection as weapons with which to fight other males for access to the females. The mandibles in several species can be so enlarged that they resemble the antlers of male deer, hence the common name stag beetle. The female we found was on a rotting tree stump by the roadside, no doubt in the process of laying her eggs.

Carol had the good sense to turn back at the stage where the track begins the first of many steep ascents through the White Horse Hills. According to *A Guide to the Bibbulmun Track*, this is another of the more challenging sections. Too right it was, especially with the increased pack weight. The 100 metre ascent of Boonerring Hill was steep and arduous, and the fact that we were walking much later in the day than usual, due to our restock at Wearne Road, meant that it was also incredibly hot. The track here was also poorly signposted; Waugals were few and very far between. This would not ordinarily be a problem because the track is well trodden, but so too were several tracks over which the Bibbulmun crossed. Thankfully, Freddy's trusty Garmin kept us from wandering off course.

The views back to Mount Cooke and Mount Dale from the top of Boonerring Hill were spectacular, and the granite clearings across its saddle were brilliant yellow, bedecked with dense stands of Yellow Featherflower. From Boonerring Hill the track descends 200 metres to a dry plain. This had recently been burnt, and the track followed dusty roads that offered little shade and little to distract our attention from the searing heat. Boonerring Spring was little more than a stagnant puddle. The Dementors seemed to be particularly abundant through this stretch, which turned into an onerous route-march that seemed to go on for hours. The track guide describes this section as an attractive Wandoo flat, which it may well have been before it was burnt.

Eventually we left the burnt area and began our 150 metre ascent of Kimberling Hill. Now physically drained, it was hard to keep going. Nonetheless there were some treats, including Oak-leaved Grevillea, no longer flowering but easily identified from its characteristic leaves; and the extraordinary Bookleaf Pea, with its seed pods encased between two modified leaves. Two species of acacia were also abundant, Prickly Moses (mindaleny) and Net-leaved Wattle. Finding new plants by the wayside provided a distraction from the uphill slog, which eventually abated at the granite summit of Kimberling Hill with spectacular views north to Boonerring and the Monadnocks beyond. Finally we descended through Wandoo woodland to White Horse Hills Hut, totally exhausted. Too many hills, too late in the day, and just too damned hot. That evening we were in our sleeping bags by six-thirty.

13

The next morning offered a pleasant walk along the granite ridge of the White Horse Hills. What a perfect way to start the first day of the Noongar season of birak, season of the young. The track passed through patches of Jarrah and Sheoak, skirted several granite flats with fine views to the north and east, and wound its way through massive granite boulders as it ascended to the granite dome of the southern peak of White Horse Hills. From here we began our descent through the Jarrah forest.

At a clearing about halfway down, we paused for a while to identify some of the many birds that were flitting through the low shrubs: Weebills (djiyaderbaat); a Western Rosella (bardinar); a Striated Pardalote (wida-wida); and a magnificent male Western Spinebill (booldjit), with its long curved bill, black-and-white-striped face, deep rufous throat, and white and black breast bands. There were five or six spinebills in this clearing, darting out from their perches to snatch insects in flight, and calling to each other: *chri-chri-chri-chri-chip-chip*. Shortly after leaving the clearing we flushed an Emu (wetj), which rushed off into the woodlands in alarm.

Once down from the White Horse Hills, the going was pretty flat for some 10 kilometres or so as we passed through the Jarrah and Sheoak woodlands towards the foothills of Mount Wells. According to the track notes, we had another 'quite challenging' climb to look forward to. As the track started gently upward, we happened upon a pair of Southern Boobook owls (nyawoo-nyawoo) perched on a log on the ground. The pair took flight up into a Western Sheoak (kondil) at the side of the track, and watched us as intently as we watched them. What a treat; these birds are often heard but seldom seen, being active mostly at night.

Like most owls, Boobooks are nocturnal predators, honed by natural selection to detect and swoop silently down on their unsuspecting prey. Their vision and hearing are second to none. Unlike other birds, but just like us, owls' eyes are forward-facing. This provides them with binocular vision, allowing them to accurately judge distance. Their eyes are very large, so they can capture even small amounts of light, and the retina is densely packed with rods, which detect low light but not colour, facilitating far better night vision than our own eyes, which have

more colour-detecting cones. Coupled with an ability to turn their heads through more than 250 degrees, this means they have the capacity to see prey from every possible angle without moving from their perch.

Their adaptations for hearing are even more remarkable. The face of an owl has the appearance of a flat, perfectly round disc. The facial disc serves as a sound detector in much the same way as a satellite dish serves to detect radio waves from space. The facial disc can be made more or less concave to focus incoming sound, which is directed to the ears that lie on the sides of the head, covered by the rim of the facial disc. Extraordinarily, the ears are asymmetrical, the left ear being positioned higher on the side of the head than the right. This asymmetry provides the owl with an almost three-dimensional hearing system, allowing it to pinpoint both the direction of the sound source and its approximate distance. And as if this battery of sensory weapons doesn't make an owl dangerous enough to small prey, its flight feathers have a serrated edge and their surface has a downy covering, both of which dampen the sound of airflow that is generated by the flight feathers of regular birds.

When an owl takes flight, then, it does so in complete silence, with detailed knowledge of the location of its target. This, coupled with its powerful talons and hooked beak, means small mammals stand little chance. The talons and beak of owls are identical to those of kites and eagles, though owls are completely unrelated to these diurnal birds of prey. This is another example of convergent evolution, as in the labellum of flying duck and Elbow Orchids, whereby a similar trait arises independently in two unrelated groups of organisms in response to the same selection pressure: in the case of the orchids' labella, to mimic the females of their pollinating male wasps; and in the case of the talons and beaks of owls and raptors, to capture and consume prey.

Watching the Boobooks was an absolute treat, and left us in good spirits for the impending ascent of Mount Wells. Turning left onto the old vehicle track and looking ahead our hearts sank, the gravel road rose impossibly steeply ahead of us. Nothing for it but to put our heads down and march forward, one step at a time. The vehicle track got steeper and steeper with every step – 'quite challenging' was an understatement. The gradient eventually started to lessen and we finally reached the saddle, but the hut was nowhere to be seen. After a short flat walk, the track left the road and headed

into the Jarrah forest, up an even steeper climb. We were not at the top at all, and would not reach the top for another fifteen minutes of brutal climbing. When I eventually reached the hut, which is perched right on the top of Mount Wells, it was to collapse with overheating and thirst, my clothes absolutely saturated. That had to be the hardest section of the entire track thus far. Freddy was struggling far behind me; his pack had given him large pressure sores on his hips over the preceding days, and the climb was aggravating them terribly. When he finally arrived, he was besieged by Dementors. Sooty Tim had left a comment in the logbook – 'I hate mountains' – and had apparently gone straight through Mount Wells without overnighting. Better man than either of us. We could not take another step.

Mount Wells Hut is unlike any other on the Bibbulmun, having been converted from the old cottage where the watchmen would live while on duty, watching day in day out from the adjacent fire tower for signs of fire in the surrounding forest matrix. It felt strange to be indoors after so long. The view from the platform was spectacular, and the natural history of the hilltop, for an entomologist, unique. For hilltops such as Mount Wells are, quite literally, breeding grounds for insects. The males of many species of bee, wasp, ant, butterfly and fly, will aggregate at the top of hills and wait there for females, which come to these conspicuous locations in the landscape specifically to find a mate. In the 1960s, American entomologist Oakley Shields demonstrated with his work on butterflies that hilltops are sexual rendezvous for insects. He found that butterflies aggregated on hilltops were more likely to be males than females, that females arriving at hilltops were generally unmated individuals, and that when mated and unmated butterflies are released some distance from hilltops, unmated females are more likely to travel to the hilltops than mated ones.

Butterflies that use hilltops as sexual rendezvous in Western Australia include the Painted Lady that had been so abundant on the grasstree inflorescences through the Jarrah forest. My colleague John Alcock has spent many years studying the mating system of Tarantula Hawk wasps and other insects on Usery Peak in Arizona. These wasps set up territories on hilltops and defend them vigorously against neighbouring males, maintaining these same territories for weeks on end. Likewise, Alcock found that Australian male Painted Lady butterflies defend territories on hilltops in order to secure matings with the females that travel there to meet them.

But in species that occur in very high numbers, defending territories is not a practical option. While on the viewing platform of the fire tower, we observed a large swam of midges rising and falling in the air column, moving sideways back and forth, but maintaining its general position above a single landmark, the water butt adjacent to the hut. Many hilltopping insects will aggregate in this way, rather than try to defend exclusive territories. Females will enter a swarm of males and be immediately seized and flown off to the surrounding vegetation where the pair will mate. Often there is structure within a swarm of midges, impossible for the human eye to detect. The swarm as we see it, is the emergent property of males jostling for the best position in the swarm, which will be the location where females are more likely to enter, perhaps determined by the prevailing wind or some feature of the landmark over which the swarm oscillates. Males better able to hold the best position, due to their size or flying ability, will be over-represented at the prime site.

Another American entomologist, Randy Thornhill studied the structure of mating swarms in a species of Mexican fly known as the Lovebug, finding that swarms were stratified by male size, with the largest more competitive males controlling access to the bottom of the swarm where females typically enter. For midges, British entomologists Rachel Neems and Athol McLachlan found that the smallest individuals were more successful in seizing and flying off with arriving females, perhaps because of their greater flying agility. Sexual selection in midge swarms might thereby favour smaller male body size. Their research also showed, however, that larger males have greater stamina, can remain in swarms for longer, and have a greater lifespan. Consequently, lifetime reproductive success was found to be greatest for males of intermediate size. In midges, then, sexual selection favours both large and small body size for different reasons, preventing average male body size from increasing or decreasing.

Another group of flies that adopt hilltopping are the tabanids or horseflies. Tabanids will hover on hilltops or perch on surrounding vegetation, awaiting females. Not a good place to be in horsefly breeding season, as we discovered. That afternoon as we sat in the porch of the hut, we were forced to simply sit and keep watching our legs, as the tabanids arrived at a rate of one or two per second and needed to be dealt with swiftly before they managed to cut into our skin to draw blood. At one stage I counted the pile of

TOP: Ornate dragons, *Ctenophorus ornatus*, are endemic to the granite outcrops of WA. They blend perfectly into the lichen-covered granite surface and so avoid detection from aerial predators. The clearing of native vegetation throughout the south-west has restricted the degree to which dragons can disperse between outcrops, with the result that they are becoming inbred and vulnerable to extinction. Leigh Simmons

MIDDLE: Blue-banded Bees, *Amegilla cingulata* are solitary, though they nest in dense aggregations, typically in dried soaks or riverbeds close to their host plants. A large colony of bees were foraging close to Nerang. These bees buzz to encourage the release of pollen from flowers. Leigh Simmons

BOTTOM: A female Christmas Beetle, *Lamprima micardi*, found south of Gringer Creek. So named for the time of year when it is abundant, it is in fact a species of stag beetle. This female will lay her eggs in rotting wood on which the larvae feed for at least a year before emerging as adults the following summer. Freddy Simmons

dead tabanids at my feet, which numbered in excess of seventy flies, and that was just my collection. The meat ants (karirt) were not complaining, dragging the carcasses off to their nests almost as quickly as we were providing them.

On the plus side, track elves were also hilltopping that day. Shortly after our arrival, but not so soon as to witness our complete and utter exhaustion, a guy turned up with his young son, on a day hike to see the fire tower. After chatting for half an hour or so he stood to leave, withdrew swiftly from his pack an ice-cold beer, which he slammed on the table, and wished us good luck on our trek. Was that the best beer ever consumed or what?

14

That night the wind whistled through the struts of the fire tower, and a loose corrugated-iron panel on the cabin at its summit flapped and crashed. The air inside the hut was stale, and we got little sleep. No matter, the forecast was for temperatures in the forties by noon the following day, with thunderstorms predicted for the afternoon, and so we had planned to rise at four-thirty to walk the 15 kilometres to Chadoora Hut before it became impossible.

As we descended Mount Wells in the cool morning air, walking was easy and pleasant. The atmosphere in the forest changed, subtly but perceptibly, as we headed south. The humidity rose and we passed through the first sections of forest in which the forest floor was dominated by Bracken (manya). The track was mostly flat, with enough undulations to make it interesting without being taxing. Thankfully, the mountains really were behind us now, as were the ticks, which had miraculously disappeared, never to be seen again. After our descent we crossed Wells Formation and began travelling along a long-disused vehicle track that would take us all the way to Chadoora.

You spend a lot of time watching the ground when walking, or at least I do. Perhaps it's because I am always on the lookout for insects or orchids. But today the number of ant lion pits was quite striking. These amazing insects have two distinct life stages. As juveniles they live in the soil, engineering the most remarkable traps with which to capture their prey, ants. If ever you notice a perfectly circular dimple in the sand, this is most likely to be an ant lion pit. The ant lion

lives in the base of the pit, where it lurks under the surface of the soil. As it digs its pit, it kicks sand upward and outward to form the funnel walls. The pit is thus lined with ultrafine dry soil that is very loose underfoot. When an ant happens to walk over the edge of the pit, it will soon lose its footing, tumbling down into the base of the pit, upon which the ant lion lunges from beneath the surface with its formidable jaws, grasping and dragging the ant underground and consuming it. This ferocious and quite ugly creature emerges as a beautiful adult insect with an elongated body and lace-like wings, not dissimilar in appearance to a damselfly, though it is nocturnal, often found on flyscreens at night, attracted to artificial light.

As we walked along the forest road, we came across a Western Grey Kangaroo (yonga) that had kangaroo blindness, its eyes clouded white and unseeing. Kangaroo blindness is a viral disease that is transmitted by midges and results in retinitis and retinal degeneration. The poor creature could sense that we were present, and hopped randomly about in circles, crashing into bushes and trees. We tried as hard as we could to pass without scaring it too much. If susceptibility to kangaroo blindness has a genetic basis, then this individual would not be passing it on to future generations, as it would be highly unlikely to breed. In this way natural selection favours the evolution of resistance to disease, weeding out those individuals that are susceptible to infection.

The last 3 kilometres of the track passed along Swamp Oak Brook, where the vegetation was quite stunning. We walked through long avenues of tall Bull Banksias (mungitch) in full bloom, their crowns meeting above the track to form long shaded archways. Chadoora Hut is set in a stunningly beautiful location, amid tall Marri and ancient Grasstrees (balga). We arrived by 10.30 am and not a moment too soon, as by noon the temperature had soared rapidly to the mid-forties. Sooty Tim had passed right through here too! His note in the logbook: '32km already, but can't stop now Dwellie TOO CLOSE BABY.' All the way from White Horse Hills, over Mount Wells and on another 20 kilometres to Dwellingup seemed like madness to us. We cowered in the shade of the hut for the rest of the day, along with several million blowflies (noordoo) that were also seeking respite from the heat. One slight movement sent them buzzing angrily around the hut in their millions. The promised thunderstorms did not arrive, and it took a long time after sunset

to cool sufficiently to sleep. Thankfully the flies abandoned the hut as soon as darkness fell, only to be replaced by a plethora of mosquitoes. Thank goodness for mosquito nets.

15

And so the final 20 kilometres to Dwellingup. We were not at all sorry to leave Chadoora – the bushflies, horseflies and mosquitoes were unbearable, which was a shame because the location itself was quite beautiful. As we continued south the change in the forest became even more marked. The odour had shifted from the dry herbaceous smell of the northern Jarrah forest to the damp, humus smell of the south. Bracken (manya) became more persistent, and patches of green moss edged the track. Spurred on by the promise of a hot shower and a cooked breakfast, we soon arrived at the disused Boddington railway, which we followed into town, arriving in just under five hours, our fastest pace on the track thus far, no doubt drawn to the excellent breakfast and coffee at the Blue Wren Café. Along the way we picked up a few birds: White-breasted Robin (boyidjil), Yellow-rumped Thornbill (djida), Ringneck Parrots (doornart), and in town the inevitable Australian White Ibis (ngalkaning).

DWELLINGUP TO COLLIE

DWELLINGUP TO COLLIE

1

It was a short 13-kilometre trek to Swamp Oak so we had a late start the following morning, taking the opportunity for a second visit to the Blue Wren Café. The weather was set to be pretty cool, and with freshly laundered clothes and a hearty breakfast we left the sleepy town of Dwellingup behind us. It was great to be in town for the luxuries of hot water and soft bedding, but strangely comforting to be back on the track again. The first 6 kilometres through Archies Brook to Nanga Road were not particularly pleasant, travelling through an area of forest that had burnt less than a week before, the heat still radiating from the ashes and some large logs on the forest floor still smouldering. Either side of Nanga Road were stretches of unburnt woodland with fine stands of flowering Holly-leaved Mirbelia, but we were soon to enter the environmental disaster that is Murray Plantation, with its sterile understorey of dead pine needles and out-of-control invasive blackberry.

We stopped briefly at River Road beside Davis Brook, before climbing up and eventually out of the pine plantation into Jarrah forest that had been burnt some months previously. While there was little regrowth to speak of, there was beauty in the freshly sprouting Grasstrees (balga) with their jet-black trunks. And even in the most unlikely places nature presents us with its wonders. We had clearly just missed seeing an Emu, a large pile of droppings

having been deposited in the middle of the path. Much of my research has focused on dung-breeding insects, so I am always eager to inspect closely any fresh dung that might provide entertainment. This morning I was not disappointed, for the Emu dung was the site of an intense ongoing battle between sepsid scavenger flies *(Parapalaeosepsis plebeia)* that had arrived to feed and lay their eggs.

We generally think of reproduction as a harmonious venture between the sexes, but, in reality, it is rife with conflict for most species. Females need to mate in order to obtain sperm so that they can fertilise their eggs, and they will go to great lengths to find the best male available to father their offspring. In general, however, females only need to mate with one male to realise their reproductive potential. After all, they have just a few eggs to lay and need only a single sperm per egg. Males, on the other hand, can increase the number of offspring they produce by fertilising the eggs of many females; the more females a given male can mate with, the more females will produce offspring fathered by that male.

This difference between males and females in the benefits of multiple mating is generally why males are the competitive sex while females are the choosy sex, and so why sexual selection typically acts on males to be aggressive and showy in order to monopolise access to many females; male reproductive success is maximised by quantity while female reproductive success is maximised by quality. While mating many times can bring a reproductive bonanza for a male, it can be very costly for a female, exposing her to increased risk of sexually transmitted diseases, costing her time and energy that is better spent producing and caring for offspring, and even subjecting her to harm inflicted by a male during mating that can reduce her life expectancy. In these scavenger flies, Swiss evolutionary biologist Wolf Blanckenhorn has shown how the male's penis, which is covered in hardened spines, will damage the internal reproductive tract of the female with the result that the more frequently a female mates the shorter her lifespan. Not surprisingly, female scavenger flies are reluctant to mate, and will resist male mating attempts by violently shaking their bodies when mounted, like a rodeo contest between rider and bull.

This battle of the sexes is expected to generate cycles of coevolutionary change in males and females in much the same way as parasites coevolve with their hosts in the battle over virulence and resistance. Any trait that allows males to subdue resistant females will increase in frequency in the population because such

males will leave more offspring, offspring that will bear the trait that allows them to mate with reluctant females. But any trait in females that allows them to better resist male mating attempts will also be favoured by selection, because these females will avoid the harm caused by excessive mating and leave more offspring with the trait that resists male mating attempts. This form of sexual selection is known widely as sexually antagonistic coevolution, or sexual conflict. In these sepsid flies, the males of most species have evolved modified front legs that are endowed with interlocking spines allowing them to clamp the female's wings, all the better to maintain position on the female during her mate rejection attempts. Female resistance behaviours and male grasping legs represent resistance and persistence adaptations in females and males respectively.

Evolutionary biologists Oliver Martin and David Hosken showed how sexual conflict in scavenger flies can drive the evolution of their behaviour. Working with a European species of scavenger fly, Martin and Hosken established laboratory populations that were breeding under different intensities of sexual conflict. Some populations allowed multiple and frequent interactions between males and females, and thus conflicts over mating, while others prevented such interactions, essentially removing sexual conflict. After thirty-five generations the researchers assessed female resistance to mating and male mating success, finding that females from populations that had evolved with sexual conflict were more likely to resist male mating attempts and far less likely to actually mate when presented with a male. Conversely, females from populations that had evolved in the absence of sexual conflict were unlikely to shake when mounted by a male and were far more likely to accept mating. These laboratory evolution experiments show us just how quickly organisms can change under sexual selection.

Sexual conflict is a widespread phenomenon in the animal kingdom, and has resulted in some extraordinary adaptations in males and females to best ensure their own reproductive success. In vinegar flies *(Drosophila)*, for example, males transfer seminal fluids to females that contain a substance known as sex peptide, which has the effect of making females increase the number of eggs they lay and reject the sexual advances of other males. While this might be in the males' best interests, sex peptide is toxic to females, reducing their lifespan. American geneticist Marianne Wolfner and her colleagues have discovered that female vinegar flies have

evolved proteins in their reproductive tract that can neutralise male seminal fluids; in vinegar flies, then, males and female appear locked in chemical warfare over when, with whom, and how much females should invest in producing offspring.

As fascinating as the scavenger flies on the emu dung were, there was little else in these burnt woodlands to hold our attention. Thankfully, we soon reached unburnt woodlands at the rim of the Murray River Valley, where things got far more interesting. As we descended into the valley, we came across a huge Rosenberg's Heath Goanna (yongki; *Varanus rosenbergi*), standing in the middle of the track, blocking our passage. Much larger than the Gould's Goanna (kaarda) we had encountered in the north, this individual had no intention of letting us pass. Freddy walked slowly towards it, upon which it puffed up its neck, raised itself on its muscled front legs and looked us squarely in the eye as if to say, 'You shall not pass.' This was somewhat awkward, as the vegetation either side of the path was rather dense, leaving us little choice but to try to pass the beast. Freddy bit the bullet and made a dash for it, and was almost bitten for his audacity, the goanna lashing out at him as he comically tried to jump out of its way with his 20-kilogram pack on his back. I was not game to try the same manoeuvre given how worked up the goanna now was, so I gave it a wide berth by bushwhacking. *A Guide to the Bibbulmun Track* says quite definitively not to walk off the track, even asking that when the track is flooded, walkers wade through. It does not, on the other hand, suggest how one should deal with a recalcitrant Heath Goanna.

On arriving at Swamp Oak Hut we were surprised to see that there was no entry in the logbook from Sooty Tim, but we could see that Jens, who we had met at Hewett's Hill, was now a full week ahead of us. The resident bird at Swamp Oak Hut was an Australian Raven (waardong), which seemed pleased to see us arrive, screeching at us at the top of its voice, *aairk, aark, aaarh* and wailing *aaieerk*, its cries echoing through the valley. That afternoon we strolled the remaining 1 kilometre down the forest road to the Murray River, where a large flock of Red-tailed Black Cockatoos (karak) were feeding on gumnuts in the tall Marri that line the banks of the permanent pools through this stretch of the river. This was the start of a wonderful section of the track, and we were both excited at the prospect of following the Murray over the coming days.

TOP: Nyawoo-nyawoo or Southern Boobook, *Ninox novaeseelandiae*. Named for its calls *boo book ... boo book*. Owls are exquisitely adapted for capturing their prey. Not only do their forward-facing eyes afford them excellent binocular vision, they can also hear in 3D, their facial disc providing a parabolic reflector to intensify the slightest rustle in the undergrowth and send it to their asymmetrically placed ears, allowing them to pinpoint their prey. And then their soft feathers are adapted to pass through the air soundlessly, so that they can swoop down on their prey unheard. Leigh Simmons

MIDDLE: Balga or Grasstree, *Xanthorrhoea preisii*, are a rich source of pollen and nectar for insects, like this Painted Lady, *Vanessa kershawi*. This species is one of the most common native butterflies found throughout the Australian continent. The males gather on hilltops such as Mount Wells, to which females travel to meet and mate with them. Freddy Simmons

BOTTOM: Deep in the base of this ant lion pit lurks a ferocious predator, poised to grasp and consume any ant that slips down the loose sandy slopes of the pit it has constructed. The adult is a large nocturnal flying insect, resembling to some extent a damselfly, and is most often seen when attracted to lights at night. Leigh Simmons

2

We woke next morning to heavy rain, and a poor bedraggled Splendid Fairy-wren (djer-djer) bobbing about under the outside bench taking shelter. Time to break out the wet-weather gear. Freddy impatiently took over as I struggled to put the rain cover on my pack, irritated by my apparent incompetence. For all the world it seemed two sizes too small. I felt totally vindicated, however, when it took him nearly twenty minutes to fit his own rain cover! It's a knack, of course, and once learnt the work of but a few seconds. And so we set out in the rain. Ascending the first hill in wet-weather gear was hot and steamy, but the smell of petrichor was quite wonderful.

The walk along the old rail formation above Swamp Oak creek passed through extensive Western Sheoak (kondil) woodland and was quite delightful, soft and springy underfoot from the thick layers of sheoak needles. Some challenging climbs lay ahead, first over a ridge before a very steep descent to Yarragil Brook. In the rain, the narrow track that hugged the edge of the steep drop into Yarragil Form was quite treacherous. The views across the form were stunning, however, and the conflict between admiring the view and ensuring our footing made for slow progress. Of course, as soon as we made it to the brook crossing, so began the steep ascent to Loop Road. Fortunately, the ascent is half as steep on the southern side of the form, so we were thankful that we were heading south rather than north.

After taking us through extensive Marri and Jarrah woodland with views across the Murray Valley, the track finally descended to the river, along which it travelled to Murray Hut. The last 2.5 kilometres along the riverbank seemed to take forever, ascending away from and then descending back to the river on far too many occasions, and never actually getting close enough to the water's edge to give us a good view. Along the banks there were extensive stretches of Branching Fringe Lily, and we came across one that had white flowers. Albinism occurs in both animals and plants, and is caused by a mutation in the genes that control pigmentation. Single mutations occur all the time when strands of DNA are replicated, but these mutations are generally only expressed when an organism has the same mutation in both copies of the same gene, one from its mother and one from its father.

Because such mutations are mostly detrimental to an organism's reproduction and survival, individuals with double mutations will be lost from the population. A plant with white flowers, for example, would struggle to attract a pollinator attuned to a population of purple flowers, so that occurrences such as our white fringe lily are rare in nature as they fail to reproduce.

We covered the 19.6 kilometres from Swamp Oak Hut to Murray Hut in just over six hours. The hut sits high on the banks of the Murray, overlooking a permanent pool on the river, and we took the opportunity of rinsing off in the surprisingly cold water. As we splashed in the shallows, Little Black Cormorants (koordjokit), perched some way off on the tree snags that emerged from the water, and watched our every move lest we come close, and a pair of Australasian Grebes (ngoonan) dived repeatedly in search of food in the cold depths of the pool.

We were to share the hut that night with Jason, only the third time since we had set out that we would share a hut. It turned out that Jason had been waiting at Murray River for Sooty Tim. Apparently they had been at school together, but had not seen each other for thirty years. A mutual friend had told Jason that Tim was walking the Bibbulmun and so Jason had planned his walk from Dwellingup to Collie so they would meet. We explained to Jason that there had been no sign of Sooty Tim's whereabouts since his epic march from White Horse Hills. We assumed that Tim had ended his walk in Dwellingup, as he would surely have passed through Murray River by now, given how far ahead of us he had been. Jason seemed disappointed, and resolved to walk on the next day. It seemed we would be walking together as far as Collie.

3

The next morning the pool was glassy still, shrouded in a thin blanket of early morning mist. The Little Black Cormorants (koordjokit) on the emergent tree snags were joined by a single Little Pied Cormorant (kakak), and the Australasian Grebes (ngoonan) on the water surface by a pair of Pacific Black Ducks (ngwonan). The stillness of the morning was captivating. As we headed off along the banks of the Murray, we passed first through the riparian zone, that strip along the banks of rivers that remains

moist and cool, is relatively protected from fire, and harbours very different plant species from the dryer elevations of the Murray Valley.

The cool mist drifted through thick stands of Wiry Wattle. This remarkably graceful wattle is completely leafless, having, as its name would suggest, long slender silver–green wiry stems that drape like willow. The plants were heavy with seedpods and morning dew, which accentuated their weeping habit. Interspersed with the Wiry Wattle were tall Albizia, with their feathery bright-green leaves and considerably larger seedpods. The chatter of Grey Fantails (kadjinak), the shrill call of a Horsfield's Bronze Cuckoo (koodooban), and the melody of Western Whistlers (bidilmidang) filled the air. Soon the track turned left, ascending out of the riparian zone up onto the high slopes of the Murray Valley. The slopes were thick with Bookleaf Peas, still in full bloom, and the understorey was a tangle of Coral Vine and Dodder.

Eventually the track descended again to travel along the banks of the river. We paused at a pool for second breakfast, and enjoyed watching a family of Splendid Fairy-wrens (djer-djer) hopping through the undergrowth at the pool's edge. The track along the riverbank was at times almost impassable, requiring a fair amount of bushwhacking through the thick Water Bush. We finally managed to reach Driver Road, from which the final steep ascent to Dookanelly Hut was along a forest road through burnt woodlands. Jason was already at the hut when we arrived, and had a billy boiling over a small but very smoky campfire. Just the day before, a walker had noted in the logbook that they had seen a Short-beaked Echidna (nyingarn) in the woodlands close to the hut, so we spent the afternoon strolling the paths in the hope of seeing one too. Alas we were not so fortunate, but it was fun trying nonetheless.

4

From Dookanelly we passed through burnt Jarrah forest down to the new Murray River footbridge. Named the Bilya Djena Bidi (swinging river footbridge) by the Gnaala Karla Booja traditional owners, this suspension bridge replaced the Long Gully Bridge in Lane Poole Reserve that was destroyed in 2015 by bushfire.

Bilya Djena Bidi is an impressive structure; spanning 92 metres and suspended between two 12 metre towers, it crosses the Murray River 6 metres above the summer river level. It blends beautifully into the forest, being constructed of rusting steel that complements the hues of the surrounding trunks of Marri and Jarrah. Built at a cost of $850,000, it reminds us not to take for granted the Bibbulmun Track Foundation and all of its supporters, who provide this track, its overnight huts and its river crossings at no charge to users.

After crossing the Murray the track turns left onto a forest road that follows the river some 10 kilometres to the Harvey Quindanning Road. The forest road was edged by stands of Wiry Wattle, Sticky Hopbush (waning) and Drummond's Eggs and Bacon Pea, and passed many permanent pools along the way, almost all of them frequented by flocks of Red-tailed Black Cockatoos (karak). We stopped at one pool that was obviously a well-used camping spot, as it came supplied with white plastic garden chairs! Sitting on the bank of the pool in the shade of the mature Swamp Paperbarks (yowarl), we watched Tree Martins (kabi-kalangkoorong) hunting insects in the canopy of the surrounding forest and swooping down to the water surface to take those that had become trapped there. Mostly they would barely touch the water surface, leaving a small wake where their bill plucked a floating insect from the pool. On occasion they would make a big splash and then soar high into the air, perhaps taking the opportunity to bathe – or could it be they were just having fun?

Tree Martins nest in small colonies, in the tops of tall dead trees that offer hollows for building nests. This colony must have contained fifty or more birds, which chattered amongst themselves – *chwip-chip-chzeit-chwip* – as they swooped in turn low over the water and high into the canopy. We took the opportunity to bathe ourselves in a pool just before Harvey Quindanning Road, the water refreshingly cool in the rising heat of the day. Shortly after crossing the road, we passed beneath the Worsley Alumina conveyer that transports bauxite mined at Mount Saddleback 50 kilometres to the Worsley refinery, and when it does so the noise is truly deafening. We were to hear the conveyer running each morning as we headed south, as far away as Harris Dam, a distance of some 40 kilometres.

We do not generally think of noise as pollution, but its effects can be just as damaging as any chemical pollutant. Many animals rely on

acoustic signalling for social communication, as we had witnessed earlier in the day when observing the Tree Martins. Males use their calls and songs to attract females, and in their turn females use those calls and songs to assess the relative merits of potential mates. Both sexes will use acoustic signals to defend their territories from rivals, or to warn other members of their social group, and other species around them, of the danger of approaching predators. But increasingly, researchers are finding that animal communication channels are seriously disrupted by anthropogenic noise. The males of many acoustically communicating species, including birds, frogs and mammals, will call more loudly when competing with anthropogenic noise, a phenomenon known as the Lombard effect. Birds will also increase the pitch of their calls to try to avoid overlap with the low-pitched rumble of mechanical machinery, and they will adjust the timing of their singing to avoid regular periods of anthropogenic noise. The dawn chorus near airports, for example, has been found to occur earlier in the morning, before the daily aircraft noise begins.

Remarkably, insects too have been found to be sensitive to anthropogenic noise. One study of European grasshoppers found that, like birds, males will alter the pitch of their calls so as to avoid overlap with the pitch of road traffic, and anthropogenic noise has even been shown to affect the contemporary evolution of grasshopper populations. German evolutionary biologist Ulrike Lampe found that grasshoppers from populations close to roads evolve differences in call pitch and in the total amount of sound produced per unit of time. These changes in acoustic signalling arise as individuals are selected by their noisy environment to be heard over the source of anthropogenic noise. Nevertheless, evolutionary changes in acoustic signalling may not be sufficient to avoid the detrimental effects that noise can have. In crickets, for example, American behavioural ecologist Robin Tinghitella and her students have shown that females take longer to respond to male calls when exposed to noise, and take longer to actually locate them when they do respond.

But the effects of noise can be far greater than delaying mate location. Anthropogenic noise as been shown to affect the speed at which crickets grow to adulthood, and to reduce their adult lifespan. Noise increases the amount of time birds spend vigilant and decreases the amount of time they spend foraging, the number of eggs they lay in a clutch, the amount of care they provide for

their young, and consequently the number of young they fledge. Noise decreases the ability of birds to detect alarm calls that alert them to approaching predators, with obvious consequences. Physiological responses to noise include increases in the levels of circulating stress hormones, which have negative effects on survival and reproduction. The accumulation of such studies over the last ten years has been overwhelming, pointing to anthropogenic noise as a serious pollutant in our environment, and yet its consequences are not widely appreciated. This evidence surely calls for action to reduce anthropogenic noise, particularly in natural areas set aside for wildlife protection and conservation.

After passing under the conveyor, the track rose steeply, as did the temperature, and walking became tough going. The pods of Brown's Wattle exploded in the heat. Explosive dispersal is seen in many acacia and pea species. Moisture is drawn slowly from their drying pods, building tension in the joints between each wing of the pod as it shrinks, and eventually, on hot dry days, the membranes break and the pod snaps open, each wing of the pod curling explosively and flinging the seeds several metres from the parent plant. All around us on the climb could be heard the *snap-snap-snap* of exploding pods.

No sooner were we at the top, than the track plummeted 100 metres before ascending a second peak. We sheltered in the shade of a large Grasstree (balga) at the summit of the second peak, trying to cool off, and watched a Nankeen Kestrel (mardiyet) stationary in the sky, searching the ground from on high for tasty morsels. Down again to Bell Brook through open Jarrah forest before a third, this time shallower but consequently longer climb back to our starting elevation. By the time we finally reached Possum Springs Hut, elevated above a small Wandoo-lined creek, we were hot, thirsty and exhausted. It had taken us more than eight hours to travel the 23.5 kilometres from Dookanelly. We were surprised to have arrived before Jason, though pleased to have the hut to ourselves for a while so that we could wash in our litre of water with some privacy. Jason had spent some time on one of the peaks where he had a phone signal, arranging for a pick-up at Harris Dam the following day, so this would be our last night together.

5

We were awoken at dawn to the rumble of the Worsley conveyer. The 19 kilometres to Yourdamung Hut were relatively flat after the previous day's trials, and the track passed through some spectacular changes in habitat. We first ascended into mixed Jarrah and Marri woodlands, with the usual smattering of Western Sheoak (kondil) and Bull Banksia (mungitch), before descending into a large section of low winter-wet swamplands known as the Plonkhole. Through here were stands of Two-sided Boronia with their pink flowers and flattened stems, some bright-orange Star Guinea Flower, graceful Golden Spray covered in their red-centred yellow flowers, and yellow Preiss's Wedge-pea. Larger shrubs and trees included Grey Stinkwood, Swamp Paperbarks (yowarl), and some ancient Grasstrees (balga) and Swamp Banksia (pungura). The Plonkhole is quite the most extraordinary area.

After ascending again into mixed Jarrah woodland, we turned left onto Wilshusen Road. And so began a long 6-kilometre stretch that was largely flat and shaded. The road was bordered on either side by thick stands of Heart-leaf Poison. Growing above head height, it had the appearance and feel of a neatly kept hedge. The leaves of Heart-leaf Poison contain the chemical fluoroacetate, from which 1080 baits are made. Our native mammals have a long evolutionary history with Heart-leaf Poison and have long since become resistant to the poison in its leaves and seeds, being completely unharmed by it. But consumed by an introduced species such as a cat or fox that has not coevolved with the plant, the poison results in certain death. Thus, baiting using 1080 has become the frontline weapon in Western Shield, the Western Australian Department of Biodiversity, Conservation and Attractions' large-scale eradication program aimed at protecting our native wildlife from introduced predators.

During baiting seasons, planes fly some 50,000 kilometres across the landscape, dropping baited meat sausages, approximately 900,000 of them each year, a task that takes around eight months to accomplish. Without these efforts we would surely have lost all of our native mammals to feral cats and foxes. We are unlikely ever to eradicate these introduced pests from our landscape – at least for cats, there is a constant inflow into the feral population from domestic animals – but the baiting program may at least

help us keep their numbers down, at least until such time as they themselves evolve resistance to the toxin.

We eventually came to a second large winter-wet swamp just after Trees Road, which was dominated by much lower shrubby vegetation. It seemed strange to us that the track should turn left along Trees Road for a kilometre or more before doubling back upon itself, but it soon became clear that in winter this would be the only way through the swamp, as the track passed over a slightly raised section in the otherwise flat depression in the landscape, with several stretches of boardwalk to aid traversing the swamp at its narrowest point.

After crossing the swamp, the track ascended again, passing into mixed woodland that featured many large mature Western Australian Christmas Trees (mooja), though none showed any signs of flowering. And so we arrived at Yourdamung Hut in just over five hours, having enjoyed a far less strenuous walk than the day before. To our surprise, Sooty Tim arrived at four that afternoon, having walked 42 kilometres from Murray Hut. It transpired that on arriving in Dwellingup after his mammoth hike from White Horse Hills, he had developed septicaemia from infected blisters on his feet, and had been rushed back to Perth where he had spent the week on his mother's couch on high-dose antibiotics watching movies. That explained his sudden disappearance from the logbooks. The tale of the hare and the tortoise flashed into my mind as he spoke of his trials and tribulations. But not to be defeated he was back on the track as soon as he had finished his course of antibiotics and been cleared by the doctor to do so. We had fun exchanging tales that afternoon; remarkably, he too had been accosted by the recalcitrant Heath Goanna at Swamp Oak!

6

The following day was a pleasant short walk, just 14 kilometres to Harris Dam Hut. Sooty Tim, of course, intended walking straight through to Collie where he had a rendezvous set up with Jason, so we bade him farewell once more. This section of the track passes through the Collie Conservation Zone and State Park, and is walk trail all the way, with no vehicle track at all. Soon after we left

TOP: This recalcitrant yongki, or Rosenberg's Heath Goanna, *Varanus rosenbergi*, became highly aggressive as we passed through its territory, blocking our path to Swamp Oak Hut. Freddy Simmons

MIDDLE: Waardong or Australian Raven, *Corvus coronoides*. Another classic Australian sound of the bush and city, is the strong muffled groan or gurgle *aairk, aark, aaarh, aargargh* and wailing *aaieerk*. Noongar stories tell of two brothers, the waardong and koolbardi who were prone to quarrelling over who had the purest white feathers. One day during a particularly escalated fight, the two brothers fell into thick black mud. While the koolbardi only slightly stained his feathers, the waardong became covered in the mud. Leigh Simmons

BOTTOM: Ngoonan or Australasia Grebe, *Tachybaptus novaehollandiae*. This tiny Grebe was frequently seen on the still waters of the Murray and Collie rivers.

Yourdamung, a pair of Australian Owlet-nightjars (yaartj) flew low across the path ahead of us and landed on a fallen tree. This was my first, and as it turned out only, life-bird – the birding term for your first in-the-flesh sighting of a species – along the Bibbulmun. Owlet-nightjars are small grey birds with a long tail, impossibly large dark eyes on rounded owl-like faces, and long whiskers either side of a hooked bill. Though common throughout Australia, they are rarely seen, being strictly nocturnal forest birds. Known colloquially as moth owls, these birds hunt moths and other insects at night, their behaviour not unlike that of flycatchers, which fill this same ecological niche during the day. This pair of birds was up late, or were we up early? We seemed to have switched to a somewhat crepuscular circadian rhythm in our attempts to walk in the coolest part of the day. Regardless, I was excited by the opportunity to finally see these birds. Both Red-tailed (karak) and Carnaby's (ngoolyak) Black Cockatoos followed us through the forest, which was filled with the deep melodic calls of Western Grey Shrike-thrush (koodilang). We had a very pleasant walk, passing through areas of winter-wet swamplands before re-entering mixed Jarrah woodlands and arriving at Harris Dam Hut in just over four hours.

As we sat that afternoon in the cool of the forest, a pair of Emu (wetj) walked slowly past, oblivious to our presence in the deep shade of the hut. Emus belong to an ancient lineage of birds, the ratites, which branched off very early in the avian evolutionary tree. The ratites were abundant on the heart of the ancient continent of Gondwana, and were carried to their current geographical locations when the Gondwanan continent broke up and drifted apart to form Earth's contemporary landmasses. They are now represented by just a handful of species: three species of cassowary, one in Australia and two in New Guinea; five species of kiwi in New Zealand; the Ostrich in Africa; two species of rhea in South America; and the Emu in Australia.

Emus are unusual in their breeding biology. Typically we expect males to compete for access to females, and to be the showy and aggressive sex. This is because males invest less in reproduction, and so tend to be available to breed in greater abundance than females. The reverse appears to be the case in Emus. It is the female who will call to attract males, inflating air sacs in her neck and producing a deep drumming *boom-boom-boom*. When a male is attracted she will circle him, remaining some metres away, and

continuing her *boom-boom-boom*. The female also has distinct feather ornamentation, developing in the breeding season jet-black feathers on the head and the neck, which is edged by a bright white ruff. These ornaments are the products of sexual selection that we generally expect to see in males rather than females.

Once a male and female pair bond is established, the two will travel together through the forest, generally within a distinct home range. The pair we observed from Harris Dam Hut were engaged in this exact activity. When the female eventually lays her eggs, it is the male who will gather them up and incubate them. Females can produce a clutch of around seven eggs every three days, but it takes a male some fifty-six days to incubate the clutch, and once he starts to incubate he will rarely stand or move away from his clutch. And so the female will seek additional males to incubate the additional eggs she can produce. In Emus, then, it is the females that can increase their reproductive success by increasing the number of incubating males they can monopolise, and they will compete aggressively with other females, chasing and kicking each other with their powerful limbs, in order to both monopolise their own incubating male and obtain additional males. This so-called reversal in sex roles and the direction of sexual selection occurs because males, rather than females, provide the majority of parental care, and critically this care makes them unavailable for additional breeding attempts.

7

We awoke the next morning to the now distant drone of the Worsley conveyor. Extraordinary how far the noise carried across the landscape. The final 22 kilometres into Collie would take us just over five hours. The track passed through now familiar mixed Jarrah woodlands, passing below Harris Dam and across a well-used area of bushland with many vehicle and bicycle tracks. Just south of Harris Dam stood a huge Candlestick Banksia (piara) in full bloom, and Blue Dampiera carpeted the forest floor in several sections of track.

I gave pause, on several occasions, to reflect on how approaching civilisation was actually more like approaching anarchy, as we were forced off the trail by mountain bikers, or had to pick our way

TOP: Karak or Red-tailed Black Cockatoo, *Calyptorhynchus banksii*. Flocks of these magnificent cockatoos are a constant companion when walking through the forests of the south-west. Typically in the tree canopy, they feed on the honky nuts of the Marri, and keep in constant communication via their *karraak karrark airrk kreeeeeik*.
Leigh Simmons

MIDDLE: Bambon or Rufous Whistler, *Pachycephala rufiventris*. Another common bird in mixed woodlands, this male is searching for insects in a Sheoak. The voice is strong and loud, *cheWIT-chWIT-chWIT-chWIT eeeee-CHIEW*. Leigh Simmons

BOTTOM: Doolor or Silvereye, *Zosterops lateralis gouldi*. Large flocks of these nomadic insectivorous birds scurry through the canopy in the forests, or the low undergrowth of coastal heaths, in search of food. A very abundant bird, they constantly chatter with their fellow travellers *tsweeip-cheeip, peeip-a-chweip, cheeip*. Leigh Simmons

through piles of horse droppings, despite clear signage that such usage of the track was not allowed, and despite the many bridle paths and the Munda Biddi Trail for cyclists literally a stone's throw from the Bibbulmun. Still, we smiled politely as sage advice was handed down upon us, about bushfires and snakes, and how we should not be walking the track at this time of year. I was pretty much over town before we even arrived. Nonetheless, it was good to get a hot shower and to launder our clothes, and the breakfast at the Colliefields, and the chicken parmie that night at the Collie Ridge Motel made it all worthwhile.

COLLIE TO BALINGUP

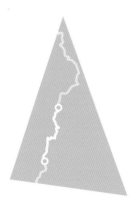

COLLIE TO BALINGUP

1

Our packs restocked and a full English inside us, we set off along the Collie spur trail back to its junction with the Bibbulmun Track. The area west of Collie is a white sandy heath with stands of Paperbark and Sheoak, an abundance of Mangles Kangaroo Paws, long since finished flowering, and clumps of Drumsticks, a tufted plant with grass-like leaves and distinctive spherical white flowers borne on long brown stems that look just like drumsticks. There was also a new fringe lily (tjunguri) scattered through here, the Sand Fringe Lily (adjiko); it has the familiar purple flowers with fringe-edged petals but they are borne on very tall leafless stems almost to waist height. This would be a great area for orchids in the spring.

It felt good to rejoin the Bibbulmun and head south, descending into the Collie River Valley. After an hour or so we heard behind us a familiar voice: 'Thought they were your footprints'; Sooty Tim joined us once more. He had taken a day off in Collie, finally catching up with his old school chum Jason. Sooty Tim walked with us as far as the banks of the Collie River, chattering away about his time in Collie, and extolling the virtues of the Collie campgrounds. We stopped to check out the birdlife on the river, partly because I wanted to see if there was anything new, and partly because we rather enjoyed the quiet of the bush and rarely spoke when we were walking. Sooty Tim, not one to linger, left us by the riverside.

It was a beautiful spot, with Swamp Paperbarks (yowarl) along the riverbanks, and Pacific Black Ducks (ngwonan) and Australasian Grebes (ngoonan) on the water. Along the flood plain of the river, tall clumps of Evergreen Kangaroo Paws (koroylbardany) were just beginning to open their flowers.

After crossing the Collie River, we ascended into mixed Jarrah forest once more, and arrived at Mungalup Dam, the halfway mark of the day's trek. Here we sat on the beach and just took in the peace and tranquillity of the forest. It felt so good to be away from town again, and what a perfect day for walking – mid-twenties and a wonderfully cool breeze off the water. Along the edges of the track, Book Triggerplants grew in dense clumps, with their bright-pink flowers a splash of colour against the rusty brown gravel, while Bull Banksia (mungitch) flowers played host to swarms of tiny orange-rumped native bees of the genus *Euhesma*. Given there are eighty-three described species of these bees across Australia, we had little chance of identifying which species this might be, although Australian entomologist Terry Houston suggests that different species may specialise on specific host plants, with *Euhesma walkeriana* having been collected mainly from banksia flowers in the south-west of Western Australia. In the forest that morning we saw our first snake, a beautiful Dugite (dobitj), brown with a black nape, that slithered gracefully through the undergrowth, oblivious to our presence as we rested on the stump of a felled Jarrah.

It took us just over six hours to cover the 19 kilometres to Yabberup Hut. Sooty Tim had been there for some time when we arrived, and we spent much of the afternoon in conversation. Well, to be fair, we mostly listened. He did like to chat, did Sooty Tim! Late that evening, just before dusk, Geoff arrived and set up his tent a short way from the hut. Geoff very quickly acquired the track name of GFP because everything he owned, from sleeping bag to beanie, was high-visibility fluorescent green. Green fluorescent protein (GFP) was first isolated from jellyfish and is frequently used to label tissues in biomedical studies. In my own field of research, the gene for the protein has been grafted into the genome of vinegar flies in order to make their sperm glow green, all the better to see them swimming around inside the female's reproductive tract. But GFP is most likely to be known outside of scientific laboratories from Alba the glowing bunny, an artistic work by the artist Eduardo Kac purportedly produced in collaboration with the geneticist Louis-Marie Houdebine, who genetically engineered a white

rabbit to express GFP in its skin and fur. It transpired that GFP was walking the track in sections, as many do, and would be our hut companion through to Balingup. Like Alba, he would be very difficult to lose in the woods.

2

We had by now settled into a daily routine. Up at first light, just before five, we would start the day with a small breakfast consisting of a shared energy bar and a coffee; we carried enough coffee bags for just one each morning.

After breakfast we packed up our gear, filled our water bladders and bottles from the tank, hoisted our packs and set off. Our packs felt reasonably comfortable for the first half-hour or so. The first pains of the day came from the ITBs, the iliotibial bands that run between the hip and the knee, which I didn't even know could hurt until we set out from Kalamunda. Thankfully by now we were becoming reasonably track fit, so that this was relatively short-lived, but at the start it was pretty full-on pain for most of the day. *A Guide to the Bibbulmun Track* recommends that you rest with packs off each hour to delay the onset of fatigue. Sound advice indeed, and we would generally stop after the first 5 kilometres for second breakfast, a handful of trail mix followed by a coffee candy, which was remarkably efficient at warding off the caffeine cravings, I must say.

Typically, walking became harder from then on, though not because of the walking per se. It is one thing to walk 10 kilometres, but is another to carry 18 kilograms for 10 kilometres. After a couple of hours, our shoulders began to ache, and eventually cramps between the shoulder blades called for a stop for morning tea, a shared muesli bar and a second coffee candy. The rationing was tiresome, to say the least. An hour later would be a stop for first lunch, another handful of trail mix and yet another coffee candy.

We would generally arrive at the hut anywhere between 11 in the morning and 2 in the afternoon, depending on the distance travelled. On arrival, our most pressing task was to release our feet from our shoes, put on our thongs and wash – well, more accurately wipe down with a cold wet flannel. Freddy would prepare second lunch, which consisted of noodles, while I would write up my track notes. Our afternoon would then be spent setting up our sleeping

gear and reading books on our smartphones. What a wonderful invention the smartphone is. How did we keep these charged, you might ask? The marvels of modern technology – we both had mini solar panels hanging from the back of our packs, and the good old Western Australian sun never let us down. Afternoon tea was at four, and then at five we would eat dried chickpeas while doing the *Guardian* quick crossword.

Freddy would 'cook' at six – or rather add water to our freeze-dried dinner – and we would be in bed by dusk. The simplicity of our routine, rising and retiring with the passage of the sun, was just so wonderful. I think that feeling of freedom and release from modern living provided by a simple routine dictated by the rising and the setting of the sun is something that most long-distance walkers cherish the most. Certainly, it was commonly commented upon by those that had entered their thoughts in the hut logbooks.

The walk to Noggerup Hut would be one of our longer days at just under 20 kilometres. We delayed our departure that day, allowing Sooty Tim to head off before us, but were still away before GFP emerged from his fluorescent tent. The track took us through Jarrah forest, around Glen Mervyn Dam, and then along a beautiful forested ridge above a tributary of the Preston River. The track eventually descended into the Preston Valley, and emerged into cleared agricultural land through which runs the Boyup Brook Road. According to *A Guide to the Bibbulmun Track*, 'the Mumballup Tavern owners welcome walkers, and this is a trail stop with a growing reputation'. We had been practically hallucinating about bacon and egg sandwiches and a latte for first lunch, and were eager to reach the tavern. Our disappointment in finding it locked up and deserted cannot be adequately described. We arrived by ten-thirty, but the tavern did not open until twelve-thirty. There are so few opportunities for luxuries like a cooked meal on the track, and the thought of passing one by was torture, but there was no way we could hang around and wait, because temperatures were tipped to be in the high thirties by noon and we had a steep ascent to tackle on the other side of Preston Valley. Dejected, we pressed on, crossing the Boyup Brook Road and following the old railway track through the valley.

The environs through here were rather depressing. This was once a heavily wooded valley through which flowed the Preston River, but now it is almost completely cleared and the land turned over to raising a few hundred head of cattle and 20 billion bushflies. This

was one of the rare occasions when we were forced to wear fly nets. But the open grasslands did yield a new cohort of birds. Willie Wagtails (djidi-djidi) perched on the fence wires, wagging their tails and flying out to capture bushflies – no shortage of food for them through here. The Noongar name for these birds perfectly describes their vocalisations. There was also a flock of Australian Wood Duck (marangana) on a dam at one of the smallholdings, and as we walked along the disused railway, edged by Bull Banksia (mungitch) and Jarrah, remnants of the forest that once was, we stumbled into the midst of full-scale battle between neighbouring groups of Western Australian Magpies (koolbardi). Apparently the rail line was the boundary between territories and it was under dispute, with six or so birds on either side of the track facing each other off, flapping their wings furiously at one another and emitting harsh *acht acht eeeear, acht acht eeeear* vocalisations.

Australians have a love–hate relationship with magpies. They were voted Australia's bird of the year in both 2017 and 2018. Their carolling calls are a quintessential sound of the Australian bush. But many also dread the onset of the breeding season, when some magpies will swoop cyclists or pedestrians that stray near their nesting sites, which in cities and towns are often on cycle paths and pedestrian walkways. According to the Magpie Alert website, magpie attacks peak in mid-September, with cyclists being the main targets. Some 14 per cent of attacks can involve serious injuries, as magpies target the eyes with their sharp bills and claws. When Freddy was 4 years old, we bought him his first bicycle for his birthday, 19 September. Our friend Peter Walley, the Peter of Jean and Peter who had met us at Abyssinia Rock, is an avid cyclist and had advised us not to put training wheels on Freddy's bike. The idea was that if we instead found a gentle hill and just set Freddy off down it, he would get the knack immediately. And so we went to the central strip in Kings Park and did just that. It worked a treat – he was cycling like a professional within seconds.

Off he went down the hill, but then, when he was some 200 metres ahead of us, a magpie swooped, knocking him off his bike and repeatedly flying at his face. Horrified, we ran down the hill screaming and shouting at the bird. Other walkers too ran to Freddy's aid, but the bird would not be dissuaded and continued its attacks, despite four grown adults striking at it and trying to shelter Freddy from its repeated swoops. It was completely uninterested in us, but intent on gaining access to Freddy. Only after we had run

some 50 metres from the original attack site did the bird leave us and return to its tree. We were fortunate; the numerous bleeding scratches to Freddy's face were around the eyelids and cheeks, but his eyes thankfully were unharmed, protected as they were by his sunglasses. Others are not so lucky, and attacks can cause permanent eye damage and even blindness.

Despite this, we nonetheless have an immense fondness for magpies, as do most Australians. They attack to protect their young from potential predators, and their territories from neighbouring groups. Freddy's crash helmet was white and relatively small, given it was a child's helmet. And it travelled at reasonable speed, less than a metre from the ground. To a magpie this would have had the appearance of the white back of an intruding bird flying into its territory. No wonder it attacked. We purchased a nice red helmet after that and were never troubled again.

Magpies, like kookaburras and bee-eaters, are cooperative breeders. They are remarkably long-lived birds, living up to twenty-five years and forming groups of three to more than fifteen birds that jointly defend their territory from other birds year round. Many of the birds in a group will be the offspring of the dominant female, but not all birds are because unrelated birds can join a group and cooperate with the female and her offspring. My colleague Mandy Ridley and her students have been studying groups of Western Australian Magpies (koolbardi) around the campus of the University of Western Australia and the Perth suburb of Guildford. Ridley's work is revealing some fascinating insights into the benefits of group living in Western Australian Magpies. Unlike many species of cooperative birds, it is not just the dominant female who will attempt to breed, and there can be several nests in a territory. But if a female's breeding attempt fails she will help other females in her group that have been successful in hatching their chicks. Helping is more common in smaller groups, and occurs mostly when chicks are at the fledgling stage, when they first leave the nest. Males will rarely help, but this is perhaps understandable since they are unlikely to be related to any of the juveniles in the group.

Using DNA fingerprinting analysis, Brisbane-based ornithologist Jane Hughes found that males from other groups sire 82 per cent of the offspring within a group. By extension, males within a group will obtain their evolutionary fitness by mating with females from other groups, and are most likely too busy on forays outside the territory seeking mating opportunities to have time to help feed fledglings in

their own group. And, assuming the breeding female is their mother, they would have to successfully help to rear at least two half-siblings to obtain the same fitness as siring one offspring in a neighbouring group. This is because they will share only 25 per cent of genes in common with half-brothers and half-sisters, while they will share 50 per cent of their genes with their own offspring. Male fitness among magpies is best served, therefore, in seeking matings elsewhere rather than helping.

The only option for females that have experienced a failed breeding attempt is to help other females in the group to raise their offspring. Because both males and females tend to remain in their natal territories for many years, groups will tend to consist of full and half-siblings, so it also makes sense for magpies to breed with individuals from outside their group, because by so doing they will avoid the detrimental effects that would come from inbreeding.

Magpies, as many of us suspected, are really smart. Ridley's group have conducted repeated cognitive testing of the birds they have studied, challenging them with a battery of different tasks to obtain a food reward of mozzarella cheese. For example, using a spatial memory task, they hid a cheese reward in a single covered well within a grid of eight wells and tested the bird's ability to find the cheese with the fewest mistakes. A bird is shown on one day which well contains the reward; the fewer wells it searches on subsequent days before finding the reward, the smarter the bird is in terms of its spatial memory. It seems that cognitive performance increases with group size; the more birds in a group the smarter the individual birds within that group are. Juveniles at 100 days old were found to have limited cognitive capacity, but by 200 days they had developed a cognitive performance that was dependent on the size of the group in which they lived.

These findings provide evidence that living in larger groups presents birds with social challenges that promote the development of cognitive capacity. And being smart can have significant consequences for individual fitness, because female magpies with greater cognitive performance were found to have a greater number of surviving fledglings each year. This link between cognition and reproductive success means that cognitive ability is under selection, and that group living is likely to have favoured the evolution of intelligence in many social animals, including ourselves.

After leaving the magpies we soon turned off the rail line and headed up a 4-kilometre dirt road that ascended the southern slope

TOP: Marangana or Australian Wood Duck, *Chenonetta jubata*. This common duck is often seen in the vicinity of dams and lakes. The pair nest high in tree holes but when the chicks hatch they must leap to the ground below where their parents call for them. Leigh Simmons

MIDDLE: Djidi-djidi or Willie Wagtail, *Rhipidura leucophrys*. Noongar names often reflect the sounds made by birds, and the Willie Wagtail is a clear example. The European name is equally appropriate, as this flycatcher wags its tail constantly to startle flies into flight so they may be seized and swallowed. Willie Wagtails are common residents of farmlands were flies are abundant. Leigh Simmons

BOTTOM: Koolbardi or Western Australian Magpie, *Gymnorhina tibicen dorsalis*. Magpies must be Australia's most loved and hated bird. Their powerful voice, with its complex and melodic vocabulary is a quintessential sound of the Australian bush. They live in groups and cooperate in the rearing of offspring. But when they are nesting they will attack anyone and anything that comes into their territory, especially if riding a bicycle. Leigh Simmons

of the Preston Valley, servicing the numerous smallholdings on its slopes. The road was steep and dusty, in direct hot sun, and the bushflies were abundant. The walking was very unpleasant and it was with great relief that we finally reached the rim of the valley and entered Greater Preston National Park. We descended through the cool shaded Jarrah forest to a creek that ran parallel to an old rail formation, which we followed for about a kilometre before reaching Noggerup Hut, perched on the hillside above the creek. Butterflies (boornarr) were abundant along the rail formation; we saw three species: the Western Xenica *(Geitoneura minyas)*, the Marbled Xenica *(Geitoneura klugii)* and the Lesser Wanderer *(Danaus chrysippus)*.

Speaking of wanderers, Sooty Tim had stopped at Noggerup for lunch but had continued on; we would not see him again although we remained in SMS contact for the duration of our journey. GFP arrived mid-afternoon; we could see him coming along the rail formation positively glowing in the shade of the forest. He had an old aluminium teapot that hung from the back of his pack. GFP's routine was to first set up his tent, this time inside the hut given it was just the three of us, and then make himself a brew in his teapot. This foul-smelling potion seemed to consist of a tea bag and hot water, with the addition of a teaspoon of Vegemite and one of peanut butter. I swear we did not witness him consume any solid food the entire time we spent with him; rather, he seemed to subsist on this concoction, which he brewed each day.

3

We were up extra early the following morning because, once again, temperatures were predicted to reach the high thirties by noon, and we wanted to cover the 22 kilometres to Grimwade Hut before it became too hot to walk. Away by five-thirty, we enjoyed the relatively level walking through the beautiful Greater Preston National Park. The track crossed several creek beds that feed the Preston River. These creek beds were bone dry at the time of our journey, but stepping logs across them foretold the running streams the winter walker would encounter. The forests through this section of the track are highly variable: the familiar dry mixed Jarrah and Marri woodland on higher ground gave way in the creek beds to

dense stands of Peppermint (wanil) understorey, their vibrant-green fresh growth glowing in the sunlight penetrating the tall Blackbutt (dwutta) canopy.

After 8 kilometres or so the track ascends into an area of old-growth Jarrah, with its magnificent mature trees and relatively open understorey. Here we paused for second breakfast and soaked up the ambiance of the pristine forest. After descending again and crossing the Lowden-Grimwade Road, we enjoyed the long stretch of raised railway formation that offered level walking. The elevation afforded by the rail embankment provided a wonderful perspective on the surrounding forest, and allowed us to come fairly close to a pair of Emu (wetj) travelling along the forest floor below. Through here the flowers of the Graceful Grasstrees (mimidi) were fresh, with creamy-white stamens emerging from chocolate-brown stems. The inflorescences were providing ample nectar for the Green Forester Moths *(Pollanisus cupreus)* that swarmed over them. These strikingly beautiful day-flying moths meet and mate at food resources at the warmest time of the day. At first glance they appear black, until the sunlight catches their metallic green wing scales and they appear iridescent.

When the track finally returned to the level of the forest floor, it was to be edged by thick stands of Spiny-leaved Flame Peas that were covered with their vibrant orange/red flowers. We rested among them briefly but pushed on as the day was becoming unbearably hot. By the time we reached Grimwade Hut at 11.30 am it was 38 degrees Celsius. We arrived to find a member of the state fire crew cleaning the area around the hut and installing fire-ban signs. He took one look at us and said, 'You boys look like you could do with a swim.' Yeah, right, like that was going to happen! Grimwade Hut overlooks a steep valley, which we had just ascended in the searing heat, with stands of mature Blackbutt, Jarrah and Marri.

Despite the heat, the birdlife here was rich; Red-tailed Black Cockatoos (karak) and Rufous Treecreepers (djini) we had seen at previous huts, but new for us here were Varied Sittella (koomaldidayit), competing with the Treecreepers for insects that crawled on the bark of the Blackbutt and Jarrah. So too were the Red-winged Fairy-wrens (djoordjilya) and their brood parasite the Fan-tailed Cuckoo (djoolar). The Fan-tailed Cuckoo has a distinctive and haunting call that carries far through the forest, a mournful trill with downward inflection – *wh-phweeeee* –

repeated over and over again. The bird at Grimwade Hut was to continue its cry for most of that afternoon.

And so we spent the afternoon birding, trying as best we could to keep cool with the help of the trusty wet flannel. Not quite a swim, but effective to a degree. Thankfully, the weather broke in the night, with a thunderstorm and downpour that freshened the air and brought the promise of more comfortable walking the following day.

4

The smell of petrichor the following morning was wonderful, a mix of damp humus and eucalyptus oil. The Red-winged Fairy-wrens (djoordjilya) hopped around the periphery of the campground, and our friend the Fan-tailed Cuckoo (djoolar) took up its mournful trilling. GFP emerged early that morning too, so we had the opportunity to chat while packing up our gear. He was due in Balingup by noon, to be picked up by his wife and whisked back to Perth, another section completed. GFP had long been an avid hiker, having walked the Larapinta in the West MacDonnell Ranges among other trails. There was much discussion of the various options for hiking in Tasmania, where Freddy was to move to take up his position as a veterinary surgeon the following February. It is always a joy to discover how much one can have in common with complete strangers.

From Grimwade the track headed steeply uphill into heavily logged forest for the first 4 kilometres or so. Although the trees had reached their natural height, they were young and had thin trunks. A recent burn meant that the understorey was sparse and open, and the walking, once we were on the crest of the hill, was reasonably level going and pleasant. We stopped for second breakfast on a fallen tree by a Snottygobble (kadgeegurr) that offered an attractive display of tiny yellow flowers. This was not the Spreading Snottygobble we had seen in the old-growth forests of the Monadnocks, but a second species that has long slender leaves and is far more common through the Jarrah and Marri forests. Other than the Snottygobble, there was little of note in flower through these regrowth forests.

After crossing the main Kirup-Grimwade Road, however, the track descended into a low-lying wet forest populated by an array of new plant species. Swamp Peppermint and Tassel Flowers dominated the

understorey, which also included Common Hovea, stands of Two-sided Boronia with its pink star-shaped flowers, and Hairy-leaved Tremandra with its flowers of pale mauve. But the highlight was a large colony of Slipper Orchids, with their large deep-green leaves and tall flower spikes. The first flowers of the season were freshly opened, perhaps stimulated by the previous night's downpour. Like the Elbow Orchids of the granite outcrops, these forest-dwelling orchids are also sexually deceptive, tricking male ichneumonid wasps into collecting and delivering their pollen to neighbouring flowers. But their deception is far more extreme than the temporary entrapment of male thynnine wasps by Elbow Orchids.

Like other sexually deceptive orchids, Slipper Orchids attract their pollinators by emitting airborne compounds that mimic the sexually attractive pheromone of female wasps. In the case of Slipper Orchids, also known as tongue orchids, five species share the same pollinator, the ichneumonid wasp *Lissopimpla excelsa*. The blend of chemical compounds that attract the male wasp have recently been characterised by chemical ecologist Björn Bohman and his colleagues. They found three volatile compounds with impossible-sounding names: (S)-2-(Tetrahydrofuran-2-yl) acetic acid and the ester derivatives methyl and ethyl (S)-2-(Tetrahydrofuran-2-yl) acetate. Put simply, biochemical names such as these describe the chemical structure of the compounds concerned.

But the contrivance by which this orchid achieves pollination requires far greater manipulation of the wasp than a simple attraction. On arrival, the male wasp will orient itself on the flower so as to insert its abdomen into the base of the labellum where the male and female parts of the flower reside, then proceed to copulate vigorously. Behavioural ecologist Anne Gaskett has studied these interactions extensively, and found that the male actually ejaculates, leaving its sperm mass on or near the stigma, along with any pollen that it may have delivered attached to its abdomen from previous sexual encounters with other orchid flowers. The orchids' mimicry of the female wasp must extend beyond simply smelling right to elicit such a strong response from the male. Gaskett has indeed found that aspects of the flower's shape mimic the shape of the female wasp. In particular, the 'heel' of the 'slipper' mimics the shape of the female wasp's thorax, promoting correct orientation by the male on arrival, and the colour of the flower coincides precisely with the colour of the female wasp. If it looks like a female, smells like a female and the genitalia fit snuggly, it must be a female. There is

a wonderful image of a male ichneumonid wasp having its wicked way with a slipper orchid in the third edition of Noel Hoffman and Andrew Brown's *Orchids of South-West Australia*.

Sexually deceptive orchids like the Elbow Orchids and flying duck orchids typically have very low rates of pollination, because the male insects they dupe into pollinating them rapidly become habituated. They are attracted to the flowers but they fail to be rewarded by copulation. Not so the Slipper Orchids, which have the highest rates of pollination of all sexually deceptive orchids. Gaskett reports rates as high as 70 per cent, compared with more typical rates of 20 per cent for other sexually deceptive orchids. There are two possible reasons for this. First, the male is obviously rewarded for being attracted to the flower. To all intents and purposes, it has successfully mated with what it 'believes' to be a female wasp. But there is perhaps a more sinister twist to this story. By promoting ejaculation in the male wasps, orchids could actually manipulate the pollinator population to their own advantage.

Ichneumonid wasps are parasitic; the female has a long hypodermic ovipositor with which she injects her eggs into the caterpillars of moths. When the egg hatches, the wasp larva feeds on the caterpillar's internal organs, eventually killing the creature when it is time for the mature wasp to emerge. Parasitic wasps, like all hymenopteran insects, have what is known as haplodiploid sex determination. When a female ichneumonid lays an egg, she can choose to fertilise it using sperm stored in her sperm storage organ or she can lay it unfertilised. Fertilised eggs will be diploid, meaning they have a copy of genes from their mother and a copy of genes from the male that provided the sperm; they will develop into female offspring. Eggs that are laid unfertilised are haploid, meaning they have only one copy of DNA, half of the mother's complement, and will develop into male offspring.

Now, sperm production is costly, and the males of most species will become depleted of ejaculate following copulation, so that when they copulate a second time the numbers of sperm they deliver will be greatly reduced. As a result, after mating with a slipper orchid, should a male find and mate with a female wasp, he will deliver a greatly reduced number of sperm. Given that females mate only once, their limited sperm stores will be rapidly exhausted so that they can produce only male offspring. The result will be a population of wasps in the next generation that is male-biased. While this may be costly for female wasps because their sons will have little

chance of finding females with which to reproduce, it will be highly beneficial for the orchids because the population will be flooded with an excess of pollinators that are ignorant of the contrivances by which the orchids achieve pollination. The intimate coevolution between Slipper Orchids and their ichneumonid pollinators, as Darwin noted succinctly for orchids generally, surely 'will exalt the whole vegetable kingdom in most persons' estimation'.

Sadly, the wet forest we were passing through was all too short, but it did give promise of what was to come in the weeks ahead. We soon ascended again into dryer forest. Thunderstorms rolled in by mid-morning, but it was just too warm to put on rain jackets so we put up with getting wet. As we ascended towards Ammon Road, the forest floor was thick with Yellow Flags. Most had finished flowering, with just the odd plant or two revealing their final flowers of the season. It would have been a spectacular scene through here just two or three weeks earlier. Eventually we emerged from the forest into the cleared agricultural land that surrounds the town of Balingup. We descended steeply along the edge of the forest towards Grimwade Road, high above a dam populated by Australasian Coot (kidjibroon), Grey Teal (kalyong) and a White-necked Heron (djilimilyan). A Little Crow, for which there is no Noongar name, flew across the valley calling *uh-uh-uh-uh-uh*.

From Grimwade Road the track ascended once more, before plummeting down into the valley along the edge of a pine plantation. The track down was severely eroded and treacherous, especially so as it was wet from the morning's thunderstorm. It was slow and careful going, but we eventually made it down to Jayes Road, along which the track meanders into the town of Balingup. I have to say that the walk along Jayes Road was quite depressing. Balingup really is an environmental disaster. The clearing of native forest has made way for an aggressive invasion of weeds. Balingup Brook is choked with brambles, feral pines seeded from the nearby plantations line its banks, and feral grasses and thistles abound. The sky was dark with thunderclouds and we were somewhat bedraggled and tired after the 23-kilometre hike from Grimwade Hut. And so we were delighted to finally arrive at the Balingup Visitor Centre to a warm welcome from Raelean, who, if she is not Track-Elf-in-Chief, should be promoted immediately.

Raelean enquired where we were staying that night. We had booked to stay in the Post Office, accommodation that offers dormitory-style rooms to Bibbulmun Track walkers. But we had

received an email while on the summit of Mount Cooke, informing us that they could no longer accommodate us as they were closing for renovations. Carol had therefore booked us into an Airbnb. When we told Raelean where we were staying, she somewhat worryingly told us how nice the view was from up there, as she looked out of the window at the approaching thunderstorm. She told us to leave our packs and head off to the tavern for a beer and some lunch. We did not need to be told twice – indeed, it was uncanny how she had read our minds. Oh, the joy of fresh food and beer; everything seems to taste orders of magnitude better after you have been deprived for several days. After lunch we visited the pharmacy for advice on treating Freddy's increasingly alarming pressure sores, leaving with dressings that we hoped would provide extra padding where his pack sat. Then to the grocery store for supplies, including some fine cheese, prosciutto and wine for supper. And finally we returned to the Visitor Centre.

Raelean called our Airbnb to arrange for a pick-up. The phone call did not go well: 'Well, of course not, they don't have a car!' Silence. 'WELL, I'LL BRING THEM UP MYSELF!' The phone returned to its cradle with some considerable force. Raelean closed the centre and bundled us into her ute. Thank goodness, too; the Airbnb was about 5 kilometres out of town, north along the South Western Highway, and at an elevation of 160 metres, straight up. And it was tipping it down by this time. Apparently the owner was not even in town and had expected us to walk there. It was advertised as perfect for walkers on the track, which it most definitely is not. Sure, the view of Balingup way off in the valley below is pretty enough, and it was very comfy, but without Raelean the entire affair would have been a nightmare. I reiterate, walking 5 kilometres is one thing, but doing it with 18 kilograms on your back up a 20 per cent incline in the pouring rain is another.

When Raelean dropped us off she kindly offered to pick us up that evening and take us to the tavern, which we declined, although we did accept her generous offer to pick us up in the morning and take us back to the Visitor Centre. Raelean really was the most warm and welcoming person we met on our entire journey, and incredibly generous. She took great pride in the fact that the Bibbulmun went through her town, and treated its walkers like her family. God bless you, Raelean.

BALINGUP TO PEMBERTON

BALINGUP TO PEMBERTON

1

We left Balingup in the rain for a wet walk through the Golden
Valley Tree Park. This arboretum is planted with hundreds of
specimen trees from Europe and North America, and the homestead
offers a history of the area. On our way through the park we saw
White-faced Herons (wayan) in the ponds and a Brown Falcon
(karkany) soaring high above the open fields. Beyond the park the
track ascends steeply along the stony Old Padbury Road, which runs
through a pine plantation to join an old rail line beyond Padbury
Reservoir. At the summit, the track turns right into Jarrah forest
where it shares its route with the Greenbushes Loop trail, following
the rim of the valley with views across the agricultural lands below,
before descending through the forest to pass along the edge of
Mount Jones Dam. We paused to photograph an ancient River
Banksia that grew close to the dam, which must have been 20 metres
or more tall. There were also some ancient Marri growing through
this short stretch of forest.

All too soon we emerged once more into cleared agricultural
land and followed the Spring Gully Road steeply down into the
valley. This area is heavily grazed with cattle, the consequence being
a substantial population of bushflies. Thankfully, that day was cool
and damp, and the flies had sources of water other than our eyes.
On crossing Norilup Brook and joining Southampton Road the

track soon took us into a large field of cattle that grazed a particularly steep slope up which the track ascended. As a distraction from the strenuous climb – well, to be fair, I would have done this anyway – I turned over a few dung pats to see who was home. I was delighted to find dung beetles doing their work in this pasture. Most dung pads were little more than patches of dried dust and grass residue, their contents devoured or buried by the resident dung beetles. The predominant species in this field was the Bull-horned Dung Beetle *(Onthophagus taurus)*, a species native to the Mediterranean regions of Europe and North Africa that was introduced into Australia in the 1970s as a biological control agent to control bushflies.

Dung beetles are an ancient group of insects with their evolutionary origins, like humans, in Africa. They have spread across the globe and speciated alongside the mammals, often each species of beetle specialising on the dung of just one or a few species of mammal. The genus *Onthophagus* has more individual species than any other animal genus on Earth, which begs the question as to why we should need to introduce dung beetles into Australia. The answer, of course, is that native Australian species of dung beetle coevolved with the continent's marsupials, and so feed only on marsupial dung. When Europeans brought their cattle to the continent, there was nothing that would eat cattle dung except bushflies, which were delivered a bonanza of resources that allowed them to breed unhindered in their trillions of trillions of trillions. The consequence was the archetypical image of the Aussie male, his hat fringed with hanging corks to ineffectually ward off the flies. Europe does not have this problem, because dung beetles there have coevolved alongside human pastoralists and their cattle.

In 1960, entomologist George Bornemissza, working in my own school at the University of Western Australia, had the idea of collecting dung beetles from Europe and Africa and introducing them to Australia, to provide a community of beetles that would deal with the copious volumes of dung produced by the Australian cattle industry. Research laboratories were established by the CSIRO in France and in Southern Africa, and beetles were collected, bred and shipped to Canberra, where they were held in quarantine and bred further so as to avoid the introduction of any other organisms that might be associated with cattle dung. Eventually they were released at locations across the Australian continent. Fifty-five species of dung beetle were imported, of which thirty-four were released and twenty-three have become successfully established.

The Australian dung beetle program is acclaimed as the most successful biological control program ever. The beetles are effective in removing dung from pastures. The fact that they bury it has the effect of enriching the soil and promoting pasture productivity while at the same time preventing bushflies from breeding. Indeed, introduced dung beetles are credited with facilitating the development of our modern café culture, which before their introduction was impossible due to the bushfly problem. If you have any doubt about this claim, go to Margaret River on a warm October weekend before the dung beetles become fully active and you'll appreciate what life was like in the 1950s before dung beetles were brought to Australia.

As a behavioural and evolutionary ecologist, my own research interests have long focused on dung-breeding insects, and I began working on the introduced Bull-horned Dung Beetle when I arrived in Australia from the UK in 1995. This species has a remarkable breeding biology. The beetles arrive at a fresh dropping within minutes of it hitting the ground. The females excavate tunnels in the soil beneath the dung pat and build chambers to which they carry dung from the pat and package it into large balls about the size of an almond. They hollow out a chamber in each dung ball into which they deposit a single egg that is held on a fine stalk so as to prevent it touching the surface of the dung and rotting. When the egg hatches, the larva feeds on the dung and grows for about two weeks before turning into a pupa. The pupa transforms into an adult beetle, which tunnels its way to the surface some three to four weeks after it hatched as a larva. The beetles then disperse, feeding on fresh dung before they become sexually mature, and the cycle begins again. It is this utilisation of dung for breeding and feeding that makes dung beetles so useful as a biological control agent.

The males of most dung beetles in this genus exhibit a suite of behavioural and physical traits that characterise alternative mating tactics. In the Bull-horned Dung Beetle some males, referred to as major males, grow a pair of head horns that resemble those of bulls, hence both their common name, Bull-horned, and their scientific species name, *taurus*. Major males will assist females in provisioning their offspring, bringing parcels of dung from the pat and delivering them to their mate to be packed into the brood balls. They will also patrol their tunnels and block the entrance to any other males that might try to usurp the owner and mate with his female. Fights between major males involve trials of physical strength as they lock

TOP: Wayan or White-faced Heron, *Ardea novaehollandiae*. A very common resident in wetlands, especially fond of human-made dams and lakes where it hunts for small fish and frogs or other tasty morsels. Leigh Simmons

MIDDLE: Kidjibroon or Eurasian Coot, *Fulica altra*. Perhaps our most common and easily recognised water bird. The white face shield has evolved as an aggressive signal assessed by competitors during conflicts over territorial boundaries. If disputes are not settled by the relative sizes of the birds' white shields, they resort to all-out physical aggression. Leigh Simmons

BOTTOM: Bull-horned Dung Beetles, *Onthophagus taurus*. These beetles were introduced from Europe to Australia to control bushflies that would otherwise breed in cattle dung. They have a remarkable mating system in which horned major males fight for access to females while small minor males sneak matings and gain paternity through sperm competition. Leigh Simmons

horns and push one another, the interloper attempting to enter and the resident to push the intruder from the tunnel entrance. Bull-horned Dung Beetles have a maximum pulling strength of up to 0.5 Newtons, the equivalent of a human pulling a double-decker bus! And when males are exposed to rivals during their development, they bulk up by increased feeding in anticipation of the trials of physical strength they expect to endure.

A second cohort of males, referred to as minor males, are smaller in body size and do not develop horns. Rather, they resemble females and dig side tunnels that intercept breeding tunnels defended by the major males. Minor males sneak into breeding chambers and mate with females while the major males are collecting dung or engaged in battles with other majors. These so-called sneaky males have to compete for fertilisations because females will have sperm in their sperm storage organs from mating with their major male breeding partner. To engage in sperm competition, minor males have larger testes than major males, capable of producing greater quantities of sperm, all the better to dilute out those from their major male rivals when it comes to fertilising eggs. Who would imagine all this was going on beneath a pile of cow dung?

On reaching the top of the cattle field, we crossed a stile and continued the steep trudge up a track through pine plantation. It began to rain heavily at this point, forcing us to put on our rain gear. Eventually the track levelled off after Hillview Road, and followed the ridge of the Blackwood Valley to Blackwood Hut, perched high on the edge of the valley with commanding views to the river below.

2

Shortly after we left Blackwood Hut the following morning, the track plummeted steeply down into the Blackwood River Valley. *A Guide to the Bibbulmun Track* refers to this climb as 'Cardiac Hill', which I can well believe would be a very apt description if you were travelling from south to north. With great caution we proceeded along the track that follows the Blackwood River past several homesteads, as Sooty Tim had kindly texted us to advise of a loose dog from one of the homesteads that had attacked him

when he passed through a few days earlier. Thankfully we did not encounter the beast.

After crossing the river at Southampton Bridge, we began the long and very steep ascent of the southern slope of the Blackwood Valley. The day was cool with a light drizzle, which helped. Entering the Jarrah forest after Millstream Dam was a joy. It seemed an age since we had emerged from the forest north of Balingup, and now, once again, we were away from human agricultural landscapes and had that sense of remoteness finally restored. The forest here had changed distinctly from that in the north. It seemed darker somehow, and Native Willow joined the understorey's plant community; this beautiful pea with deep green willow-like leaves was just starting to display its golden yellow flowers.

The track from here continued with some serious descents and ascents for the remaining 14 kilometres to Gregory Brook Hut. One arrives from above and descends to the hut on the edge of the brook whose name it bears. When we arrived it was to the frightful drone of a leaf-blower echoing up the valley. The guy from the fire crew who we had met at Grimwade three days previously was putting up fire ban signs and cleaning the campground. I admire immensely the efforts put into keeping the huts clean and comfortable for walkers, but really do question the utility of using power and energy to blow leaves in a forest. He was great, though, stopping the wretched blower immediately on our arrival, and leaving us to the peace and tranquillity of Gregory Brook Hut, one of the best-located huts on the track, situated as it is in a dip in the forest and surrounded by large River Banksia and mature Marri. There were excellent birds to be seen too: White-breasted Robin (boyidjil), Western Rosella (bardinar), White-browed Scrub-wren (koorkal), Australian Ringneck Parrot (doornart) and the Jacky Winter flycatcher. We spent the afternoon watching the beautiful Gilbert's Honeyeaters (djingki) feeding on the abundance of flowers in the canopies of the Marri that surrounded the hut, their deep melodic *wherrt-wherrt-wherrt* echoing up the valley.

3

The following day our 21-kilometre walk to Donnelly River Village was simply magical. We started early, wanting to arrive in good

time for first lunch before our friends arrived. For we had booked a cottage at Donnelly River Village, and Carol was coming down with our good friends Win and Ruth for a three-night break to celebrate Christmas, albeit a week early.

The first 3 kilometres had some ups and downs to contend with, but the majestic River Banksia and mature Marri scattered through the forest were just beautiful. And at Karri Gully we entered Karri forest for the first time. Much as anticipated, the first Karri we encountered was simply massive, its tall straight trunk reaching 80 or more metres into the sky. Karri are the tallest trees in Western Australia and among the tallest in the world. They grow in the wetter soils of the south, which also harbour a host of other unique plant species. The understorey through Karri Gully featured Native Willow, River Banksia, Oak-leaf Chorilaena, Wild Plum (koolah), Hooded Lily and Cut-leaf Hibbertia. And crawling across the damp woodland paths were bright-yellow Canary Worms *(Fletchamia sugdeni)*, a species of planarian flatworm. Little is known about these flatworms, though their extremely bright yellow colouration is likely to be a warning to forest birds and small mammals not to eat them.

Many species of invertebrates that harbour toxins sequestered from the plants on which they feed, or manufacture them de novo, have evolved what is called aposematic colouration, typically bright yellows, reds and sometimes both, which make them highly conspicuous. You would think that being conspicuous to a predator would be a bad thing. But predators learn very quickly to avoid foods they find distasteful or that make them sick, so warning colourations can be adaptive in prey because they deter predatory attack. Some species can evolve colouration that mimics the colours of toxic species with which they co-occur. Because predators have an evolved learning response to avoid conspicuously coloured toxic prey, other species can exploit the predator's phobia of brightly coloured prey by evolving conspicuous colouration even though they are themselves perfectly palatable. But the benefits of mimicry can collapse if mimics become too common. The costs to predators of eating conspicuous prey will be greatly reduced if they are more often palatable than not, and predators may start to specialise on eating brightly coloured prey as they will be easier to find. Mimicry, then, is only beneficial when mimics are rare and toxic prey common, a phenomenon called frequency-dependent selection.

It was Henry Walter Bates, a naturalist and contemporary of Darwin and Wallace, who discovered this form of mimicry, which

is commonly referred to as Batesian mimicry. Bates and Wallace travelled to South America in 1848, and together explored the Amazon, sending collections of insects and other animals home to England. Darwin benefited greatly from Bates's observations on the Amazon, which provided considerable evidence in support of his own emerging ideas on the origin of species by natural selection. Darwin is said to have described Bates's narrative *The Naturalist on the River Amazons* published in 1863 as 'the best work on natural travels ever published in England'. For reasons unknown, Bates and Wallace parted company a year after arriving in Amazonia and Wallace returned to England alone in 1852, losing his collection en route when his ship caught fire and sank in the North Atlantic. Wallace thankfully survived, and later went on to travel as a naturalist through the Malay Archipelago. Bates meanwhile remained in Amazonia, returning to England in 1859 after eleven years of exploration, having collected 14,712 species of which nearly 8,000 were new to science. Those were the days, when you could make a living travelling through the bush collecting and observing animals and plants new to science.

After the Brookman Highway, the track first passed under the Yarnup–Nannup transmission line, where we encountered a male Emu (wetj) wandering along the clearing in the forest, followed closely by three stripy chicks. Walking along the Willow Bridge rail formation alongside the Donnelly River was delightful. River Banksia lined the river gully, and the forest transitioned back and forth between wet Karri and dry Jarrah, with numerous crossings of tributaries joining the Donnelly River, which we finally crossed at Demo Road. The final 2 kilometres to Donnelly River were hard going, but not because of any hills. On the contrary, the old rail formation provided easy, level walking for the entire journey to Donnelly River Village. Rather, a considerable number of Karri had fallen across the track through the final section, which, given their massive girths, took some considerable efforts to climb over – no easy feat with a heavy pack.

Donnelly River Village, a township officially named Wheatley, is the site of an old timber mill established by the Wheatley family in 1912 to manufacture telegraph poles from trees cut in the forest. Bunnings ran a profitable milling business there from 1951, and the village grew around it until it was closed in 1978. The cottages are now individually owned on a leasehold basis, and Donnelly River Village has become a popular tourist retreat. The general store

TOP: Ngowonan or Pacific Black Duck, *Anas superciliosa*. Far from the cooperative monogamous pair they appear, ducks generally are locked in an extraordinary coevolutionary arms race as males and females evolve ever more complex genitalia to control when and with whom to mate. Freddy Simmons

MIDDLE: Bamboon or Western Yellow Robin, *Eopsaltria griseogularis*. A common resident of the Jarrah forests. The western form differs from the eastern states' form in its grey breast. Like other robins it forages for insects in the leaf litter on the forest floor. Freddy Simmons

BOTTOM: Wetj or Emu, *Dromaius novaehollandiae*. The largest Australian bird. They come from an ancient group of flightless birds the ratites. They show sex role reversals in that it is the male who incubates the eggs and rears the young, while females compete aggressively for access to males and their parental care. Leigh Simmons

makes an excellent coffee, and we sampled their breakfast offerings and sat in their comfy armchairs, glowing in the knowledge that we had made it halfway. Spending two days without having to carry a pack, drinking fine wine, dining on home-cooked food, and wearing a pair of jeans, cotton T-shirt and comfy sandals was a real treat. I was rather startled, though, to find that my civvies were all rather large. I had to tighten my belt an extra two holes to stop my jeans falling around my ankles.

4

We set off again on 21 December, without quite the haste of our departure from Kalamunda it must be said. Indeed, getting into my track clothes and hoisting the pack onto my back was something of an emotional challenge. Sure, I was fit enough by now, but it would have been so easy to just jump in the car and go home for Christmas.

The track south from Donnelly River Village was closed at Jeffries Road, a prescribed burn planned for the area in the coming days. This was a great shame because the track winds its way through magnificent Karri forest along Yanmah Brook before heading south along the Donnelly River, passing through, according to *A Guide to the Bibbulmun Track*, 'some of the best blackbutt in the south-west' in the Blackbutt Nature Reserve. The description of Tom Road Hut, set on 'a lovely permanent pool by the river, with granite boulders and massive karri trees' sounds quite wonderful. Not for us, alas.

We were detoured down Gregory Road and then along Paganini Road to cleared agricultural land where there was a temporary campground – well, a portaloo on a trailer and a picnic bench. It was just too depressing to stay there overnight, and so after a relaxed lunch and a snooze, we continued on steeply up Paganini Road to reach Graphite Road, along which we had to contend with speeding traffic for the 6 kilometres down to One Tree Bridge. We had covered just over 19 kilometres by that time and had little appetite to walk further, so we set up camp near Glenoran Pool, a delightful permanent pool on the Donnelly River that offered an arresting dip in its icy water. The beautiful sunset over the mature Karri, the clear and starry night sky, and the chorus of Slender Tree Frogs *(Litoria adelaidensis)* all combined to reinforce in us the importance of completing the journey to which we had committed. Despite the

human impact on the environment through which we had passed, we still managed to add to our bird list: a pair of Magpie-larks (diliboort) duetted in the hedgerow that edged Paganini Road – *qwoo-zik-wheeik...qwoo-zik-wheeik* – and Yellow-billed Spoonbills (kaaka-baaka) and Straw-necked Ibis (nankiny) waded along the edges of a large dam nestled in the dip between two gently sloping pastures. We slept well that night, knowing that the following day we would return to the forest.

From One Tree Bridge the track followed the Donnelly River all the way to Boarding House Hut, some 13 kilometres south. We set off at 6.15 am; the high was predicted to be 38 degrees Celsius and, of course, we wanted to reach Boarding House Hut before it became too hot. The morning was fresh and cool, and the forest delightfully damp as mist rose from the surface of Glenoran Pool. There were many opportunities to stop by the river as it cascaded over its rocky bed. Along the banks grew Karri Sheoak, Karri Hazel (djop born), Native Willow, Water Bush and Peppermint (wanil). The Bracken (manya) in places grew as tall as 3 metres, and Maidenhair Fern (karbarra) gave a fresh vibrant-green cover to the track edges in the darker damper sections where the majestic Karri blocked much of the sunlight.

At second breakfast a group of White-browed Babblers (ngowan) passed us, travelling from tree to tree, about 1 metre from the ground, chattering incessantly to each other as they moved through the understorey – *squarrk-squarrairk, wheeit-wheeit, chur-r-r-r-, tchuk*. Another of Australia's cooperatively breeding birds, White-browed Babblers are always found in large family groups, where helpers assist in rearing young produced by one or more breeding females. Babblers generally can have a remarkable repertoire of vocalisations. The phonetic transcriptions of birdcalls give us an idea of how those calls sound, but they tell us nothing of their meaning. Indeed, whether animals actually communicate with one another in the same way we humans do, by combining sounds to make meaningful phrases, is actually a hot topic in animal behaviour research. Is there meaning in the babble of babblers?

As humans, we utter sounds that are combined to make meaning. In English, the sounds /c/ /a/ and /t/ can be combined to form words that convey a specific meaning, such as 'cat' or 'act'. But other combinations 'cta' and 'tca' are meaningless. Our language is said to be combinatorial, as it consists of many distinct sounds (the alphabet) that are combined to form meaningful words and phrases.

Babblers, it turns out, are no different. Behavioural ecologist Sabrina Engesser and her colleagues have studied the way South African Pied Babblers combine their apparently meaningless sounds, and have established that the order of sound production can in fact have significant meaning for other Pied Babblers. Male Pied Babblers combine two distinct raucous 'cry-like' vocalisations that end with repetitions of a single note or double notes. When a male produces a 'cry' it serves to alert the family group and initiate movement. Very different behavioural responses are elicited, however, by the single-note repetition, which elicits a 'come to me' response, and the double-note repetition that elicits a longer-distance 'come with me' movement response. There is meaning, it seems, in the babbling of babblers.

By mid-morning we reached the official halfway marker, a 3-metre tall red pole topped with a giant Waugal. Ironically, we placed little significance in this landmark at the time, though we did ask ourselves why the Waugal should be so large, and indeed why it was on a metal pole and not nailed to the adjacent tree like all the other Waugals! It only occurred to us that this was a significant landmark later, after we had arrived at Boarding House Hut. For us, the halfway mark had been achieved and celebrated back at Donnelly River Village, and so we were not anticipating coming across a marker. But there we were, 501 kilometres from Kalamunda, with 501 kilometres to go. Mind-boggling. I have since found images of this marker on the internet, with distance pointers to Kalamunda and Albany. I guess these pointers have since been stolen.

Beyond the halfway marker we came across several stands of Club-lipped Spider Orchids growing in the middle of the track. Spider orchids are an immensely abundant group of orchids whose taxonomy is not yet well established. Noel Hoffman and Andrew Brown report some 240 described species globally, the vast majority of which are endemic to Australia. With more than 150 species endemic to Western Australia, spider orchids form the single largest group of orchids in the region. But they are a highly variable group, both in their detailed structure and how they are pollinated. Some, like the Pink Fairy and Cowslip orchids, have brightly coloured flowers that attract pollinators seeking nectar rewards, though they provide none; they mimic the flowers of nectar-rewarding plants. Others, like the slipper and Elbow orchids, are sexually deceptive, attracting male thynnine wasps with scents that mimic the pheromones of female wasps.

Club-lipped Spider Orchids are among the sexually deceptive species, with swollen clubs at the tips of the drab green petals and sepals that emit signalling chemicals mimicking the wasp's sex pheromone. The fact that so many closely related species of spider orchid exploit such different mechanisms to achieve pollination provides a classic example of divergent evolution and speciation, driven by competition for a limited supply of pollinators. We were fortunate to see this orchid, as most spider orchids have long since finished their flowering season by December.

We arrived at Boarding House Hut by 11 am, having crossed the Donnelly River via the large fallen Karri that has been used to form a footbridge. The hut lies along a spur trail, perched high on the banks of the river where the old bridge once stood. It was so hot by midday that we scrambled down the bank to some small flowing pools between rocks and fallen trees and just sat in the cool water, entertained by curious yabbies that ambled across the sandy bottom to nibble at our toes. The new bird for our list at Boarding House Hut was a Black Kite that circled high above us in the heat of the day.

5

My heart sank when I looked on the Bibbulmun Track map at the terrain profile for the following day's walk. *A Guide to the Bibbulmun Track* says 'this is one of the more challenging sections'. There would be some serious ups and downs to contend with, that much was clear, as the track climbed in and out of the Donnelly River Valley. But on the map, around the 11-kilometre mark, there seemed to be an impossible gouge in the topography, a sheer descent followed by an equally sheer ascent. Okay, the fine print on the map says that 'a vertical exaggeration of five to one has been used to simulate the walker's experience', but surely this must be a printing error! One of the inkjet nozzles must have been blocked – yes, that was it, it could not possibly be that steep. We packed the map away and set off.

We walked along the banks of the Donnelly River before crossing Palings Road, then headed steadily uphill along Wirraway Form to an elevation of around 200 metres. The form is cut into the steep slope of the valley and afforded a relatively level 4-kilometre walk

along the 200-metre contour. The views down into the valley were stunning. We were above the understorey canopy of Karri, Sheoak and Peppermint (wanil), yet below the upper canopy of the old-growth Karri – a natural 'tall-trees' walkway. Total silence, other than the Donnelly River trickling cool and dark below, *whit-whit-whit-whiet-wheet qWHIT* from Western Whistlers (bidilmidang), *ai-whiieer-la, ai-whIIIeeeeer-la* from a flock of Carnaby's Black Cockatoos (ngoolyak), and the melodic *quorra-quorra-quorra, WHIEET-CHIEW* of the Western Grey Shrike-thrush (koodilang). It was simply magical.

Eventually we descended to cross the Donnelly River on the Lease Road Bridge, where we stopped for second breakfast, before climbing again along Lease Road and turning off, back into the Karri forest, where Morning Iris, Scaly-leaved Hibbertia, Milkwort and Karri Dampiera provided splashes of colour along the edges of the track. Large fallen Karri were covered thickly in verdant moss within which clumps of Snail Orchids grew, their flower spikes long since dried and brown.

Soon the track started to descend again. It was then that we realised there was nothing wrong with the printer used to produce our map. We plummeted 110 metres before climbing immediately around 140 metres while covering a linear distance of just 1 kilometre! The climb down into the valley was loose under foot, with steep steps in places presenting more of a scramble than a walk. On the other side of the stream that fed into the Donnelly River, the track was thankfully firmer underfoot, but the haul up was one of the hardest stretches of the track thus far. We were exhausted when we finally reached the top, only to drop down to the river valley again some 3 kilometres further on. Why on earth did they not simply route the track along the river, around that massive hill?

The trail along the river to Beavis Hut was level going from there on in, and it was a blessed relief to have cleared all the major climbs of the day. We spooked a huge black-and-white feral pig along this section; it resembled a giant panda plummeting into the bush, crushing everything in its path. It had clearly been digging for roots along the riverbank, which was heavily 'ploughed'. It took us just over six hours to walk the 20 kilometres to Beavis, and our relief at sighting the recumbent walker icon that indicates a soon to be reached campground was immense.

Beavis Hut is a wonderfully remote camp in the depths of Greater Beedelup National Park, surrounded by mature Karri and with a

small dam in its front yard from which we could collect water to wash ourselves and our clothes, which after the day's exertions were in desperate need. The dam attracted good birdlife too, with Red-winged Fairy-wrens (djoordjilya) coming down to the water's edge to drink, Silvereyes (doolor), White-breasted Robins (boyidjil), Grey Fantails (kadjinak), White-browed Scrub-wrens (koorkal) and a Little Eagle. Our arrival had obviously caught some of the residents in compromised positions; as we sat quietly birding and recovering in the shade of the shelter, a large King's Skink (wandy; *Egernia kingii*), scuttled across the front porch and under the bridge that spanned the overflow for the dam, so fast that it left a cloud of dust behind. And a native Bush Rat *(Rattus fuscipes)*, dropped from the ceiling of the hut onto the sleeping platform; with its legs pumping fast to gain traction on the varnished surface, it made more noise than forward motion. Eventually the panicked creature found a footing, overshot the edge and fell comically to the ground before disappearing into a hole between the corner of the platform and the hut wall.

Bush Rats are not to be mistaken for the invasive rats that arrived on ships with early settlers and plague our homes and gardens. No, Bush Rats are endemic, native Australian mammals descendent from rodents that arrived in Australia 2 million years ago. Unlike invasive European Black and Norwegian rats, our endemic Bush Rat does not carry disease and will not be found around our cities and towns. Rather, it is restricted to and dependent upon our native forests, feeding on insects, fungi and plants. Darwin was the first European to collect this species, when he visited Albany on his voyage around the world, in a trap baited with cheese that he had placed in bushland south of Mount Melville. It was first described by the zoologist George Waterhouse in Darwin's edited volume *The Zoology of the Voyage of H.M.S. Beagle*. Bush Rats fall easy prey to introduced cats and foxes, and though currently not in danger of extinction, their protection is just as important as that of our more charismatic Western Quoll (chuditch), because they are an important food source for these native carnivores.

It was a privilege to share Beavis Hut with its resident rodent, though Freddy was not best pleased in the morning to find that it had chewed at the zip of his pack, no doubt attracted by the odour of second breakfast. Our own fault – we should have placed all food items in the plastic containers provided. We would not need to be reminded of that again.

6

Christmas Eve. It would be another long day, as we had 21 kilometres of ground to cover, but the track to Beedelup Hut passes through Karri Valley Resort, nestled in the Karri forest on the shore of a beautiful lake formed by the damming of Beedelup Brook, and we were hopeful of a good meal and a beer at lunchtime. We passed mainly through wet Karri forest, with occasional stretches of dry Jarrah and Marri on the higher ground. Higher ground, of course, meant that we had a roller-coaster of steep ascents and descents to tackle.

Though still tough going, it was not quite as bad as the previous day's march from hell. Through the sections of Jarrah forest were fresh Pale Rainbow Sundews (boon), climbing through the skirts of Grasstrees (balga). These extraordinary plants, like their Pretty Sundew cousins we saw in the northern Jarrah forests, are insectivorous. They capture and digest insects with the sticky tendrils that cover their leaf surfaces. But unlike Pretty Sundews, Pale Rainbow Sundews have two types of sticky trap. Some are on short stems and serve to entrap and digest their insect prey. Others are on the tips of long stems and are used to grasp and form strongholds on neighbouring vegetation, allowing the plant to climb to considerable heights above the forest floor. These plants have extremely thin and spindly stems that would be unable to hold them upright, but their sticky traps allow them to grow up to 2 metres through the surrounding vegetation so as to present their pretty white flowers in the flight paths of passing insect pollinators.

After about 5 kilometres, we climbed out of the Donnelly River Valley, crossed Seven Day Road and joined a forest track that travelled alongside Carey Brook. The forest was still and quiet, with the exception of the ever-present *twitch-twitchit* of the Grey Fantails (kadjinak) and the perfunctory whistle of the Western Gerygone (waralyboodang). But at precisely 9 o'clock, ticking cicadas *(Physeema latorea)* abruptly started their incessant *tick...tick...tick... tick...tick...tick...tick*. Here at last was the sound of summer forests that brings such fond memories of summer trips to the southern forests of Walpole and Nornalup. The morning thus far had been cool and overcast, but the clouds had now parted and the sun drenched down into the forest, warm and bright. The sunlight had triggered the onset of the cicada noises, a hypothesis I would test

over the coming days. Indeed, the cicada chorus was always delayed on cloudy days but started very early on cloudless days, typically around 7 am or even earlier when hot, sometimes before we had started our day's walking.

That day, as we climbed through the forest along the edge of Carey Brook, we were to witness an extraordinary event – a mass emergence of cicadas from the forest floor. Cicadas spend most of their life underground, sucking sap from the roots of trees and growing in body size until they are large enough to emerge as adults. When summer arrives, they dig out of the ground, crawl across the surface and climb the first stick or branch they encounter. They will stop about 50 centimetres from the ground to moult into an adult cicada, leaving empty brown husks of their former juvenile selves like ghosts clinging to the vegetation. The newly moulted adult is soft and pale and must pump blood into its crumpled wings to expand them. They remain motionless in the warm sunshine as their cuticle hardens, and once it has they fly up to join the chorus in the forest canopy. As we walked along the track that day we saw an abundance of empty skins and many newly emerging adults. We were in peak emergence, but the ticking chorus above us was still small relative to what it would become over the coming days and weeks.

Life for an adult cicada lasts just a few weeks, assuming they do not fall immediate prey to awaiting butcherbirds and currawongs. The males spend their days calling from the forest canopy to attract females. Cicadas produce their sound in a very different way from the ground crickets we saw at Mount Cooke. Back in the 1980s, David Young, an entomologist from Melbourne University, discovered how cicadas produce what is the loudest sound made by any insect. Within the cicada's abdomen lies a cavernous air sac that takes up a large part of the insect's body cavity. On the body surface, just behind the base of the wings, lies a pair of stiff horny plates, the tymbals, which buckle under the strain generated by contraction of a large muscle. When the tymbals buckle they generate a click that is amplified by the internal air sac. The sound-production mechanism is analogous to an empty jam jar with its lid on; pressing the safety button in the centre of the lid will cause it to buckle and produce a click that is amplified by the empty jar acting as a Helmholtz resonator. In cicadas this sound is transmitted to the outside world through the insect's ears, which lie behind the tymbals. The ears, then, both receive and radiate sound.

The loud, throbbing *tick...tick...tick* that we hear in the south-west forests is the combined output of hundreds and thousands of individual cicadas calling in synchrony. American evolutionary biologist Michael Greenfield has shown that the synchronous chorusing of singing insects is an emergent property of the intense competition among males to attract choosy females. The female's hearing system is such that on receipt of a sound stimulus there is a temporary inhibition of the sensory neurons that receive the stimulus, so that any further sound arriving in her ear is muted; her response, then, is tuned to the first sound she hears, and she will be attracted to the male that first stimulates her ear. This phenomenon is known as the precedence effect in sound localisation; when bombarded with sound it is easiest to locate the source of the very first sound you hear.

Female choice through the precedence effect generates sexual selection on males to be the first to call, so as to inhibit the female's perception of their rivals' calls. Male cicadas, then, compete with one another to produce their clicks before those of a nearby rival, and they need only be milliseconds ahead to win the attention of females. What we hear as a highly synchronised chorus of *tick...tick...tick* is in fact the overlaid ticks of rival males, ever so slightly out of phase to a female cicada's ears – *TtIiCcKk...TtIiCcKk...TtIiCcKk* – leading her to fly to the leading male to mate.

We soon arrived at Carey Brook Falls, where we rested for first lunch. We had a long climb ahead of us over the ridge to the Karri Valley Resort, but were spurred on by the prospect of our Christmas Eve lunch. We soon arrived at the shores of the lake, the resort beckoning from the far side. It would be an extra 2 kilometres' walking but would be worth it. Freddy called ahead to make sure the restaurant was open, and that they welcomed non-residents, and thankfully it was and they did. We were surprised to find the restaurant empty apart from us, which was probably a good thing, given it was quite fancy and we were not exactly dressed for the occasion. Nevertheless, the staff welcomed us warmly and we feasted on steak sandwiches and English bitter. What a treat. When we left around 2 pm it had become quite hot. We generally avoided walking in the heat of the day, so the steep 2-kilometre climb to Beedelup Hut was harder than it should have been. Never mind, we had a great day. Beedelup is a beautiful hut, perched on the edge of Beedelup Brook, and was a wonderful spot to spend Christmas Eve. Freddy picked a branch of Karri Sheoak that served as a Christmas

tree, decorating it with baubles made of Marri nuts and sheoak cones, and we dined that evening listening to a medley of corny Christmas hits from Spotify. A Christmas Eve to remember.

7

We were up early on Christmas morning. Another hiccup in our plans meant that we had to be in Pemberton by noon. We had booked a self-contained cabin in the Pemberton Caravan Park, but had been bumped again at the last minute. It turned out that the caravan park changed hands, and the previous owner had put his cabins on the back of a trailer and driven off into the sunset, leaving us high and dry. Finding accommodation on Christmas Day with just a few days' notice was challenging, but thankfully a delightful couple on Airbnb agreed to take us in, and even invited us to join their family dinner given nothing would be open in town. We declined this kind offer, not wanting to invade their family Christmas any more than was necessary, but promised to arrive before lunchtime. With 24 kilometres to walk, we set off at the crack of dawn. The Christmas medley the previous night was a big mistake. Those Christmas number-one hits are composed to worm their way into your brain, annoyingly playing over and over in your head until they drive you insane. My brain was infested with earworms that would take weeks to shift.

The track headed straight uphill from Beedelup Hut, but soon reached a plateau with relaxed walking through the Karri forest. We crossed Channybearup Road just a kilometre from Truffle & Wine Co., where we had gone for lunch while staying at Donnelly River. That drive had taken just thirty-five minutes, but walking here had taken us four days; that put the scale of our journey into perspective. After crossing and passing briefly through agricultural land we re-entered the forest and travelled along Fly Brook, through some fine stands of mixed Karri and Blackbutt (dwutta). We were to see some equally fine orchids that day. The first of these, a Potato Orchid (koon), was growing at the base of a large Blackbutt. Potato Orchids get their common name from the large tuberous root eaten by the Noongar. These fascinating orchids belong to a globally widespread genus that can be found throughout India, Malaysia, New Guinea, New Zealand and Australia. We have seven

TOP: Canary Worms can be found on the damp paths through the Karri forests around Pemberton. Little is known of the biology of these planarian flatworms, but their bright yellow colour is likely to signal their distastefulness to would-be predators. Freddy Simmons

MIDDLE: Koorkal or White-browed Scrub-wren, *Sericornis frontalis*. Common in the south-west of Western Australia, on heaths and in forests alike. While this species has its own distinctive calls, *ch-weip, ch-weip, ch-weip*, it also mimics other species, making it difficult to identify by call alone. Freddy Simmons

BOTTOM: Koomool or Brushtail Possum, *Trichosurus vulpecula*. Wildlife abounds around the forest village of Donnelly River. This nocturnal visitor is predominantly folivorous, but will eat small mammals or the eggs of birds if the opportunity arises. Introduced into New Zealand in the 1850s to establish a fur industry, the species has become a pest, as often happens when exotic species are released from the natural selection pressures that moderate populations in their native range. Freddy Simmons

species in Australia, of which just one occurs in the south-west of Western Australia, between Bunbury and Albany.

Potato Orchids lack any chlorophyll, appearing brown to off-white, have no leaves, and their flowers are simple white bell-shaped structures, giving them their other common name, bell orchids. In appearance, Potato Orchids are really quite ugly, but like all orchids their biology is fascinating. Like other orchids they exploit others around them, but in this case not to achieve pollination. Indeed, Potato Orchids are quite ordinary in their pollination biology, for like other flowering plants, their flowers are scented and offer nectar rewards to their pollinators, which include native bees, flies and beetles. Where Potato Orchids exploit others is by their parasitic lifestyle, for they obtain all of their nutrients from fungi that are themselves parasitic on trees and shrubs; Potato Orchids are parasitic on parasites. Now there's justice for you.

We were also to see large stands of Club-lipped Spider Orchids and White Mignonette Orchids on the tracks through the Arboretum just before we reached Big Brook Dam. We stopped briefly here to watch a pair of Black Swans (maali) swim past, and to take a welcome and refreshing swim. The last 6 kilometres into Pemberton were a slog, especially after leaving Big Brook Park, as the habitat along Lefroy Brook is seriously degraded, choked with brambles and other invasive weeds. By the time we reached town it was in the high thirties, and the walk up Pemberton's steep main street with the heat bouncing off the tarmac was unpleasant. But we reached our Airbnb in good time and received a warm welcome from our generous hosts.

The accommodation was in a self-contained building, so we were able to keep to ourselves and not impinge on our hosts too seriously. And the good thing was that we had already done the steep slog through town, so that setting off the next morning would be a breeze. What's more, the track elves had been here the week before and left an assortment of goodies to provide Christmas cheer, and importantly supplies for the next leg of our journey. We even had a roast chicken supper; just add boiling water and let sit for ten minutes – delicious.

PEMBERTON TO NORTHCLIFFE

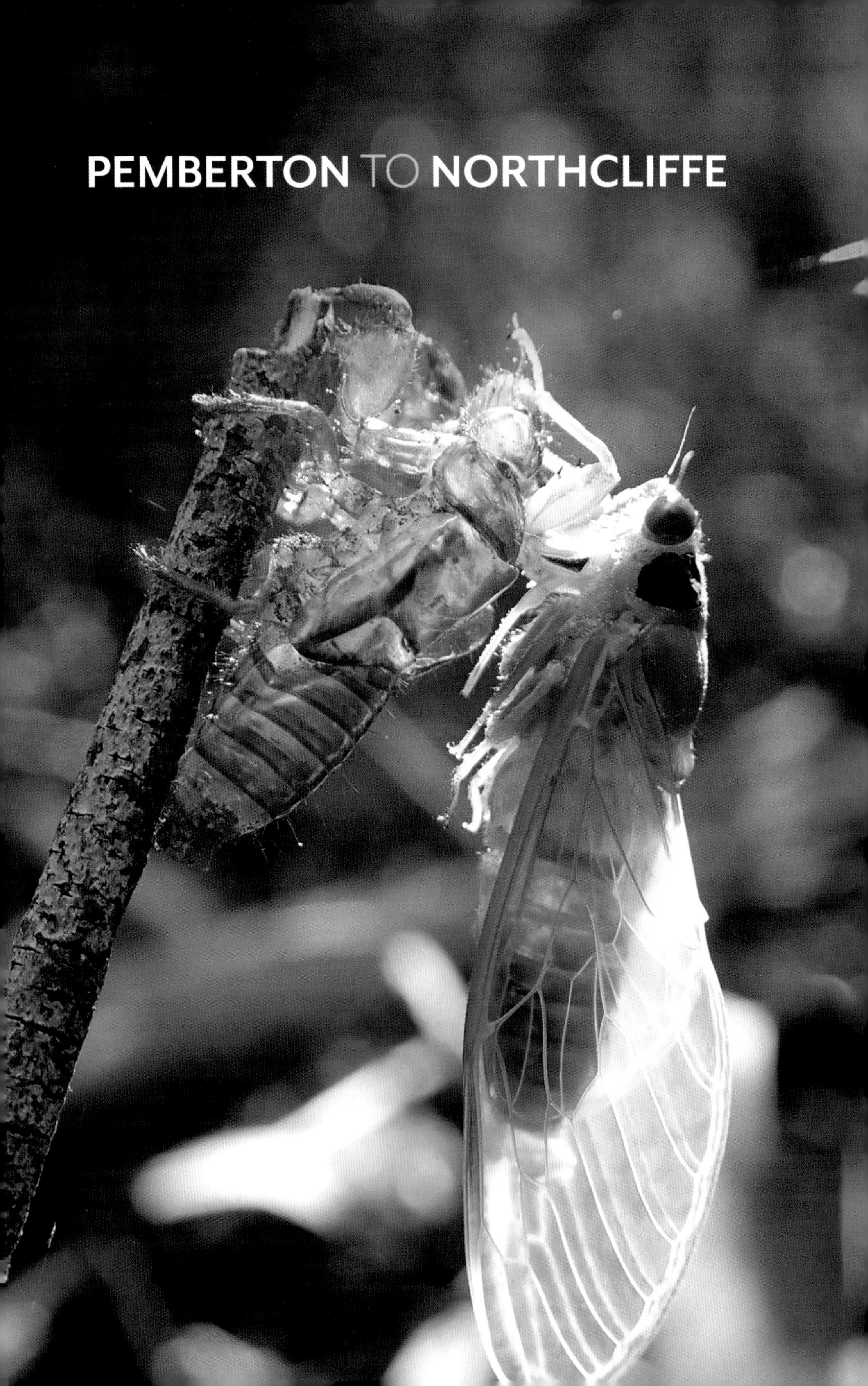

PEMBERTON TO NORTHCLIFFE

1

Our first stop out of town was the Gloucester Tree. Oh, for the vigour of youth; although we had 20 kilometres to walk that day, Freddy nonetheless felt compelled to climb the 58 metres to the top. The Gloucester Tree is a giant Karri, and the tallest fire lookout in the world. It was used between 1937 and 1952, along with seven other trees in the area, to scan the surrounding forest for fire. Three such lookouts remain today and can be climbed, the Bicentennial Tree and Diamond Tree being the other two. Each tree once had a small wooden cabin built in its crown within which the lookout would sit. Thankfully, the wooden cabins are no more, replaced with safer steel and aluminium cages. But access to the top of the Gloucester Tree is not for the faint-hearted; 153 spikes spiral the tree's 7 metre trunk. These spikes are widely spaced and some less firmly embedded in the trunk than one would like. A warning sign at the base alerts unsuspecting visitors of a 'Tree Climbing Risk'. No kidding!

On Freddy's return to terra firma, we descended the steep slope through the Karri forest down to East Brook. The understorey of Cut-leaf Hibbertia, Water Bush and Karri Hazel was barely visible in parts, acting as a scaffold for dense cover of three species of climbing plants: Native Wisteria, Coral Vine and Common Clematis. These climbing plants had long since finished flowering,

but the fluffy white seeds that give the clematis its other common name of Old Man's Beard were very evident. These fluffy seeds are swept up by the wind and carried hundreds of metres through the forest before they settle on new ground to germinate. The Coral Vine and Native Wisteria are both in the pea family and have the same explosive seed-dispersal mechanisms we experienced on our way to Yourdamung. But these different plants have converged on the habit of climbing through the understorey to reach higher into the forest in order to gain access to the limited light they require for photosynthesis, although to do so they have evolved distinctly different mechanisms.

Darwin was fascinated by climbing plants. He spent many hours in his greenhouse at Down House observing their movements, and used these observations to support his general theory of adaptation by natural selection. In his volume *On the Movements and Habits of Climbing Plants*, Darwin described how the young leaves of clematis have sensitive leaf stems that when touched lightly with a twig will bend in the direction of contact over a period of several hours, but will return straight again if no anchorage is found. If a solid structure is encountered, the leaf stem will wind itself around the anchorage and become toughened so that it is extremely difficult to release it. Darwin referred to species of clematis, such as Old Man's Beard, as leaf-climbers. In contrast, Native Wisteria and Coral Vine are what he termed twiners. As these plants grow, their leading shoots move in a circular or elliptical manner, so that on encountering any anchorage – a twig or stem of a neighbouring plant – the shoots wind around it, so growing up through the surrounding vegetation. Once they establish a stronghold, the grip of twiners can be so tight as to distort the growth of the plant about which they are twined, as is often seen on the stems of Karri Hazel bound by Native Wisteria.

Darwin's studies of both climbing plants and insectivorous plants led him to research more widely the ability of plants to move, which formed the subject of his final major work on plants, published in 1880, *The Power of Movement in Plants*. Sensitivity and movement had often been argued to be the distinguishing feature that separated the animal kingdom from plants. But Darwin's work showed very clearly that plants can have both faculties. Indeed, Darwin concluded that 'It should rather be said that plants acquire and display this power only when it is of some advantage to them; this being of comparatively rare occurrence,

as they are affixed to the ground, and food is brought to them by the air and rain'. In this, he was asserting that if natural selection favours the power of movement and sensitivity in plants, then there was every reason to expect these traits would evolve.

Darwin would have loved the work of Monica Gagliano, a former researcher in the Centre for Evolutionary Biology at the University of Western Australia. Working with garden peas, Gagliano presented seedlings with two natural environmental stimuli: light and a breeze emanating respectively from a lamp and a fan placed at the end of one arm of a Y-maze. The position of the combined light and fan were randomised each day for a period of three days. Pea seedlings naturally grow towards light, as do all plants, because they need the light to produce sugars via photosynthesis. After training peas, Gagliano presented just the fan and found that the peas would grow towards the fan even though no light was present. This form of associative learning has long been thought unique to animals, and was first demonstrated by Pavlov in his now classic experiments with dogs, where dogs learnt to associate food rewards with the sound of a bell. It appears from Gagliano's work that plants, too, can learn, casting doubt on yet another distinction between animals and plants.

During September, the forest around the Gloucester Tree is a riot of colour: white, red and purple from the climbing plants that cover the understorey. But there was little evidence of this spectacle when we walked through the forest surrounding the Gloucester Tree, other than the wispy grey of the Old Man's Beard. Having descended into East Brook Valley, we walked along the banks of East Brook on the elevated railway form through an avenue of Karri Hazel. Along this stretch we saw our first Tiger Snake (moyop), its beautiful glossy black back blending to a peachy orange–yellow belly as it slithered through the undergrowth along the side of the track. After ascending a small hill, we came to a sign to the Cascades and decided to abandon our packs in the bushes and head down to the river for second breakfast. There we sat by the cascading brook in the sunshine, watching the Blue Skimmers patrolling their territories.

Blue Skimmers are a widespread species of dragonfly (*Orthetrum caledonicum*) that can be found on still and flowing streams throughout the Australian continent. The resident males must have emerged over the last week or so; their black juvenile skins were left clinging to the reeds along the edge of the brook.

The life cycle of dragonflies is not too dissimilar to that of cicadas in this regard, where juvenile and adult occupy very different habitats. As juveniles, dragonflies are fully aquatic, living among the submerged vegetation where they sit and await their prey. For they are ferocious predators, seizing passing tadpoles or small fish that they devour with their razor-sharp mandibles. After a year or maybe two, when they have grown sufficiently, they crawl up the stems of reeds and break out of their nymphal skins, taking on their adult form. On emergence they fly into the forest, where they spend their days hunting for other insects, seizing them in flight and then alighting to consume them. Only when they are sexually mature do the males return to the streams from which they emerged and establish their territories. As we sat at the Cascades we watched males settled on strategic vantage points, typically rocks that emerged from the cascading water, occasionally taking flight to patrol their territory boundaries and battle with their neighbouring rivals, all on the lookout for females returning from the forest to lay their eggs in the stream.

Darwin believed that sexual selection acted on male characteristics that gave them an advantage in gaining access to females, and assumed that sexual selection ceased once mating was achieved. Perhaps inhibited by the social mores of his time, he did not consider that females might mate with more than one male, and therefore he did not appreciate that sexual selection would continue to act on males even after they had successfully mated. It was not until 1970 that my good friend and colleague Geoff Parker discovered that because female insects will mate with many different males and store the sperm they receive from them in structures within their reproductive tracts called spermathecae, a male's battle to become a father would involve his sperm outcompeting the sperm of his rivals. To this end, Parker argued, sperm competition would favour counter-adaptations in males, both allowing them to pre-empt any sperm stored by females from their rivals, and preventing their own sperm from being pre-empted by any future male the female might meet.

We now know that sperm competition has favoured a dazzling array of morphological, behavioural and physiological traits that are sexually selected after mating. Dragonflies offer us a fascinating example of both morphological and behavioural traits that are the product of this post-mating sexual selection. When a female arrives to lay her eggs, she will have sperm stored in her spermathecae

from her previous visit, when she would have mated and laid a clutch of eggs. On arrival, a male will first seize the female behind the head using appendages at the tip of his abdomen. He will then loop his abdomen around to reach his secondary genitalia, which lie at the base of his chest, and ejaculate into a sperm reservoir. Next, the female will bring her abdomen to engage the male's secondary genitalia, forming the 'wheel' position in which they mate. The pair will fly or perch in this position for some time. The male's secondary genitalia are remarkably complex structures, with inflatable sacs and spines that fit into the female's reproductive tract like a hand into a glove. The spines on the male's genitalia entrap and remove most of the rival sperm, while the inflatable sacs pack any remaining rival sperm into the far reaches of the female's reproductive tract, from which they are unable to gain access to eggs. Only once the rival sperm have been thus displaced will the male deliver his own ejaculate. This male adaptation to sperm competition allows the male to father almost all of the eggs the female will lay.

Once mating is accomplished, the female disengages her genitalia from those of the male and the pair fly down to the stream where the female lays her eggs. But the male does not release the female. If he did, he would run the risk of a rival male seizing his mate, removing his sperm from her sperm stores and replacing them with his own. And so a second male adaptation to sperm competition, mate guarding, ensures that the female lays all of her eggs before she is released. Thus the male flies in tandem with the female, alighting on floating vegetation so that she can deposit her eggs.

Some species of dragonflies will adopt non-contact mate guarding, flying close to the female and chasing rival males away should they approach her. Still other species will adopt both contact and non-contact mate guarding, depending on the immediate risk posed by other males; they will remain close to the females when there are few rival males around, but will remain in contact when many rivals are present. This plasticity in mate guarding behaviour allows males in low-density populations to mate and guard several females at once, which is not possible when they remain in contact with a single female. While sperm removal by secondary genitalia is mostly restricted to dragonflies and damselflies, mate guarding is a common adaptation to sperm competition and is found in many animals, from insects to birds and mammals. None of the Blue Skimmers found a female while we watched, but as we left

the Cascades a second species of dragonfly, a Western Darner (*Austroaeschna anacantha*), was lucky enough to meet an incoming female and flew with her into an overhanging Peppermint (wanil) tree, where they engaged in the 'wheel' position.

On re-joining the track, we descended into and ascended out of gully after gully, down which flowed the many tributaries of East Brook. Some streams were narrow, crossed by stepping logs, others wider and crossed by footbridges. The gullies were thick with cushions of green moss, and the track passed through extensive carpets of creeping Hairy-leaved Hibbertia. We were surprised to find, in the gully just north of Raspy Road, huge stands of Tree Ferns. Tree Ferns, of course, are not native to Western Australia, and these, we assume, must have derived from spores brought on the wind from domestic gardens, where they are often planted as ornamentals. Though alien to the Karri forest, they nevertheless gave a wonderful Jurassic ambiance to the dark damp gully.

Eventually the track descended into the Warren River Valley, following the river and affording a few welcome kilometres of level ground. There were many stands of both Club-lipped Spider and Slipper Orchids along the river, and some magnificent stands of Warren River Cedar, a species of tree found nowhere else on Earth. After Collins Road, the track ascended steeply back into Karri forest and brought us to what was for me the most beautiful and tranquil campsite of the Bibbulmun, Warren Hut, perched at an elevation of 100 metres, with magnificent views down through the Karri to the Warren River below. Rufous Treecreepers (djini) picked insects from the bark of the Karri; Western Rosellas (bardinar) were nesting in a tree hole just metres from the hut; Red-winged Fairy-wrens (djoordjilya) hopped through the understorey; and Dusky Woodswallows (kayibort) swooped through gaps in the canopy, snatching insects from the air.

As I sat that afternoon writing up my notes in the dappled sunlight pouring through the Karri canopy, Freddy called in a loud whisper, drawing my attention to a Mardo, or Yellow-footed Antechinus (*Antechinus flavipes*), that was tugging at the waist-strap pocket on my pack, no doubt trying to gain access to the trail mix within. This was my first ever sighting of an antechinus, though I have written about them often, for they offer an extreme example of the consequences for males of sexual selection via sperm competition.

The Mardo is a small carnivorous dasyurid marsupial, related to quolls and the Tasmanian Devil. What makes them extraordinary is their breeding biology. They breed for a very short period at the start of summer, when there is an abundance of insect prey, which forms the bulk of their diet. All females in the population become sexually receptive at the same time, for a very brief window, a matter of weeks, and will mate with any male they should meet. In consequence, sperm competition among males to father just the handful of offspring that a female will produce is intense.

One of the most general patterns seen across the animal kingdom, from parasitic worms to primates, is that males from species where females mate with multiple males invest more in sperm production, and therefore testes size. Parker likened sperm competition to a lottery for males: the more tickets a male has in the draw, the more likely he is to win the prize. Thus, multiple mating by females, and the sperm competition that it generates, results in sexual selection on males for increased sperm production. The extreme multiple mating by female antechinus has selected for suicidal investment in sperm production by males. Male antechinus invest so much of their energy reserves into sperm production that they have nothing left to support other bodily functions – their immune system collapses, their fur falls out and they develop gastrointestinal ulcers that result in them bleeding to death. Male die-off after the brief and frenzied mating season leaves a population dominated by single mothers and their offspring.

But why should females mate with so many males and generate such intense sperm competition? Queensland ecologist Diana Fisher discovered the answer to this question in her studies of the Brown Antechinus. Fisher found that males successful in sperm competition fathered offspring that had a greater chance of surviving to weaning, and a greater chance of surviving as independent offspring to the following year's breeding season. Males capable of investing the most in sperm production appear to carry the genetic material that allows their offspring to survive and reproduce. By inciting sperm competition, then, female antechinus are able to ensure that their offspring are fathered only by males carrying good genetic material, a form of cryptic female choice that occurs after mating.

2

We had to drag ourselves away from Warren Hut next morning; it is such a beautiful location. As the sun rose, shafts of light penetrated through the Karri, igniting their trunks with a rich golden glow. But leave we had to. We reaped the rewards of our steep climb to the hut the previous day, as the first part of the 21-kilometre hike was downhill all the way to the historic River Road Bridge. This wonderful old structure was built in the 1930s as a crossing for the log-hauling railway. The track then followed the Warren River, ascending and descending the many gullies that run into the Warren, or travelling low and flat along the river's edge, but always surrounded by majestic Karri.

We had two stops, the first on a fallen Karri that spanned the river where we had second breakfast, and the second at Blackberry Pool for morning tea. Here, we walked out into the middle of the dry riverbed, and sat on the large rocks taking in the view of the deep pool as it travelled west through the forest. We had hoped our vantage point might provide us with some good birding while we rested, but the morning had now become overcast, and after five minutes or so it began to drizzle. It soon became evident that a heavier shower was imminent, and so we stood to retrieve our wet-weather gear from our packs. But the drizzle had turned the surface of the rocks to slime, and it was impossible to remain upright; we slipped and skated briefly before falling. Rather than take the full force of a fall onto the rocks, I managed to turn gracefully into a body roll. No serious damage, thankfully, though I did manage to take a chunk of skin off my knee. We must have looked so comical as we clambered our way over the rocks to the firmer footing of the sandy riverbank, keeping our centres of gravity low, each of us with one hand firmly planted on the slimy rocks for support and dragging our packs as best we could. Lesson learnt there!

At the western end of Blackberry Pool, we turned south, ascending for the last time out of the Warren River Valley and eventually reaching the Wheatley Coast Road. After crossing the road, the track heads back into Karri forest for a short distance before reaching cleared farmland, passing along two sides of a large paddock, and then re-entering a stretch of Karri forest before reaching Schafer Hut. In this last section of forest, we were fortunate to flush a pair of Tawny Frogmouths (djoowi) that had

been perched on a low branch, at head height, right alongside the track. We would have passed them by without noticing had they not flown from their perch, such is the perfection of these birds' camouflage. Tawny Frogmouths are large nocturnal birds, related to the Owlet-nightjar (yaartj) we saw at Harris Dam. Often mistaken for owls, they do not have the same flattened facial disc or forward-pointing eyes. They have converged, however, on the same adaptation that owls use for silent flight, with the same serrated edges and downy covering to their flight feathers that dampens any sound that might otherwise be generated by their beating wings, and allows them to swoop down unheard on ground-dwelling insects, lizards and small mammals.

But the most remarkable adaptation of the Tawny Frogmouths is their ability to remain hidden in plain sight. For they perch on open branches, their tail and flank feathers flush against the tree making the join between bird and bark invisible, they also stretch their neck upward, pointing their bills to the sky and appear for all the world like a broken branch. Their feather patterns complete the masquerade, with black and brown streaking appearing like fire-charred bark, and the occasional grey or white blotch providing the appearance of lichen growing on the stump. And there they sit, motionless like living statues, all the while observing the environment around them through the slightest of cracks between tightly closed eyelids. We must have practically touched these birds for them to have broken their cover and flown off as they did. Indeed, they exploded from a branch close to our heads, giving us quite a start. Neither bird flew far, but we could find only one of the pair at its new perch, the other vanishing into the form of the tree on which it had landed.

3

Schafer Hut sits on the edge of a large dam, with a roped section available for walkers to enjoy a refreshing swim. On a hot day we could have spent some time enjoying the private pool, but by the time we arrived it had clouded over again and become really quite cool. Although we did go for a dip, we were driven more by the desire to be clean than cool. We spent that afternoon sheltering in the hut, listening to the heavy rain falling on

the tin roof. It continued to rain heavily throughout the night, and was still tipping it down when we packed up the following morning. Fortunately, it was also quite cool, so that wearing wet-weather gear was not as uncomfortable as it could have been. And the 14 kilometres into Northcliffe turned out to be much more enjoyable than we anticipated initially when setting off in the rain.

After travelling along the Schafer vehicle access track for just over a kilometre we came to a large flooded depression, vegetated thickly around its edges with reeds and home to a large chorus of Clicking Froglets *(Crinia glauerti)* that were clearly enjoying the rain. Shortly after the pool, we turned off into a fragment of forest that must have been burnt the previous summer, for it had an abundance of verdant regrowth that included Tall Banjine and two species of orchid, the Scented Mignonette which only flowers after fire, and King Leek orchids. The King Leeks were taller than either of us, almost 2 metres, and covered in fresh flowers. Leek orchids do not deceive their pollinators as is the case for most orchids, but rather attract them with masses of flowers that emit alluring scents and offer rewards of nectar. They mostly attract wasps, bees, flower beetles and flies, which carry the orchid's pollen packages in exchange for the nectar reward.

On this day, however, there was a resident on one of the King Leek inflorescences that is a master deceiver of insect pollinators: a White Flower Spider *(Thomisus spectabilis)*. Flower spiders, also known as crab spiders, do not spin webs to capture their prey; rather, they are sit-and-wait predators, capturing insects that arrive at flowers to collect nectar. And they have remarkable adaptations for avoiding detection by their prey, for they are completely white and choose to settle on white flowers, where they blend in perfectly. Or at least they do from a distance. Sydney-based behavioural ecologist Marie Herberstein and her colleagues have found that Australian flower spiders reflect ultraviolet light. While they are perfectly camouflaged from a distance, when a bee comes close to the flower it can detect the ultraviolet reflectance of a flower spider. But rather than serving as a warning, this has the cruel consequence of luring bees to their death, because flowers too reflect ultraviolet, and bees are attracted to ultraviolet because of the anticipated reward. The spiders have adapted to exploit the sensory system of their prey, and so increase their own foraging success.

In a wonderful example of coevolution between predators and their prey, however, our native bees have evolved counter-adaptations to flower spider deception, and can detect and avoid flowers on which flower spiders are waiting with some, though not complete, success. Not so for European honeybees, which have not had a history of coevolution with these predators. European honeybees were only brought to Australia in 1822, and they have not yet evolved the ability to resist the draw of a flower spider's deceptive colouration. The flower spider that we found on our King Leek had unwittingly managed to become the carrier of the orchid's pollen bundles, which were firmly attached to its back.

After crossing Lane Poole Road, we entered Jane National Park. This is a wonderfully varied area, alternating between Karri forest and low-lying winter-wet swamplands through which run tributaries of the Gardner River. Rough Rush was the predominant species through the white sandy swamplands. Like the Zamia Palm (jeeriji) and sheoaks, these rushes have separate sexes that are only distinguishable when in flower. The male has feathery anthers that appear yellow with their abundance of pollen, while the female has fleshy pink tendrils that catch pollen as it is carried on the wind. As we passed from swamp to Karri forest, we walked through avenues of thick Fine Tea-tree.

All around us in the Karri forest, the heavy rains were stimulating Forest Toadlets (*Metacrinia nichollsi*) to produce their characteristic croak: a short sharp *arrk*. Forest Toadlets are one of just six ancient Gondwanan relict species of frog that are confined to this small area of wet forest in the south-west corner of Western Australia. This ancient lineage of frogs has remained relatively unchanged since the continents split and drifted northward. Forest Toadlets live in the leaf litter and under rocks and rotting logs, remarkably having no requirement for standing water at all. For these tiny frogs, just 2 centimetres from tip to toe, have adapted to life on land by a process of direct development; their eggs contain enough nutrients to allow tadpoles to grow and metamorphose within the safety of the egg's membrane, hatching after several months of development as tiny, fully formed and independent frogs. It was magical walking through these ancient forests in the rain, but it ended all too soon as we emerged into agricultural lands long since cleared and now used for dairy farming.

Fortunately, the rain ceased almost as soon as we emerged from the forest, and within thirty minutes the sun had appeared,

TOP: A newly emerged cicada *(Physeema latorea)* dries its wings before joining the chorus of ticking males in the forest canopy. Males compete to be the first to produce their tick, because females mate with leaders rather than followers in the chorus. Freddy Simmons

MIDDLE: The empty skin of a juvenile dragonfly, the Blue Skimmer *(Orthetrum caledonicum)*. In their juvenile stage dragonflies are ferocious aquatic predators of small fish, tadpoles and one another. Only when large enough will they climb emergent vegetation, shed their skin and begin their brief adult life. Freddy Simmons

BOTTOM: As adults, male Blue Skimmers defend territories on streams and search for females that arrive to lay their eggs in the water. During mating the pair enter the wheel position, with the female (below) engaging her genitalia with the male's (above) secondary genitalia that are positioned on his 'chest'. He will remove rival sperm from the female's genital tract using barbs and flanges on his 'penis'. Leigh Simmons

allowing us to shed our wet-weather gear. From here we travelled along Smiths Road, a farm track that winds its way steadily towards Northcliffe. The farmlands afforded a change in bird assemblage, to the Western Australian Magpies (koolbardi), Willie Wagtails (djidi-djidi) and Australian White Ibis (ngalkaning) so common in these rural environs. But a new species for the list was a small flock of Elegant Parrots (koolyidarang) that travelled with us for some distance, flying from tea-tree to tea-tree along the hedgerow that bordered the road. Eventually we reached Northcliffe Forest Park, a beautiful stretch of Karri forest through which runs the Gardner River, that morning home to a large chorus of Motorbike Frogs *(Litoria moorei)*. Through this stretch of forest, flocks of tiny Purple-crowned Lorikeets (kawoor) sped screeching from Karri to Karri, and Karri Boronia added splashes of vibrant pink amid the stands of Rough Rushes. And so, in just under four hours, we arrived in Northcliffe – 628 kilometres travelled and 375 kilometres to go. Time for a long macchiato, a big breakfast and a shower. In that order.

The moral support we received from those we met on our journey was astonishing. As we sat that morning outside the café in Northcliffe, several passers-by took the time to come over to say g'day. I guess it was obvious that we had travelled a long way – by this time we were looking pretty grubby, and there was more to old man's beard than the clematis that grew in the forest. The heavy packs discarded by our table were also a dead giveaway. The discussion always focused around fond memories of sections walked in the past, or future ambitions to walk from end to end. But above all, they were always wholeheartedly admiring and supportive, and in no small way contributed to our forward momentum.

NORTHCLIFFE TO WALPOLE

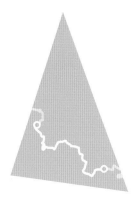

NORTHCLIFFE TO WALPOLE

1

After restocking our supplies of freeze-dried meals at the Northcliffe Visitor Centre, we set off along the rail track heading south. The first 3 kilometres of track follow the main Wheatley Road out of town. As we passed the fields surrounding the various smallholdings, we saw large mobs of Western Grey Kangaroo (yonga), and flocks of White-necked Heron (djilimilyan) and Australasian Pipit (waradjoolon). After 3 kilometres the track finally turned off Wheatley Road into a fragment of Karri forest. Here a long sand track eventually ran into walk trail that followed the Gardner River towards the Southern Ocean through D'Entrecasteaux National Park. This 118,799 hectares of wilderness is largely flat, low-lying wetlands with fragments of Karri Forest, granite, and limestone coastline. The sheer size of D'Entrecasteaux makes this the most remote part of the Bibbulmun Track, and a section we had been looking forward to since we set out.

The walking was easy, mostly flat along sand trails, crossing and recrossing the Gardner River. The riparian zone around the Gardner was vegetated with plants typical of the Karri forest, with stands of Warren River Cedar, Karri Hazel, Rough Rushes and Karri Wattle. At one of the river crossings, a Sacred Kingfisher (kanyinak) perched above the river, watching for

small fish in the clear tannin-stained water. Away from the river's edge, the vegetation was very different from what we had become accustomed to over the last few weeks – open and dry, with sparsely distributed Jarrah; a predominance of Red-eyed Wattle (wilyawa), Orange Wattle (coojong), Peppermint (wanil), Green Stinkwood, Grey Stinkwood and Fine Tea-tree; and abundant stands of Rough Rushes and Evergreen Kangaroo Paws. Drumsticks were just beginning to bloom, and as we approached Gardner Hut the edges of the track were lined with stunning displays of vivid purple Crowded Wedge-pea.

Gardner Hut is a newly constructed, rammed-earth hut perched high on a sand bank in a bend of the Gardner River. A small trail leads down to a pool deep in the shade, where you can take a refreshing dip after the heat of the day's hike. As we sat in the shade, sheltering from the midday sun, the leaves at the top of the surrounding trees began to rustle, gently at first, almost imperceptibly, but then emphatically as a fresh south-westerly breeze rolled across the landscape, bringing the cool scent of sea air and an invigorating, wakening tonic to the suffocating heat of the morning. This was the first sea breeze we had experienced since leaving Kalamunda nearly six weeks earlier, and until that moment we had not realised just how much we had missed this old friend.

Mid-afternoon we heard the voices of approaching walkers coming from the south. We had not shared a hut on the track since GFP left us at Grimwade. To our surprise, a bedraggled King Charles Spaniel gambolled up to the hut and proceeded to rub its wet fur against our legs. Its owners arrived shortly thereafter, terribly apologetic, but nonetheless did nothing to restrain the animal. They were nice enough people for sure, but really? Dogs are not allowed in national parks for very good reasons. We were mildly amused when its owner started to complain bitterly how she had been forced to hide in the bushes for almost half an hour the day before, from a ranger who had been at the hut. But then we became totally bemused at her responses when we tried very circuitously to suggest why it might not be the best idea to have a dog off-lead in the middle of D'Entrecasteaux National Park: 'You should keep a close eye on her, you know, there are 1080 baits scattered around the area, which are fatal to dogs,' Freddy offered kindly. 'Oh, she is very good, she would drop anything if I told her to.' 'Don't you worry about snakes?' I offered. 'Oh, she wouldn't hurt them, she's very mild-tempered'. Unbelievable!

Fortunately, they were camped way off in the campground, all the better to hide from the ranger, so we did not end up sharing the hut with them that night. And neither did we share with Malou, a young German woman who arrived from the north thirty minutes later. Malou had set out from Kalamunda less than two weeks earlier and was motoring on to Albany and back on a schedule of five weeks! She carried almost nothing; here she was, walking into one of the most remote regions in the south-west with little more than a 1 litre water bottle and a couple of chocolate bars. Complete madness. And so we spent the night at Gardner, effectively alone again in the wilderness, literally far from the madding crowd.

2

We were up and away early the following morning, managing to avoid our canine friend. Today's was a wonderfully varied walk into the heart of D'Entrecasteaux, across sand plains and through fragments of Karri forest. The deeper into the park we travelled, the more varied the vegetation became. Oak-leaved Banksia and Swamp Bottlebrush grew to waist height, while their understorey was thick with Rough Rush and Paper-heaths, the latter in bloom with their delicate white flowers. And along the very edges of the path, Cow Kicks, one of the largest of our triggerplants, provided us the opportunity to examine the contrivance by which these plants achieve pollination.

Triggerplants are another genus with the power of very rapid movement. The pollen-bearing stamen and the pollen-receiving stigma are both found at the tip of the flower column, which is bent back behind the petals and maintained there at great elastic pressure. When an insect lands on the flower's petals to take nectar, an action potential is generated that releases the pressure in the column and snaps it forward so as to deliver the unsuspecting insect a mighty thwack. The flower's response takes a matter of milliseconds, rendering the insect powerless to avoid the strike, and when it recovers from the blow it will be covered in pollen grains that it carries to neighbouring flowers. The trigger is reset within minutes, ready to thwack the next insect that is lured to the flower, and if that insect should be covered in pollen from a previous assault by a neighbouring flower, the flower will both deliver and

receive pollen. Another remarkable trait of triggerplants is their ability to consume insects, for some species have converged on the same sticky-trap leaves that we see in sundews, and the same ability to digest entrapped insects and absorb their juices.

As we sat on a fallen tree for second breakfast, a Tiger Snake (moyop) basked in the early morning sunshine on the opposite side of the path. This individual was only about 60 centimetres long and clearly preparing to shed its skin, for it had a milky opalescent hue to its body and eyes. Walking became uncomfortably hot by 9 am, and the cool patch of Karri forest after Chesapeake Road offered welcome respite from the mounting heat of the day. We stopped again on the banks of the Gardner River, climbing down into the riverbed and resting on a sand bank, where we watched Brown Honeyeaters (djindjokoor) feeding from the Evergreen Kangaroo Paws that edged the banks. Honeyeaters are the main pollinators of kangaroo paws, the anthers of the plant dusting the back of the bird's head as it probes the flower for nectar hidden deep within.

Eventually we turned left onto Lake Road, leaving the Gardner River for the last time and emerging once more onto exposed sand plains. In just over a kilometre, we re-entered mixed woodlands of Peppermint (wanil), Karri and Blackbutt (dwutta), through which we travelled to Lake Maringup Hut. Maringup is up there with Warren as one of the very best camps on the Bibbulmun, perched on the crest of a hill with stunning views through Blackbutt and Karri to Lake Maringup below, itself edged by Warren River Cedar and Saw Sedge. When we first arrived, a family of three were camped in the hut, literally with their tents pitched on the sleeping platform, but they left shortly after our arrival, so that once again we had the hut to ourselves. Smoke hung in the forest and obscured the view to the far side of Lake Maringup, drifting there from control burns to the north. But by one o'clock our old friend the sea breeze arrived and cleared the air within minutes, revealing the full beauty of the lake below.

There was an abundance of birdlife, both on the lake and in the trees surrounding Lake Maringup Hut. When we went for a dip in the lake, we saw circling above us a lone Wedge-tailed Eagle (waalitj), and on the lake Little Black (koordjokit) and Pied (midi) Cormorants; Australasian (ngoonan) and Hoary-headed (wyooda) Grebes; Black Swans (maali); Pacific Black Ducks (ngwonan); and the extraordinary Musk Duck (kadar). Musk Ducks are the

only living species of an ancient genus *Biziura*, which includes one other, now extinct species from New Zealand known only from the fossil record.

Male Musk Ducks are highly territorial, partitioning up areas of open water that serve as display grounds. Their remarkable displays include acoustic, visual and olfactory signals, which are broadcast in the hope of winning the affections of choosy females. Males are considerably larger than females, and during their display inflate their cheeks and pump blood into a large fleshy black lobe that hangs below the bill and becomes turgid. These morphological traits make the male highly visible as he raises his head high above the water surface. And to further draw attention to himself, he performs a spectacular splashing and whistling display.

While stationary in the water the male uses his backwardly positioned legs to project water sideways as his feet slap down into the water. At the same time he produces a metallic-sounding *ping* that carries far across the surface of the water. He will then flap his wings and utter an *ugh*, a *honk* and finally a high-pitched whistle, all the while projecting water jets sideways and slightly forward. Females are attracted to the male's antics, and when one is within a metre or so, the male also emits a distinct musky scent – hence their common name – which the females find irresistible. This showy display is the evolutionary product of sexual selection imposed by female choice of large males that possess larger lobes, display more frequently and produce more musk. Thus, only one or two of the most attractively displaying males are successful in producing offspring, ensuring the inheritance of these extraordinary sexual displays across generations.

Musk Ducks were once widespread across the entire south of the Australian continent, but genetic studies have indicated that populations in the east and west became isolated from one another during the late Pleistocene, 1.8 million to 12,000 years ago, when central Australia became arid. Interestingly, the sexual displays of eastern and western races differ, in both behavioural and acoustic elements, illustrating the power of sexual selection by female choice to drive divergence in male sexual displays and ultimately generate new species.

Mating systems like that of the Musk Duck, where males display on small territories in otherwise featureless environments, are commonly referred to as leks, and they frequently characterise those species with the most exaggerated male secondary sexual

traits. Peacocks, of course, are the classic example, displaying spectacular trains while dancing and shimmering their eyespots in front of drab choosy peahens. But the Musk Duck is the only duck species known to have a lek mating system. More typical for ducks is to form pair bonds early in the breeding season and to cooperate in the rearing of young, as do Pacific Black Ducks (ngwonan). The same is true of Black Swans (maali). That is not to say that the morphology and behaviour of these species are not also shaped by sexual selection.

Black Swans provide us with an example of a species that is under mutual sexual selection, where both males and females are selective of their mates. During their courtship rituals, male and female swans will circle each other with their wings held stiffly up, displaying their curly black wing feathers, which are completely useless for flight. Both sexes have these feathers, and they examine each other carefully as they paddle in parallel and circle each other during their dances. Males prefer females with more of the curly feathers, and likewise females prefer males with more of them. The result is assortative mating based on these sexual ornaments. Both males and females with more curly feathers are also socially dominant, and the pairing of dominant birds allows them to control access to greater resources and to be more successful in raising young than the subordinate, less well adorned birds. In this way, the reproductive benefits of mutual mate choice results in the evolution of identical sexual ornaments in both sexes.

Like Darwin, most biologists used to believe that species of birds that form pair bonds and cooperate in the raising of young, such as swans and ducks, were sexually monogamous. But the advent of molecular technologies in the 1980s, allowing us to assign genetic identity, revealed that in fact most birds seek and accept extra-pair matings. In Black Swans, for example, some 15 per cent of cygnets are not fathered by the male that tends the brood. Biologists now refer to birds as socially monogamous, knowing as we do that sexual monogamy is very rare. In some cases, females actively seek extra-pair matings, but in others they can be forced upon them by males unable to find a female with which to raise a family.

We do not generally think of ducks as having a penis. But in fact they do, and it can be twice as long as the male duck's body and coiled like a corkscrew. Ducks have a very rapid 'explosive' erection that drives the penis into the female's cloaca to deliver sperm, and

male dabbling ducks, such as the Pacific Black Duck (ngwonan), will try to forcibly mate with females, which in turn will resist copulation attempts in order to preserve the paternity of their pair-bonded mate. American evolutionary biologist Patricia Brennan has studied the size and shape of penises in dabbling ducks, and also the complexity of the internal reproductive tracts of female ducks. She has found that species whose males have large coiled penises also have females with deep counter-coiling genital openings, with blind ends that can prevent penetration by the explosive penis. Duck genitalia, it seems, have evolved through sexual conflict between males and females over which males father offspring.

The birds around the hut were no less interesting than those on the lake, and offered a classic example of niche partitioning. This term is used by ecologists to describe how a given environment can support an assemblage of animal species all exploiting the same or very similar resource. For example, species of birds will compete with one another for nesting sites or food, and a given environment may not have enough resources to sustain multiple species. Niche partitioning, however, can allow the coexistence of multiple species. Here at Lake Maringup Hut, the birds were competing for two food resources: nectar from the flowering Karri and Blackbutt (dwutta), and insect prey. And at least eight species of birds foraging around the hut that afternoon had partitioned the habitat into separate niches, broadly defined by their vertical position in the forest. At the crowns of the Karri and Blackbutt, Purple-crowned Lorikeets (kawoor) foraged for nectar, but these birds never penetrated into the depths of the canopy. Some 2 to 3 metres below the crown were flocks of New Holland Honeyeaters (bandiny) and Gilbert's Honeyeaters (djingki), which were taking nectar from flowers lower in the canopy and also gleaning insects from the leaves. Below them the Grey Fantails (kadjinak) and Western Whistlers (bidilmidang) captured insects on the wing and on the trunks and lower branches of the trees. Lower still, White-breasted Robins (boyidjil) perched, occasionally dropping to the ground to take insects from the forest floor. And on the forest floor, Red-winged Fairy-wrens (djoordjilya), White-browed Scrub-wrens (koorkal) and White-browed Babblers (ngowan) turned over leaf litter in search of insects hiding beneath.

Niche partitioning arises as an evolutionary product of competition among species, allowing an assemblage of birds to coexist in relative harmony while maximally exploiting the

TOP: Djoowi or Tawny Frogmouth, *Podargus strigoides*. Hidden in plain sight, this nocturnal predator sits out in the open during the day, masquerading as a dead branch in order to avoid detection. Unrelated to owls, the same soft downy feathers that allow it to fly silently through the night provide an example of convergent evolution of traits that aid in prey capture. Leigh Simmons

MIDDLE: This King Leek Orchid has attached its pollen sacs to the back of a White Flower Spider, *Thomisus spectabilis*. Flower spiders are cryptic and await the arrival of pollinators to the flower where they ambush and consume them. Like many flowers, spiders are highly ultraviolet reflective. Introduced honey bees are strongly attracted to ultraviolet and therefore vulnerable to predation. Native bees that have coevolved with the spiders are less likely to fall victim. Freddy Simmons

BOTTOM: Djindjokoor or Brown Honeyeater, *Lichmera indistincta*. One of our smallest honeyeaters often seen feeding from Evergreen Kangaroo Paws, and indeed is one of the principal pollinators of this species. As the Honeyeater penetrates deep into the flower to suck nectar, the anthers of the Kangaroo Paw dust pollen onto the back of the bird's head so that often they seem to have a yellow crown. Leigh Simmons

resources available. Later that night, as we fell asleep listening to the roar of the ocean just a few kilometres to the south, a second example of niche partitioning, again spatial, was evident in the chorus of Motorbike Frogs *(Litoria moorei)* in the reeds surrounding Lake Maringup, and the equally loud chorus of Slender Tree Frogs *(Litoria adelaidensis)* some 100 metres or so away from the lake edge in the gully adjacent to the hut. Lake Maringup really is a naturalist's paradise.

3

We woke at four-thirty to a cacophony of birdsong, a spectacular dawn chorus the likes of which I have rarely experienced. Sound carries particularly well in the still cool air of early morning, and many have hypothesised that birds sing at dawn because of the sound transmission properties of the morning microclimate. Others have argued that birds have little else to do at this time of day, given their inability to find food in the dim light of early morning. While these suggestions may contain a kernel of truth, dawn singing would only evolve if it increased the reproductive success of the choristers.

The dawn chorus, it seems, is a spectacular product of the ubiquitous competition between males for access to females. Male birds sing both to attract females and to defend their territories from neighbouring rivals. Many studies of songbirds, including our own fairy-wrens, have found that the dim light of day, when visibility is poor, is the time when males sneak into the territories of their neighbours to copulate with the resident females. And early morning is the time when mating is most likely to lead to successful reproduction, because females fertilise their eggs early in the day, before the egg is laid. Resident males, then, are at the greatest risk of cuckoldry in the early morning, when detecting interlopers is difficult and their mates are at peak fertility. Danish evolutionary biologist Anders Møller has found that intrusion rates on male territories are lower for territory owners that produce song. The dawn chorus, then, is best explained as an adaptation for the avoidance of sperm competition; male songbirds guard their mates from sperm competition rivals by defending their territories when the risks are greatest, at dawn.

The dawn chorus is also highly affective as an early morning alarm call for walkers. We were up and away by five-thirty, facing our longest day on the track thus far – ahead of us lay 26 kilometres to Dog Pool Hut. Although we were reticent to leave this magical spot, the day would yield many highlights that would compensate. Lake Maringup is, literally, a turning point on the track. After many weeks of heading south, from here on we would be heading predominantly east towards Albany. The first part of the day's walk was through magnificent Karri forest with a thick understorey of lush green Karri Wattle bearing feathery leaves and delicate yellow blooms at the tips of slender stems. We crossed several low-lying areas with boardwalks or stepping logs; in winter, walkers must wade knee-deep through these flooded plains. 'Seasonally inundated' it says on the map, and in parts it was still quite muddy. I think we picked the right time of year for our end-to-end, despite the few hot days in the north, as walking was now easy, the temperature mild, and the afternoon sea breezes invigorating.

After Chesapeake Road we again flushed a pair of Tawny Frogmouths (djoowi), and spent some time marvelling at their ability to merge into the woodlands unseen to all but the keen-eyed. After 8 kilometres or so we emerged into an area of elevated granite, surrounded by open woodlands of Jarrah very reminiscent of the northern sections of the track. This was followed by several long stretches of white sandy tracks that eventually emerged into open heathlands, covered predominantly by grasses and sedge, and with an abundance of flowering plants, including Paper-heath, Curry Flower, Royal Robe and Sea Celery.

We spent some time watching the insects drawn to the copious nectaries of Schauer's Astartea, including pairs of Red-legged Weevils *(Catasarcis impressipennis)*, the males guarding the females by riding on their backs and so preventing rivals from mating, and an impressive male Golden Head Rutilia (probably *Rutilia cingulata*), a large tachinid fly with beautiful iridescent turquoise patches. These flies are parasitoids, laying their larvae on those of large scarab beetles such as the Christmas Beetle we saw south of Gringer Creek. The larvae eat the beetle grub from within, emerging to pupate when they have had their fill. Along the wetter stretches of the sandy tracks grew colonies of two species of sundew new to our plant list, the Pygmy Sundew and Rosy Sundew. The latter has tongue-shaped leaves tinged fleshy red, all the better to lure carrion-feeding flies to their death. And there

were also two species of triggerplant: the Lovely Triggerplant, with its tall flower spikes covered in purple flowers; and dense colonies of the tiny Dotted Triggerplant. No taller than 10 centimetres, the Dotted Triggerplant has white flowers, each petal decorated with a small red spot.

These heathlands are perfect habitat for one of my favourite birds, the Southern Emu-wren (djirdjilya), which I was delighted to finally see hopping through the dense heathlands. Emu-wrens get their name from their tail feathers, which have the appearance of an emu feather, thin and wispy, and are next to useless for flying. Indeed, emu-wrens are very poor fliers, travelling more by hopping through the dense heathland, with only a low laboured flight when crossing a sand path through the heathland becomes absolutely necessary. Although locally common in these southern heathlands, their secretive habits mean that they are more often heard than seen, hopping up onto the exposed crowns of bushes only very briefly to broadcast their territorial song, a high-pitched, undulating *tsiee-seit-tzeet-tzeet-siee-seeit-tzeeit-tzeet-seee-seeit* barely within the frequency range of this ageing human ear. The heaths are also classic snake country, and that day we passed no fewer than five large Tiger Snakes (moyop) coiled beside the track basking in the warm rays of the early morning sun.

Snakes represent the major predator of emu-wrens, whose nests are frequently raided and nestlings consumed by these venomous reptiles. Tiger Snakes will also take fish, lizards and small mammals as prey. They hunt by scent, tasting the air with their tongues. When their target is within reach they will strike, injecting venom that paralyses the victim rapidly, allowing it to be swallowed whole. There was a single evolutionary origin of venom in the ancestors of modern snakes, followed by a series of evolutionary losses among those snakes that subsequently evolved alternative means of capturing their prey, such as pythons, which crush their victims to death before swallowing them. Among the venomous snakes there is considerable variation in the cocktail of proteins and peptides that make up the venom they use to paralyse their prey; this variation appears to have been driven by coevolutionary cycles between predator and prey.

Natural selection shapes the composition of snake venom so that it is effective at paralysing prey; individuals that are better equipped to paralyse their prey will be successful hunters, and able to grow and reproduce. On the other hand, prey that can

resist the paralysing effects of venom will escape their predators and reproduce, favouring the evolution of resistance to the toxins contained within their predator's venom. Evolved resistance in prey will in turn favour changes in snake venom that can overcome the resistance of prey. In this way, cycles of adaptation and coadaptation in predator and prey have generated an extraordinary diversity in venom complexity among snake species, and even among genetically isolated populations of Tiger Snakes in Australia.

A recent study of the venom from 132 snake species identified sixty-three different protein families, to each of which is added many different toxins – one snake's venom is not the same as another's. It is this variation that makes it so difficult to treat snakebites in humans, because the antidote to the venom of one species will not be effective against the venom of another. And it is for this reason that it is important to ascertain, if you can, whether the snake that bit you is a brown or a black snake, so that you can be administered the appropriate antivenom. Not that you are likely to get bitten, for most snakes, including Tiger Snakes, are not aggressive and will retreat quickly into the undergrowth at the slightest disturbance. In this regard, our intense fear of snakes is totally irrational. The Australian Snakebite Project found that of all cases reported between 2005 and 2015, only 100 actually involved envenomation, and among these only two deaths occurred per year. Your chances of being bitten by a snake in Australia are between three and eighteen per 100,000, which are pretty slim odds; you are far more likely to die driving your car than you are from a snakebite. The Tiger Snakes we encountered along this stretch of track retreated into the undergrowth on sensing our approaching footsteps, too quickly even for us to get a decent photograph.

The final 5 kilometres of track travelled along Dog Road to the banks of the Shannon River, where a large granite outcrop creates a permanent deep pool. Dog Pool Hut sits high on the west bank of the river, and a 36-metre bridge allows walkers to cross, with fine views upriver through the Karri that line the banks of the Shannon River. It was a relief to arrive, after seven hours of walking we were totally exhausted. As we walked down to the pool to collect water, we disturbed the largest Tiger Snake (moyop) I have ever seen, some 3 metres long, which slithered off to its lair under the footbridge. This was obviously a longstanding resident, as many walkers had written warnings in the logbook to beware of the Basilisk. What a beautiful spot to spend New Year's Eve.

TOP: A Clicking Froglet, *Crinia glauerti*. Western Australia's smallest frog, this species rarely exceeds 2 centimetres in length. Its call is reminiscent of a marble being upturned in an empty jam jar. The species is a common resident of pools and streams in Jarra and Karri forests. Leigh Simmons

MIDDLE: Nembing or Common Bronzewing Pigeon, *Phaps chalcoptera*. These solitary pigeons feed on the ground and are most often seen when flushed. The call is a slow, deep, mournful *whooo* repeated at regular intervals. Common in the Jarrah woodlands along the northern sections of the track. Leigh Simmons

BOTTOM: Djoolar or Fan-tailed Cuckoo, *Cacomantis flabelliformis*. This brood parasite lays its eggs in the nests of small birds that build domed nests, such as scrub-wrens, and thornbills. Its melancholy descending trills provide a haunting refrain in the late afternoon and early mornings in the Jarra and Karri forests. Leigh Simmons

4

On New Year's Day we had another long, though flat, walk to Mount Chance. The first half of the 20-kilometre section was along Marron Road, a white sand track that passed across some fine stretches of heath, and through several patches of now dry Jarrah woodland and the occasional stretch of Karri forest. Marron Road would be a wonderful section of the track to visit in September, for the white sand is the perfect habitat for orchids. Indeed, we passed many large colonies of now spent flying duck and hammer orchids, their pollination mechanisms still evident in their dried and shrivelled flowers that surmounted their swollen ovaries. Slipper and King Leek orchids were still flowering in the damp drainage ditches either side of the track, and there were a host of other heathland plants, including Yellow Milkwort, Common Sea Heath and Long-flowered Pimelea. In the undergrowth of the areas of Jarrah woodland we found Diverse-leaved Petrophile.

On reaching Pingerup Road we had burnt and barren plains to our right and unburnt heathlands to our left, an interesting contrast for the 3 kilometres along Pingerup Road before we turned right and headed eastward across the Pingerup Plains to Mount Chance. The track had been closed to walkers up until just a few days before. Indeed, we had been expecting to have to walk a 35-kilometre detour, putting an extra gruelling day on our journey, so we were delighted to get Sooty Tim's text message wishing us a happy new year, and informing us that the track was now open, but warning us that there was no water at Mount Chance Hut.

There was little natural history for us as we walked across the Pingerup Plains that morning. This area at any other time is a botanist's paradise, described as one of the most spectacular wildflower areas along the Bibbulmun Track. But when we passed through, the ground was bare, with blackened and charred twigs rising from white sand, and grey ash blown into little conical piles around the dead stems of Oak-leaved Banksia and defoliated tussocks of sedge. On the one hand I felt cheated, and cursed the fact that there had been a controlled burn. But on the other, I reminded myself that this is a natural phase of these habitats, and that fire is essential for the biodiversity of the plains. And there was a certain beauty to the scene: fresh green shoots were emerging from the sedge tussocks, nourished by the nutrients contained in

the ash the plants had captured at their root mounds; and
Oak-leaved Banksia cones, black and charred, had split open
to release the precious seeds that would germinate in the nutrified
soils, their spent seed cases now golden brown in the sunlight and
offering the promise of new life to come. Fresh shoots had already
sprouted from the blackened trunks of Jarrah, the leaves a blend
of green and rufous red. Life would return like a phoenix from the
fire, more beautiful than before. Still, it was a shame we had to see
it on a burning day.

Mount Chance is a granite massif in the midst of the Pingerup
Plains, forested by Jarrah and Karri. The hut is located 300 metres
up a spur trail at the base of the granite dome, the view from
which was spectacular, north to Mount Frankland on the far
horizon, south to Broke Inlet and the Indian Ocean beyond, and
east across the plains to Mount Pingerup. We often refer to the
ocean we see from the south coast of Australia as the Southern
Ocean, but technically the Southern Ocean is a thin belt of ocean
around Antarctica; the ocean lapping the southern shores of the
Australian continent is the Indian Ocean, which meets the Pacific
Ocean at Tasmania. Mount Chance that New Year's Day was a
strange and haunting place, the forest blackened, its canopy dead
and browned from the heat that had risen from the forest floor as
it burned. Everything we touched was sooty and black, for which
we could not blame Sooty Tim, and the water in the tank had
stagnated, giving off a nasty sulfurous odour that complemented
the blackened forest. It was positively Mordor-like, especially so as
it grew dusk and the orange glow of fire deep in the heart of a giant
Karri lit up the night, sending wisps of smoke drifting through the
still air.

5

What an extraordinarily beautiful scene awaited us next morning
as we descended once more onto the Pingerup Plains. The visibility
was limited by a mixture of fog rising from the damp plains and
smoke from the smouldering heathlands, but as the sun rose in the
east and cast golden rays across the landscape, the browned sedges
and leaves of the scorched vegetation began to glow a stunning
chestnut orange. The effect lasted but a few minutes and was gone.

Our journey took us another 10 kilometres across burnt plains. The track was mostly dry; the few low-lying areas still inundated were easily crossed using the stepping logs placed there by previous walkers. After skirting the base of Mount Pingerup, we crossed Broke Inlet Road, the boundary of the prescribed burn, and once more entered Karri forest. It was a relief to be back into lush green vegetation, and we were excited to see our first Red Tingle to the left of the track – a lone, outlying individual that offered a sneak preview of what lay ahead of us in the Walpole-Nornalup National Park.

The next 10 kilometres passed through pristine seasonally inundated heathlands. The contrast with this habitat's burnt state to the north-west was striking: tall grasses and sedges, among them Semaphore Sedge and Large-flowered Bog Rush, rose almost to head height, offering a scaffold for climbing plants such as Preiss's Wedge-pea, Climbing Triggerplant and Tattered Triggerplant. These triggerplants are so different in their growing habits from any other, their leaves curling and grasping surrounding grasses as their stems twine their way through the thick vegetation to present their flowers high in the flight paths of passing insects. So remarkably different from the diminutive, ground-hugging Creamy Triggerplant present on the sandy path and the Lovely Triggerplant at its edge, but instantly recognisable as belonging to the same genus of plant by the trigger pollination mechanism of their flowers.

Common Sea Heath and Curry Flower were scattered among the grasses, and Foxtails edged the sand paths across the plain, while Karri Boronia replaced them on the path as it passed through the Jarrah woodland patches that skirted granite outcrops. Albany Bottlebrush was among the largest of the shrubs on the plain, and Pretty Sundews among the smallest of plants on the damp sand tracks. The plant diversity across these plains is quite arresting, and it was difficult to keep our walking pace. I suspect it was somewhat irritating for my fellow traveller if truth be told, but my pace was to slow considerably over the next few days as we traversed this naturalist's paradise towards the coast.

Still, we covered the 21 kilometres to Woolbales Hut in just over five hours. Woolbales, like Mount Chance, is located at the base of a granite dome, in this case Dove Rock, from which there are wonderful views south across Broke Inlet to the coast and north across Frankland National Park. As we sat that afternoon

at Woolbales Hut we were privileged to witness an extraordinary scene: a female thynnine wasp from the genus *Hemithynnus* emerged from the ground, travelled some 2 to 3 metres to a small sedge up which she climbed, and sat at the very tip with mandibles spread wide awaiting a male to find her and carry her away. This species of thynnine is one of our largest, the female being in the region of 3 centimetres long, her body bright yellow with black and red banding. She did not have to wait long, for within five minutes a huge male arrived, some 4 centimetres long, flying close to the ground in a zigzagging path, homing in on the pheromone plume wafting from the female. The male sounded like a helicopter approaching from afar, a deep drone growing louder and louder the closer he came. He found her quickly, and without him stopping she grasped him around the abdomen with her massive jaws and was carried off into the surrounding bushland. This lucky male had found the object of his desire, rather than being duped by a deceptive orchid.

6

The 20 kilometres from Woolbales to Long Point must be among the best walks on the Bibbulmun Track. If you had only one day available and wished to experience an abridged end-to-end, this has to be the best section to walk, passing as it does through every habitat type in the south-west, with the exception of tingle forest. And with that habitat diversity comes a wealth of natural history.

For us, the walking conditions were perfect, with an expected high of just 22 degrees Celsius and a cool breeze. Heavy rain during the night promised to make our introduction to dune walking firmer underfoot than it might otherwise have been. Given the promise of cool weather, we had a lazy morning, setting off at seven. Somewhat counterintuitively, we first headed west in order to circumnavigate Dove Rock, before heading south through the Woolbale Hills, a collection of granite outcrops and massifs within dry Jarrah woodlands, reminiscent of the northern sections of the track. Along the track side were clumps of Prickly Conostylis with their yellow flowers, and pretty blue Karri Dampiera. We soon came across a large colony of Leopard Orchids (joobuk) on the sandy track, still sleeping. Yes, plants do sleep, a phenomenon

TOP: Maali or Black Swan, *Cygnus atratus*. Commonly found on large water bodies such as Lake Maringup. These birds exercise mutual mate choice. During courtship, male and female will circle each other with their wings held stiffly up, displaying their curly black wing feathers that are completely useless for flight. Leigh Simmons

MIDDLE: Kadar or Musk Duck, *Biziura lobata*. The males of this species have an extraordinary courtship display that includes visual, acoustic and olfactory stimuli that are used to impress the female. The male has a large leathery lobe that hangs beneath the bill and is highly visible from a distance. He will splash water sideways with his feet and utter a loud *ping* that caries far across the open water. Close up, he has a distinct odour that the female finds highly attractive. The males gather together in the middle of large lakes and perform their displays in what are known as leks, to which females come to inspect males and make their choice of mate. Leigh Simmons

BOTTOM: Kwidjar or Motorbike Frog, *Litoria moorei*. So named because its call resembles a motorbike changing gear. A large chorus of these frogs was resident among the reeds along the banks of Lake Maringup.
Leigh Simmons

recorded by Carl Linnaeus in his essay *Somnus Plantarum*, and discussed at length by Darwin in *The Power of Movement in Plants*. Many flowers close at night, only opening when the sun is high enough in the sky to deliver its warm, nourishing rays of light.

Darwin conducted many experiments with plants that close their leaves at night, concluding that they did so to protect themselves from night chills. Flowers, too, are delicate structures and probably also avoid cold damage by closing at night. Flowers are also, however, the guardians of valuable pollen packages, whose delivery to appropriate pollinators ensures the plant's reproductive success. Pollen is highly nutritious, and the source of food for many nocturnal insects such as bushcrickets, so by closing at night flowers can protect their valuable pollen packages from potential marauders. Leopard Orchids belong to a large genus of over thirty sun orchids that occur in the south-west of Western Australia, so named because their flowers only open on warm sunny days when their pollinators are available.

Sun orchids are also flower mimics; they have evolved radial symmetry and bright, contrasting colours resembling those of flowers that offer nectar to pollinating insects. But sun orchids provide no such rewards, deceiving flies and native bees into visiting them and carrying their pollen bundles to neighbouring orchids. The evolution of floral mimicry follows the same rules of Batesian mimicry that govern the evolution of warning colouration in perfectly palatable organisms that co-occur with toxic organisms and that predators learn to avoid. As long as food-mimicking orchids are rare, the sun orchid masquerade can be effective, because mostly pollinators do obtain rewards by visiting brightly coloured flowers.

In the case of Leopard Orchids, given their yellow and ruddy-brown colours, their pollinators are likely to be insects that would normally visit jacksonia flowers, or bitter peas and eggs-and-bacon peas. To identify these Leopard Orchids we had to persuade one flower to open up, but later in the morning, when the sun was higher in the sky, we came across several colonies of Chestnut Sun Orchids that were fully opened. Similar in their colouration to Leopard Orchids, Chestnut Sun Orchids differ in having very slender petals and striped rather than speckled ruddy-brown markings. The close match in colouration of Leopard and Chestnut Sun orchids would suggest that they both mimic the same rewarding flower species and dupe the same cohort of pollinators.

Our passage over the granite outcrops afforded fine views over Broke Inlet, and offered a variety of highly localised plant species, such as Granite Kunzea, Granite Acacia and Resurrection Plant. After 6 kilometres we crossed a flood plain with vegetation resembling the Pingerup Plains further to the north. In the middle of these plains ran a watercourse crossed via a long boardwalk that would keep the feet of winter walkers dry. Here the creek was lined with tall Warren River Cedar, and there were large stands of flowering Evergreen Kangaroo Paws; Blood Root (mardja), a herb widely used by the Noongar as a food flavouring; Schauer's Astartea; and Walpole Wax. Then, after crossing the flood plain, we entered a large area of cool dark Karri forest, with its now familiar understorey of Karri Wattle, Albizia, Bracken (manya) and Spreading Sword-sedge. Through here were no fewer than five species of guinea flower: Serrate-leaved, Hairy-leaved, Stalked, Cunningham's and Inconspicuous. On emerging from this species-rich patch of Karri we found ourselves at the base of a steep sand hill, which is fitted with rubber matting to prevent erosion from walkers as they ascend. This is the first ridge of the coastal dune system that runs south-west to north-east, and marks the major transition in the Bibbulmun Track to its coastal section.

And so began a series of steep ascents and descents as we walked south across the dunes. In the troughs were stands of Peppermint (wanil) offering deep shade, the footpath worn into a thick bed of Hairy-leaved Hibbertia. On the crests of the dunes we were exposed to the full blast of the wind coming off the ocean. *A Guide to the Bibbulmun Track* warns that these coastal conditions generate more strenuous walking, with loose sand, steep ridges and widespread lack of shade and shelter, but for a naturalist the dunes offered the excitement of an entirely new ecosystem to explore, with its own unique plants as well as some familiar species that grow in a highly stunted form, shaped by the prevailing winds.

On the ridges, Bull Banksia (mungitch) and Western Sheoak (kondil) that grow tall in the Jarrah forests were more like small shrubs than trees, rarely exceeding 1- to 2-metres high. The Grey Stinkwood and Cut-leaf Hibbertia were quite diminutive, little taller than 30 centimetres or so. These trees and shrubs were shorter on the crests of the dunes than on the sheltered north-facing slopes, and they became more and more diminutive the closer we came to the coast, to the extent that it was difficult to

appreciate how they could possibly be the same species as their counterparts that grow tall in the forests to the north. But they are.

Plants, and animals, are able to take on different forms in sheltered versus exposed habitats because of a phenomenon known as phenotypic plasticity. The same set of genes can produce a tall tree-like Bull Banksia and a short shrub, depending on the environment in which the plant grows. Different soil types, varying in water or nutrient content or salinity levels, can affect the way genes work, whether or not they are switched on, or the degree to which they are expressed, and so affect the development of ecologically important traits such as the thickness and shape of leaves or the length of branches. In this way a plant is able to grow in a manner that is optimal for the environment within which it finds itself: short and squat on exposed arid sand dunes, or tall and slender in damp dark forests. It is often the case that the appearance of an individual is a combination of these influences, referred to as genotype by environment interactions.

Differences in selection imposed by different environments, like coastal dunes and inland forests, can also result in fixed genetic differences between populations of animals and plants. They are said to become locally adapted. Local adaptation makes organisms perfectly suited to the environment in which their ancestors have evolved, but their offspring would be unable to survive if translocated to a different environment, because they would be ill-suited to their new environment. Understanding whether and how animals and plants respond to changes in their environment is critically important for managing populations vulnerable to extinction. For example, as appealing as it might seem, it is not always possible simply to shift a population of organisms elsewhere when you want to use their habitat for some anthropogenic purpose. The success or otherwise of a translocation will depend on the degree to which organisms are phenotypically plastic and the degree to which they have fixed locally adapted genes.

Thick-leaved Fan-flower dominated throughout the dune system, and imparted that distinct musky, herbaceous scent that always conjures, in my mind at least, images of the south-west coastal region. Scattered among the Thick-leaved Fan-flower grew a host of different species, including Scratchy Wattle, Basket Bush, Native Rosemary, the semi-parasitic Broom Ballart (djuk) or Native Cherry, and Coastal Honeymyrtle. And along the edges of the sandy track were Slender Lobelia, the small white and pink

pompoms of Coastal Mulla Mulla and the bright-pink flower clusters of Rose Banjine. Close to the coast on the crest of a dune, we encountered a beautiful Western Crowned Snake *(Elapognathus coronatus)* basking in the centre of the sandy track. This little snake, no longer than 50 centimetres, is a uniform olive green along the length of its body, with a black headband and pale blue–grey crown. While venomous, these small snakes are not dangerous in any way. This one allowed us to photograph it before it fled into the thick vegetation edging the track. And then at last we arrived at the west end of Mandalay Beach, a magnificent pristine white-sand beach bordered by high, vegetation-covered dunes and pummelled by the tumultuous turquoise waters of the Indian Ocean. The views across the thundering waves to Chatham Island were breathtaking.

Our first beach walk, though just 1 kilometre, was surprisingly tough going, as the strong winds and rough seas meant that we were forced to walk over the softest sand at the back of the beach, rather than the firm sand along its tideline. The surf was of little consequence to a lone Hooded Plover (dirl-dirl) that chased the retreating tide down the beach, gathering invertebrates dumped on the sand before running hurriedly back up the beach ahead of the next crashing wave. This beautiful little shorebird is often referred to as a 'hoody' for its black head and throat, which make its scarlet bill and eye-ring even more prominent. The southern beaches of the south-west are the last strongholds of this endangered plover found only in the south of the Australian continent. The last survey revealed that some 4,000 pairs of the western subspecies remained, and half that number of pairs of the subspecies in the eastern states; numbers everywhere are in serious decline.

The problem is that Hooded Plovers spend their entire lives on beaches, where they feed and breed. They do not build nests as such, but rather simply lay their eggs among the flotsam and jetsam thrown onto the beach by the ocean. The small speckled eggs blend perfectly into the natural debris along the high-water mark. Hooded Plovers exhibit a remarkable antipredator behaviour when disturbed at the nest. They will limp away, one wing hanging loosely, signalling to the predator that they are injured and unable to escape, drawing it away from the nest before suddenly taking flight, leaving the duped predator unable to find the perfectly camouflaged eggs among the flotsam and jetsam. Our southern beaches are immensely popular recreational areas. For reasons I have never quite fathomed, we like to drive our vehicles up and

down otherwise pristine beaches, along the high-water mark where the sand is firm. The inevitable consequence for the hoodies is that nests are destroyed, by our vehicles, our dogs and our foot traffic. Thankfully, the numbers of hoodies in Western Australia appear stable, as we have many more wilderness beaches such as Mandalay than in the eastern states. But we should all take care that the footprints we leave have not inadvertently crushed one of our most endangered waders.

At the eastern end of Mandalay we turned inland, over the low foredune and into the unique and beautiful habitat that is the backdune. Here a freshwater stream fed the swamp, where a loud chorus of Clicking Froglets *(Crinia glauerti)* could be heard rattling among the reeds. Stands of Sweet Mignonette Orchids grew in the shallow edges of the freshwater pool, and all around, the dunes were stabilised by a rich diversity of grasses and sedges, dominated by Beach Spinifex and Marram Grass. Beach Spinifex has separate male and female plants, the female plants producing the spiky balls that are often seen blowing along the sands, carrying their seeds afar. From here the real struggle began, as we ascended the steep dunes towards Cliffy Head. One step upward, half a step downward as the soft sands shifted beneath our feet. The ascent was made in sections, up one steep dune before descending into a trough before the start of the next.

The climb could have been a nightmare had it not been for the abundance of insect life to distract our attention from our labours. For the Grasstrees (balga) through the sheltered dune system were in full flower, blooms rising 3 to 4 metres into the air, magnets for day-flying insects searching for pollen and nectar. Every flower spike held something of interest. There were at least four species of thynnine wasp feeding there, including the large species of *Hemithynnus* we had seen pair up the previous day at Woolbales Hut. The males were collecting pollen and nectar from the grasstree flowers, the females hanging on firmly with their enlarged mandibles gripping the male's abdomen, their genitalia attached to those of the male. Occasionally the female would release her mate's abdomen and reach up to his mouthparts so that he could feed her the pollen and nectar that he had collected. The male carries the female from plant to plant, feeding her in this way until he has inseminated her and she is fully sated. Only then will she release herself from him, dropping to the soil surface and digging down in search of beetle larvae on which to

deposit her eggs. What a joy it was to watch these magnificent wasps, and in such abundance.

Another spectacular insect attracted to the grasstree flowers was a jewel beetle from the genus *Castiarina*. The jewel beetles, or bupestrids, are so named because of their beautiful iridescent, highly coloured wing cases (elytra) that cover their flight wings. This is a huge family of beetles, with eighty-two genera containing more than 1,200 species in Australia alone. There are in excess of 475 species in the genus *Castiarina*, and these species have diverged markedly in the patterning of iridescent green patches that occur on the glossy golden-brown, yellow or orange elytra. Or are they yellow and orange markings on a glossy iridescent green background, for each species differs in the colour that dominates.

This diversification is likely the product of sexual selection, as the beetles identify their mates based on the colour of their elytra. Entomologists Darryl Gwynne and David Rentz reported how one species of Australian jewel beetle, *Julodimorpha bakewelli*, can actually mistake discarded beer bottles for females; the colour and reflection of the glass are the same as that of the females' elytra, and the size of the bottle makes them a super-stimulus, to which males are attracted and repeatedly attempt to copulate. This species of jewel beetle will mistake the orange of high-visibility clothing worn by road workers for the reflectance of females, with unappreciated consequences. Sexual selection to maximise male mating success has tuned these beetles' visual system to the precise wavelength of colour reflected by females, making them acutely sensitive to anything that looks vaguely like a potential mate.

And finally, that day on the dunes, Southern Whistling Moths *(Hecatesia thyridion)*, could be found perched on prominent bare twigs. These moths have a number of fascinating traits, not the least of which, as their common name suggests, is their capacity to whistle. Sound production is common in many insects, like the ground crickets and cicadas we found in the north, but is not so common among butterflies and moths. The males of whistling moths will perch on dominant vegetation and raise their wings, bringing the leading edges together to make an audible click. The speed at which they bring their wings together above their body generates an audibly continuous train of clicks that sounds like a whistle.

My good friend and colleague Winston Bailey described the mechanisms by which these moths produce their whistles.

On the leading edge of each forewing is a castanet. When the wings are raised to the point at which the castanets strike each other, a cavity is formed below the castanets that amplifies and radiates the sound. Bailey described a simple mechanical equivalent as when the thumbs of the hand are struck together with both hands linked and cupped. John Alcock has studied the mating system of whistling moths in Western Australia; the males defend territories in the heathland and whistle to attract females for mating. Males will also attract other males, and prolonged chases will occur as they whistle at each other in acoustic displays over territory ownership. Females obtain no resources from a male's territory, mating and simply leaving, suggesting that the males are defending areas of the habitat that offer the best conditions for attracting females, for example sheltered areas offering warm, still microclimates through which their whistles can more effectively propagate.

Another interesting feature of whistling moths is their colouration. When at rest they are highly cryptic: their black wings with white spots and stripes allow them to blend unseen into the vegetation on which they are perched. But when they take flight, a bright-orange abdomen and hindwings are revealed. Such a colour scheme is characteristic of aposematic species that signal their distastefulness to potential predators, or those species that mimic the distastefulness of toxic prey. The caterpillars of whistling moths feed on the parasitic Dodder; every species has its burden – even parasites have predators. The caterpillars of whistling moths have black and white markings, with yellow bands, red spots around the hind end and fine white hairs, all hallmarks of a distasteful insect. And indeed, the caterpillar gut does contain significant amounts of distasteful alkaloids derived from the Dodder. However, these alkaloids are not found in the adult moths, which Bailey found to be perfectly palatable to Singing Honeyeaters.

One possible explanation is that predators avoid the brightly coloured adult moths because they have evolved to avoid their toxic caterpillars; perhaps the colouration of palatable adults is beneficial because it mimics the colour defences of their distasteful offspring. An alternative explanation for adult colouration is that it protects the moth by confusing the predator. In many highly cryptic insects, the hindwings can be brightly coloured and highly conspicuous. When disturbed by a predator and taking flight,

paradoxically the cryptic insect becomes highly conspicuous, not at all what you would think to be adaptive for avoiding predators. This 'flash behaviour' can be seen across the animal kingdom; when rabbits flee, for example, they flash their bright-white under-tail. Another insect we saw on the track was a Bark-mimicking Grasshopper *(Coryphistes ruricola)*, which on disturbance flashed its bright-blue hindwings and then disappeared into the path just as soon as it landed, returning to its stick-like camouflaged state. Flash displays can hinder the location of prey when they settle, because the predator's search image has been fixed on the colour of the display, which suddenly disappears.

It was slow going up the back of the dunes to Cliffy Head, mostly because there was so much natural history to observe along the way: two species of longicorn beetles were meeting and mating on their respective host plants, Red-eyed Wattle (wilyawa) and Berry Saltbush. But when we finally made it to the top, the views back to Chatham Island and ahead to Long Point were spectacular. No sooner were we at the top than we started back down again towards Lost Beach, traversing a long sand ridge before reaching the spur trail into Long Point Hut. The 20 kilometres had taken us six hours to complete and had provided spectacular views, and a stunning diversity of flora and fauna – one of our best days on the track.

After afternoon tea, we took the short trail at the back of Long Point Hut down to the coast, through a thick dark Peppermint (wanil) grove where Dichondra covered the ground, out onto the exposed granite slopes that plummet into the sea. Here the vegetation clung to the ground, stunted to just knee height by the gusting winds off the ocean. Coastal Pigface (bain) and Fleshy Saltbush, now all the rage in fancy restaurants, survived happily on the shallow sea-soaked soils that covered the granite slopes. As tempted as we were, it probably would not have complemented our freeze-dried spag bol. We soon made a hasty retreat back to the shelter of the hut as driving rain rolled in across the ocean from the south.

TOP: A male Golden Head Rutilia, probably *Rutilia cingulatea*, a large tachinid fly. Seen here feeding from the nectaries of Schauer's Astartea, these flies are parasitoids, laying their larvae on those of large scarab beetles. The larvae eat the beetle grub from within, emerging to pupate when they have had their fill. Freddy Simmons

MIDDLE: Red-legged Weevils, *Catasarcis impressipennis*. The male is guarding the female by riding on her back and so preventing rivals from mating. Mate guarding is a common behavioural adaptation to sperm competition found across the animal kingdom, from insects to mammals. Freddy Simmons

BOTTOM: A Western Crowned Snake, *Elapognathus coronatus*. While venomous, these small snakes are not aggressive. They will rush for cover at the slightest movement and so are rarely seen. Freddy Simmons

7

We had grown accustomed over the last six weeks to being awakened by a rich and varied dawn chorus, which was conspicuous in its absence the following morning. Rather, we awoke to the sound of thundering waves crashing over the granite slopes of Long Point. The abundance and species richness of birds on the coastal heath was lower than we had been experiencing in the inland forests. Southern Emu-wrens (djirdjilya) and Splendid Fairy-wren (djer-djer) hopped through the low heathland shrubs at the front of the hut, while Silvereyes (doolor) and New Holland Honeyeaters (bandiny) flitted through the Peppermint (wanil) trees in the gulley to the rear. But their vocalisations were few and far between, and consisted of short, sharp generic syllables: a *chip, chip* now and then, or a *tzweet*. Elaborate songs would be swept swiftly away on the prevailing south-westerly winds or drowned out by the thundering roar of the ocean crashing over the rocks, making territorial singing an ineffective paternity guard on these exposed coastal heaths. Better to remain close to your mate and physically chase off philandering rivals.

The track was just as varied in its habitats as it had been the previous day, passing as it did first eastward along the coast before heading inland across the dune system to Mount Clare at the western end of the Walpole-Nornalup National Park. We set off at five-thirty, walking down the spur trail to re-join the track on the sand ridge we had travelled along the previous day. The early morning meant that few day-active insects could yet be seen on the Grasstree (balga) flower spikes, but there remained some nocturnal visitors: a species of tettigoniid, the Common Marauding Katydid *(Metaballus frontalis)*, was up late, still feasting on the rich source of pollen.

Katydids (bushcrickets) are often mistaken for grasshoppers, having the same long hind legs that allow them to jump when disturbed. But they are easily distinguished from grasshoppers by their long filiform antennae, generally as long, if not longer, than the insect's body. It was to study these insects that I first came to Australia from Britain in the 1980s. For the south-west coastal heaths harbour a huge diversity of species, many at that time unknown to science. I spent several nights camped out on the coast at Hassell Beach, north-east of Cheyne Beach, collecting katydids

by night and sorting them by day. I was there with my colleagues Win Bailey, Todd Shelly and Nina Wedell, and accompanied by a katydid taxonomist from the CSIRO, David Rentz. I was astonished as Rentz sorted through our catch, declaring one after another as new to science. On that collecting trip we found more than twenty different species, including a new genus, and I am sure there remain many other species to discover. The species richness of katydids on the south-west coastal heaths offers yet another striking example of why it is so important to protect this region of south-western Australia.

It was the katydid mating system that I came to Australia to study. Like the ground crickets we saw at Mount Cooke, male katydids produce a call by drawing a scrapper on the right forewing over a file on the left forewing, which causes a structure on the right forewing, the mirror, to radiate vibrations into the air. As with ground crickets the rate and frequency with which the wings are drawn together determine the structure of the call produced. Females are attracted to the male's advertisement calls and will travel through the vegetation in order to make contact with him. Once contact is made, the pair will couple their genitalia. But then an extraordinary thing happens. Over a period of half an hour or so, the male will squeeze out an enormous sperm-containing package followed by an even larger sticky gelatinous mass. This so-called spermatophore can represent 20 per cent or more of a male's total body mass; the equivalent of me shedding my 18-kilogram pack, which I so wished I could. The spent male will then leave the female to feast on the gelatinous mass, which can take her several hours to consume, during which time sperm are transferred from the sperm package to her reproductive tract. The nutrients contained within the gelatinous 'nuptial gift' can be used by the female to sustain her own essential bodily functions and to produce eggs. Meanwhile, the male will need to feast on protein-rich foods, such as grass seeds, pollen or other insects, for up to a week before he is able to mate again.

Nuptial gifts are both valuable for females and highly costly for males to provide. Darryl Gwynne had observed the mating behaviours of marauding katydids around the Cape Naturaliste area north-west of Busselton. He had observed that in some populations, the slightest short chirp from a male resulted in multiple females rushing to the source of the sound. The male would be reluctant to transfer his nuptial gift, often rejecting

eager females before settling on one particular female on which to bestow it. This behaviour is the reverse of Darwin's general observations in the animal kingdom: that it is typically the males that are eager to mate and the females that are choosy. In a second population of the same species just a few kilometres away, however, the complete opposite was true: males were producing constant trains of song while females seemed oblivious to their sexual signals. And Gwynne found that he could change the behaviour of a male katydid from choosy to eager and vice versa, simply by moving him between populations. What was it about these different environments that had such a dramatic effect on the insects' behaviour?

I studied a related species, the Flower-loving Spring Katydid (*Kawanophila nartee*), which occurs in Kings Park in Perth. This species, as its name suggests, feeds exclusively on the pollen and nectar of spring flowers, and in the early spring predominantly on Mangles Kangaroo Paws. At this time of year, males are choosy and females eager to mate with males and accept their nuptial gifts. When the Grasstrees (balga) flower, however, the mating system flips completely, and males become eager and females uninterested.

It turns out that it is the availability of food in the environment that determines the mating system. When pollen is limited, nuptial gifts are essential for females to reproduce, and they will harvest them from as many males as they can find. The time it takes males to replenish their spent reserves means that there are fewer males available than there are females seeking them, so that females must compete for access to the limited supply of males, which in turn can afford to be choosy about which female they mate with, selecting those that offer the greatest number of eggs. When pollen is abundant, however, females can obtain all the food they need, and no longer require the nuptial food gifts offered by males. Males become more abundant than receptive females, allowing females the opportunity to choose among males as they compete for female attention.

These insects provided the first evidence that it is the relative investments made by males and females in their offspring that determines the extent to which each must compete for access to mates, and thereby the sex on which sexual selection will act. Typically, it is the females that invest more and choose among competitive males. But sometimes, as in Emus, the male's investment in offspring exceeds the female's and the roles

reverse. And sometimes, as in katydids, these roles can be highly flexible, depending on the environment within which animals find themselves.

The track took us towards the coast, through patches of Peppermint (wanil) before ascending the limestone ridge that runs east from Hush Hush Beach. Here we found a new species of fringe lily (tjunguri), the Hairy Fringe Lily (adjiko), very similar in appearance to the Many-flowered Fringe Lily we had seen in the north but with small white hairs scattered along its leaves. Narrow-flowered Blue Leschenaultia and Foxtails were also abundant. On turning inland and descending from the limestone ridge, we traversed dunes covered in Grey Stinkwood and travelled through dense stands of Evergreen Kangaroo Paws as we approached the junction with the Nuyts Wilderness Walk Trail. Here we rested for second breakfast at the shoe-cleaning station, and watched Western Spinebill (booldjit) as they fed on the kangaroo paws and beautiful mature Holly-leaved Banksia.

Shoe-cleaning stations have been established in many places along the trail in an attempt to ease the spread of Cinnamon Mould (*Phytophthora cinnamomi*). The genus name sums up this species quite literally: *Phytophthora* means plant killer. This species was first discovered on the bark of cinnamon trees, hence the species name. Cinnamon Mould is one of the world's most invasive species, now recorded in more than seventy countries. It is an oomycete, an alga that travels in water through the soil and enters the root systems of plants. There it grows, absorbing the host plant's nutrients and destroying its root tissue so that it becomes unable to absorb its own water and nutrients. The root of the host rots and the plant dies, a phenomenon most famously known from the Irish Potato Famine of 1845.

Cinnamon Mould was first detected in Australia in 1935 and represents a particular threat to the biodiversity of the south-west, where as many as 22 per cent of plant species are susceptible to the pathogen, resulting in significant loss of forest and heath vegetation in a phenomenon referred to as dieback. Plants from many taxonomic groups are lost to dieback; Jarrah, sheoaks, wattles, banksias, snottygobbles (kadgeegurr), grevilleas, hakeas, boronias, peppermints, tea-trees, grasstrees, Foxtails, heaths, hibbertias – the list goes on. And the consequences are devastating, not just for the biodiversity of plants, but also for the animals that rely on them for food and shelter. All those insects we saw feeding on the pollen

TOP: Dirl-dirl or Hooded Plover, *Thinornis cucullatus*. This endemic plover once widespread, is now critically endangered as it nests on open beaches which are increasingly populated by humans. They appear safe in Western Australia where remote beaches such as Mandalay remain relatively pristine. Leigh Simmons

MIDDLE: A female thynnine wasp from the genus *Hemithynnus* signals from the top of a sedge to attract a male. On detecting her scent, the male will fly to her so that she can grasp his abdomen with her enlarged mandibles. Many orchids mimic the scent of female thynnines so as to dupe males into carrying their pollen. Freddy Simmons

BOTTOM: Once the male thynnine wasp has found his mate, he will carry her to sources of pollen and nectar such as the flower spikes of Grasstrees (balga). He collects food and will regurgitate it for the female when she reaches up to his mouthparts. All this time they remain in genital contact so that the male can transfer his sperm. Once sated the female will release the male and fall to the ground, burrowing into the soil where she hunts beetle larvae upon which to lay her eggs. Freddy Simmons

and nectar of Grasstrees can be lost from the landscape when populations of Grasstrees die. The biodiversity of katydids no doubt hinges on the biodiversity of plants in the region.

Western Australian ecologist Robert Davis and his colleagues have reported losses of bird species from habitats affected by dieback, a notable example being the Western Spinebill (booldjit) that were feasting on the Holly-leaved Banksia at our rest stop. This is why it is so vital to manage the spread of the disease. As the spores of Cinnamon Mould are carried in soil, we should all be conscious of our potential to carry infected soil on our vehicles or footwear when travelling between areas of natural bushland. This is why the provision of boot-cleaning stations along sections of the track that are particularly susceptible to the disease is an important initiative, and one that we should all respect. And besides, it's a good excuse to take the weight off your feet and 'delay the onset of fatigue'.

From here we continued our journey inland, Mount Clare looming ahead of us, taunting us with the prospect of the climb up its western slope, where on the map the track runs perpendicular to the tightly packed contours. Where is that Patronus when you need it? We passed over the damp winter-wet streambeds of Crystal Brook, edged by Fine Tea-tree and home to colonies of Pygmy Sundew, and soon reached a stretch of stunted forest, initially containing Karri and Marri, and then Western Sheoak (kondil) and Peppermint (wanil) as we reached the banks of Deep River. Here we rested briefly on the banks of Deep River before crossing the suspension bridge and starting the almost vertical climb through the tingle forest to the summit of Mount Clare. We kept the Dementors at bay, reaching the hut in good spirits.

It was worth every step – what a stunning setting! Mount Clare Hut is set among majestic Red Tingle that tower hundreds of feet above the thick understorey of Karri Hazel, Karri Wattle, Oak-leaf Chorilaena and Spreading Sword-sedge. It could not be more different from the windswept, flat coastal heath setting of Long Point.

8

We had vowed at the start that we would stay in every single hut on the track. We had now missed two: Helena Valley, burnt to the ground the summer before our walk; and Tom Road, through no fault of our own, diverted due to the prescribed burn. Here we faced a dilemma. The walk into Walpole was just 10 kilometres – we could do it in a couple of hours. Awaiting us there were a beer, shower, crisp white sheets on a comfortable bed, and a parmie and chips at the tavern. On the other hand, the environs of Mount Clare Hut are stunning, and we could while away the rest of the day birding and relaxing in the dappled sunlight penetrating the tingle canopy. Animals and plants are exquisitely adapted to maximise their fitness gains while minimising the costs; any organism that prioritised cost over benefit would soon become extinct. The onset of heavy drizzle after lunch diminished the gains from staying, so we packed up our gear and set off for Walpole.

No sooner had we left than we were arrested in our tracks by a very large Tiger Snake (moyop) curled up in the centre of the track. As the air was cool, it took some persuasion to move the snake on, but after much tossing of sticks and stamping of feet it did move aside and allow us through. Not only is this section of the track short, it is mostly downhill. And it passes through three distinctly different habitat types: tingle forest, coastal heath and melaleuca swamp. The first, of course, is unique, and is why the Walpole-Nornalup National Park exists. For these cool, wet forests represent the last fragment of vegetation dating back to Gondwana, before the continents split and drifted north to their current positions. Three species of tingle occur here, and nowhere else on earth: the Red Tingle, Rate's Tingle and Yellow Tingle. These trees grow to 60 metres or more and can live for up to 400 years. The trunks of Red Tingle are buttressed to support their great height, increasing the size of these ancient giants. There is something distinctly Tolkienesque about them; they are the archetypal Ents.

The tingles are restricted to the higher elevations of the Walpole-Nornalup area where year-round drizzle keeps the soil and canopy moist, while Karri, Marri and Jarrah fill the forest in its lower elevations, and the understorey is dominated by a range of medium to low trees, shrubs and sedges, including Karri Sheoak, Karri Wattle, Karri Hazel, Leafy Thomasia, Oak-leaf Chorilaena and

Spreading Sword-sedge. More often than not, you walk through a fine drizzle that penetrates the canopy, and the soil underfoot is rich, dark and musty: temperate rainforest at its best. And these cool wet forests are home to many Gondwanan relict animals as well, including the Tingle Pygmy Trapdoor Spider (*Bertmainius tingle*).

When Freddy was little I took him along to a night-time nature walk at the Tree Top Walk Visitor Centre. I always find such events difficult; when a tour guide asks their guests what they do for a living, should I confess to being a professor of evolutionary biology? I fear that this may establish in them a sense of being under examination, or perhaps undermine confidence in some way, so that I would generally say I was a cobbler perhaps, or in finance. We were all provided with a child's insect-collecting kit – plastic jar and small scoop – and sent off to rummage in the bushes and bring back for identification and mutual admiration any items we had found. I took Freddy to rummage through leaf litter at the base of a Red Tingle. We found a Forest Toadlet and a male Tingle Pygmy Trapdoor Spider, so I sent Freddy off to report back to our nature guide. 'Oh look, everyone, Freddy has a frog and a huntsman spider,' announced our guide. 'My dad says that's a trapdoor spider,' Freddy rejoined. 'Oh no, dear, I'll take it out and show you, shall I? They're quite harmless.' Had she looked at the fangs on that thing? While trapdoor spiders are not dangerous, their bites can be very painful. Time to fess up! After a somewhat awkward discussion, I managed to retrieve the spider and release it into the leaf litter where we had found it.

On our way to Walpole we passed John Rate Lookout, with fine views out across the forest to Nornalup Inlet and the Indian Ocean beyond. Just below the lookout were stands of Much-branched Ozothamnus, with dense clusters of pinkish-white flowers that had attracted hundreds of Flower Longicorn Beetles *(Stenoderus suturalis)*, the males mounted on their females and defending them from rivals that might otherwise mate and compete for fertilisations. From here the track descends through the forest, emerging onto coastal heath where the vegetation was reminiscent of the Pingerup Plains to the west, with stands of Pink Boronia, and masses of heavily scented creamy-white flowers of the Linear-leaved Hakea, pinkish wax flowers of Schauer's Astartea, and pale-yellow flowers of the Creamy Triggerplant. After crossing Rest Point Road, we soon entered the Saltwater Paperbark

TOP: A Common Marauding Katydid, *Metaballus frontalis*. This female still has the remains of a spermatophore attached to her genital opening, upon which she has been feeding. Katydids are often mistaken for grasshoppers, having the same long hind legs that allow them to jump when disturbed. But they are easily distinguished from grasshoppers by their long filiform antennae, generally as long, if not longer, than the insect's body. Leigh Simmons

MIDDLE: A Southern Whistling Moth, *Hecatesia thyridion*. The males of this day-flying moth have castanets on the outer edges of their forewings that they bring together in rapid sequence to produce a whistle that both repels rivals and attracts females. The bright orange colouration of the hind wings and abdomen likely function in predator avoidance. Leigh Simmons

BOTTOM: Bark-mimicking Grasshoppers, *Coryphistes ruricola*, that on disturbance flash their bright-blue hindwings and then disappear into the background just as soon as they land, returning to their stick-like camouflaged state. Here a male is mating with the larger female below. This extreme sexual size difference is a common feature of grasshoppers in which the male is adapted to remain attached, sometimes for days, to prevent rivals from mating. Leigh Simmons

woodlands that edge the Walpole River and Walpole Inlet. These beautiful trees grow along the banks and in the shallow edges of the river, their white papery trunks bright against the dark, tannin-stained river.

In the thirty years we have been visiting Walpole, this was the first time we had crossed the bridge over the Walpole River, or walked along the edge of Walpole Inlet. Arriving in town was somewhat surreal. We visit every year; it is our home from home. Of all the places in the world we have visited, this is where we return time and time again. It is the only place where I truly relax. Normally it takes more than five hours' drive to get here, which is why we come only once a year – it's too far for a weekend visit. Yet here we were on our annual pilgrimage, this year having walked 760 kilometres to get here!

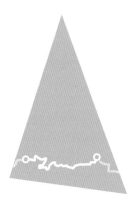

WALPOLE TO DENMARK

1

It was the right decision to walk on into town, allowing us a day's
rest from carrying our heavy packs. We had plenty of time for a
long-overdue launder of clothing, and a relaxed day restocking
supplies for the days ahead. While in the Pioneer Store supermarket
that day I recognised a fellow shopper out of the corner of my eye.
I whispered to Freddy, 'Hey, isn't that Jens from Hewett's Hill?'
'Of course not,' came Freddy's reply, 'he was a massive bloke.' 'No,
I'm sure it is. I always recognise a face. I'm going to go talk to him.'
'No, don't, you'll look an idiot. It's not him, it can't be!' But sure
enough it was Jens, now on his way north again to Kalamunda.
He was literally half the man he had been when we first met him
at Hewett's Hill!

We spent an enjoyable twenty minutes exchanging track stories,
Jens giving us tips on crossing the various inlets that lay ahead.
Apparently all the sandbars across the inlets were dry, and Jens
advised various shortcuts. Shortcuts were not for us, however;
we were determined to travel the track in its entirety, including
the various inlet crossings. But then I guess, having just completed
your eleventh end-to-end, you might be less exacting. The
transformation in Jens's physique was astonishing, and it prompted
me to examine myself in the mirror when we later returned to our
motel room. Good grief, that was a shock! No wonder my trousers

kept falling about my ankles; over the last two weeks I had started to hoist my trousers up and secure them in place using the waist straps of my pack. Now in town, without the pack, I found that I had to keep them up using my hands tucked into my pockets.

We set off the following day, rested and excited to be starting our journey through the tingle forest. This was well-trodden ground; we had walked various sections of the Bibbulmun Track between Walpole and Conspicuous Cliff hundreds of times over the years, but in all that time we had never stayed overnight in the forest. Our first pause was by the jetty on Walpole Inlet to watch Buff-banded Rails (kooli) and Purple Swamphens (kwirlam) picking their way through the reed beds, Australian Pelicans (boodalang) and Silver Gulls (djeringkara) perched on the jetty rails, and Musk Ducks (kadar) paddling on the inlet. The short walk across the wetlands on the eastern side of the inlet provided more encounters with Tiger Snakes (moyop) and Southern Emu-wrens (djirdjilya), and a new bird for the list, a magnificent Swamp Harrier (dilyordoo).

We stopped briefly at Coalmine Beach to admire the fine views across Nornalup Inlet, and to have second breakfast with one of my former students, Marianne, who was camping there with her family. But we did not linger, as we wanted to climb the 200 metres to the top of Douglas Hill before the day became too hot. After we crossed the South Coast Highway and entered the tingle forest, the walking was simply magical. There are no superlatives sufficient to describe the majestic tingles that dominate this forest and provide habitat for its abundant wildlife. High in the trees the *tick-tock, tick-tock* of the Tick-Tock cicadas *(Physeema quadricincta)*, was a constant presence. The occasional *tsweeit-tseet* of a Grey Fantail (kadjinak), and the melodic calls of Western Grey Shrike-thrush (koodilang) and Gilbert's Honeyeater (djingki), echoed through the dense forest. Western Gerygones (waralyboodang), New Holland Honeyeaters (bandiny) and Western Rosellas (bardinar) were abundant in the mid-storey of the forest. On the deeply fluted trunk of a Karri Sheoak we found a group of Feather-horned Beetles, a species from the genus *Rhipicera*, whose males have elaborate feathery antennae to detect the sexual scent that receptive females emit into the cool dark forest. This female had attracted three suitors; one was mounted and mating while two latecomers were mounted on either side of the pair, struggling to gain access to the female below the mating male.

After passing Hilltop Lookout and admiring the views across Nornalup Inlet, we arrived at the Giant Tingle, a huge, fire-hollowed red tingle that is reputedly the largest living tree in the forest. This tree looks more like an Ent than any other, with its hollowed base giving it the appearance of having legs, and the gnarled burls on its trunk are positively face-like. Of course, the boardwalk through this section of the forest is popular with daytrippers, especially at this time of year, so we passed quickly through so as to reach the seclusion of the more remote areas of the forest.

On the track east of the Giant Tingle we found a single Scented Sun Orchid. This species, like the Leopard and Chestnut Sun orchids we had seen east of Woolbales, is a food-mimic, attracting flies, beetles and native bees that would normally be drawn to the nectaries of purple flowers such as those of Purple Flags, False Blind Grass, Morning Iris and fringe lilies, to which the flowers of Scented Sun Orchid bear a close resemblance. This individual was flowering very late in the season, so we were lucky to find it.

We continued our climb up Douglas Hill and then along its ridge high above the Frankland River, which flows through the forest 150 metres below. Plant species of note included the Scaly-leaved Hibbertia; and Varied-leaved Thomasia. After walking along the ridge for about 2 kilometres, we began the long slow descent, eventually crossing Creek Road and walking along the access track to Frankland River Hut, which is perched on the banks of the river in the heart of the Walpole-Nornalup National Park. What a spectacular setting: the tannin-stained permanent pool in the Frankland River was perfectly still, reflecting the Karri and tingle on the banks of the river, like a giant watch-glass. The reflections were disturbed only by the passage of a pair of Pacific Black Ducks (ngwonan). We had been day visitors to this hut on many an occasion over the years, and were very happy to be here for the night. Amazingly, yet again, we had the hut all to ourselves.

As we sat on the shaded verandah of Frankland River Hut that afternoon, I noticed an aggregation of sand wasps from the genus *Bembix* that had taken up residence in the sandy patch in front of the hut. American entomologist Howard Evans came to Australia in the late 1960s to study the behaviour and ecology of these wasps. They are solitary, each female digging a long tunnel into the sand, the terminal end of which serves as a nursery in which she provisions a single offspring. Females hunt for flies, paralysing them

with their stings and carrying them into the nest, where the larva devours them.

Despite being solitary, sand wasps tend to aggregate in large numbers, perhaps because the perfect conditions for nesting are limited through the forest, or perhaps because there is safety in numbers. For *Bembix* wasps play host to brood parasitic flies that enter a wasp's nest and lay their own eggs, which hatch and feed on the provisions the mother wasp brings for her offspring. They are analogous to the Fan-tailed Cuckoos that lay their eggs in the nests of fairy-wrens, their young hatching to exploit the mother wren's parental provisioning at the expense of her own offspring. The more nests in a given area, the lower will be the probability that it is your nest that will become parasitised. This idea stems back to British evolutionary biologist William Hamilton's theory of the selfish herd: an individual that joins a group of its own species will dilute its chances of falling prey to the local predators.

Brood parasitism is probably also the reason behind the evolution of three rather peculiar behaviours of *Bembix* wasps. First, every time a female leaves her nest she will backfill the entrance with sand so that it is barely visible. We watched females coming and going, excavating their tunnel entrances and then refilling them. Without knowledge of the dangers a wasp faces by leaving the entrance to her nest open, an observer would think the creatures quite mad, digging a hole and then filling it in again, time after time after time! The second remarkable behaviour is that females will dig false tunnels all around their active nest, leaving these open to dupe the would-be parasite. Again, the more obvious nest holes she makes that are visible to a parasitic fly, the lower the chances are that the fly will find the real nest. The final cunning tactic the wasps employ is to mark out the sand surrounding their nest holes with what appear to be trails leading away from the active nest. Whether these trails serve as markers for the wasps themselves to find their nest entrance, or whether they draw attention of would-be parasites away from the nest is unknown. But we do know that species differ considerably in the patterns they make in the sand around their nests, which would certainly make nest location easier for those species that nest in mixed-species aggregations.

Sand wasps in the genus *Bembix* occur across the world, but in Australia they have exhibited an extraordinary evolutionary divergence. This is a recurring theme for south-western Australia, where 'mega' evolutionary divergence characterises many taxa,

from orchids to insectivorous plants, hibbertias, fringe lilies, triggerplants, banksias, katydids, and so on. When Howard Evans first came to Australia to study *Bembix*, there were about thirty-five known species. In twelve short months he collected eighty species from across the country, discovering that unlike the *Bembix* on any other continent, those in Australia had diversified in their preferred prey; typically they hunt flies, but some species in Australia will take damselflies, some ant lions, some bees, and some even other species of wasp. They can live at close quarters without competition because they have evolved to partition up their habitat by specialising on different prey items. Evans reported finding as many as six species nesting within a single aggregation. Almost no research has been done on *Bembix* since Howard's expeditions in the late 1960s, and undoubtably there are many new species to be found in the south-west of Western Australia if only we had the time and resources to look for them. Such efforts are critical. Without a thorough and accurate knowledge of the biodiversity of the region, we are unable to protect it from the effects of environmental change.

It is estimated that Australia has around 600,000 different species of animals and plants, of which only 30 per cent have been recognised, named and described. Such work is the remit of taxonomists working in museums, government organisations such as the CSIRO, and universities. But funding for taxonomy has declined significantly over the last decades; in an era of rapid developments in genomics, taxonomy is often viewed as an old-fashioned science, pushed aside as unnecessary or unimportant. We can now sequence the DNA in a glass of seawater, blast the sequences against huge databases and get a list of the animals and plants based on DNA matches. The brave new world of environmental DNA is the way of the future, right? But here's the thing. Many DNA sequences don't find matches in the database because, guess what, there are all those undescribed species out there that have not yet had their DNA sequences read and loaded into the database. Moreover, gene sequences are often highly conserved across species. That is, genes that have important biological functions, for example homeobox genes involved in development, are identical across species as varied as fungi, insects and humans. Finding such gene sequences can tell us nothing of the species represented in a sample of DNA. And a list of species generated from DNA samples is only as accurate as the original

TOP: Much-branched Ozothamnus attract hundreds of Flower Longicorn Beetles, *Stenoderus suturalis*, that feast on their nectaries. The males of these beetles remain mounted on the female after mating, and defend them from rivals who might otherwise mate and compete for fertilisations. Leigh Simmons

MIDDLE: Forest Toadlets, *Metacrinia nichollsi*, are an ancient Gondwanan relict species of frog that is confined to the wet forests of the south-west corner of Western Australia. Their eggs contain enough nutrients to allow the tadpole to grow and metamorphose within the safety of the egg's membrane, hatching after several months of development as a tiny, fully formed and independent frog. Leigh Simmons

BOTTOM: The cool wet forests are home to many Gondwanan relicts, including the Tingle Pygmy Trapdoor Spider, *Bertmainius tingle*. This male was found in the leaf litter at the base of a Red Tingle, probably in search of the more sedentary females that remain in their subterranean burrow. The species is threatened with extinction due to inappropriate fire regimes and climate change. Leigh Simmons

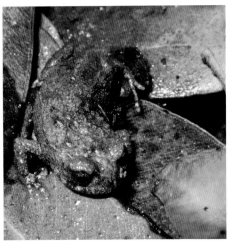

identifications made on the animals and plants from which the DNA sequences were extracted. Without a qualified taxonomist to identify the animal or plant in the first instance, environmental genotyping is a leap of faith.

Discovering new species is not just an exercise in making a list of what's out there. Many of our medicines come from animals and plants, and the discovery of new species will deliver new medicines, or replacement medicines for those to which our parasites and pathogens have evolved resistance. The work of taxonomists is essential. The Australian Academy of Science launched its decadal plan for taxonomy and biosystematics in 2018, aimed at increasing attention on the need for renewed government investment in taxonomic research. The academy rightly recognises that unless we act quickly, most of the biodiversity we have will be lost to extinction before we even know it's there, and we shall be the poorer for it.

2

The 14.5 kilometres between Frankland River and Giants Hut is perhaps the very best section of the Bibbulmun Track, passing through the heart of the ancient forest that is the Walpole-Nornalup National Park. The track meanders first along the banks of the Frankland River as it flows through the forest towards Nornalup Inlet. It then crosses the river at Sappers Bridge; a surprise for us was that Sappers Bridge was no longer the wooden bridge built by Australian Army engineers in 1982, but now a sparkling new concrete-and-steel road bridge. From here we walked up Brainy Cut Off, the source of many a joke when Freddy was little, and turned right into a wonderful section of track that winds uphill through a pristine forest of sheoak and majestic Karri and tingle.

We paused for second breakfast at my favourite spot in the forest, the crest of a hill just before Boxhall Road where stand three of the tallest Red Tingles in the forest; these trees are so tall they make you feel like Gulliver in Brobdingnag. Being in this forest brings unsurpassed peace and tranquillity, and our annual visits to this region are restorative for good reason – being in the forest triggers an innate physiological response programmed into us by millions of years of evolution.

It may come as some surprise, but the physiological and psychological benefits of forests are now well established. Finnish ecologist Eeva Karjalainen and her colleagues have reviewed studies from around the world that converge on the finding that visits to forests have the effect of lowering our blood pressure, heart rate and cortisol levels, all factors that when high contribute to stress. And a recent study by American environmentalist Gregory Bratman and his colleagues has reported that a ninety-minute walk in a natural environment such as a forest causes reductions in neural activity within the regions of the brain that would otherwise cause depression.

But why should we have such a profound physiological response to forests? The answer lies in our evolutionary response to predation. For contrary to popular belief of man as the hunter, humans in fact have a long evolutionary history of being the prey in predator–prey relationships, as Donna Hart and Robert Sussman show in their book *Man the Hunted*. Even in contemporary societies we are victims of predation: tigers in India, lions in Africa and sharks in Australia often prey on humans. While not as common as it would have been in our evolutionary past, falling victim to predators is natural for our species. Humans will also have fallen victim, and still do, to lethal attacks from individuals of our own species. Contemporary Western civilisations, while now not as susceptible to biological predation, have replaced the risk from predators with a risk of death from artificial sources, such as fast-moving vehicles. The selection pressure for constant vigilance remains with us. And the selected response in all animals to such risk is heightened stress: the increased blood pressure, heart rate and cortisol levels that will allow an animal to react quickly in escaping from a predatory attack.

An important concept in ecology proposed originally by American behavioural ecologist John Laundré is the 'landscape of fear'. Animals live in a highly variable environment, from open plains to thick forests, and these varied environments expose animals to different levels of predation risk. We can plot an animal's landscape of fear very much like we plot elevations above sea level on a topographic map, with the hills those areas of the landscape where animals have greatest fear and the valleys those areas where they have least fear. Fear itself can be measured by how vigilant an animal is, how long it is prepared to stay in a given place eating before moving on, and physiological measures of stress, such as heart rate or cortisol levels.

For our ancestors, caves and forests provided shelter and protection from predators such as sabre-toothed tigers that roamed the open grasslands. Forests represent valleys in our landscape of fear, reducing our stress levels. When you walk through a forest and feel that overwhelming sense of relaxation, you are experiencing a deep-rooted evolved response to a reduced risk of predation. And given the known mental and physiological health benefits that forests provide us, we should strive to protect what remaining forests we have. Surely the tingle forests of Walpole-Nornalup National Park should be World Heritage–listed, given they represent the last remaining temperate forests of Gondwana, and contain relict species of both plants and animals found nowhere else on Earth. And they contribute demonstrably to our mental health and wellbeing.

From Boxhall Road the track passes through the tingle forest, descending and then ascending ridges, crossing streams but generally heading down towards the Valley of the Giants. It was along this section of the track that Freddy had suggested, almost a year earlier to the day, that we do an end-to-end. The walk to Giants Hut took us just over five hours, passing the world-renowned Tree Top Walk in the Valley of the Giants. This steel walkway suspended 40 metres above the ground meanders 420 metres through the tingle canopy, affording spectacular views across the forest to the ocean. We have walked the Tree Top Walk many times over the years, so we did not stop on this occasion – well, only briefly to enjoy a long macchiato from the Tall Timber coffee cart in the car park.

The hut at Giants, set in the base of a valley whose sides are clad with huge old-growth Marri, Karri and sheoaks, was one of our top-five campsites on the track. Again, we had visited Giants on many an occasion on day walks, but never before had we stayed overnight. During the afternoon, several parties arrived and left, daytrippers from the Tree Top Walk car park who marvelled at our feat of having walked from Kalamunda. But come twilight the forest fell into silence. Remarkably, we had the hut to ourselves again that night. We had been on the track now for fifty nights, only sharing the hut on six of them. We felt especially privileged that night to have this long-cherished spot to ourselves.

3

We struck out the following morning with some reluctance. We would be leaving the tingle forest for the last time, and heading south cutting across a diversity of habitat types in our walk to Rame Head, which is perched on limestone cliffs high above the southern Indian Ocean. We would exchange the tranquillity of the cool damp forest for the wild, exposed environs of the coastal sections of the track that would lead us ever closer to our destination in Albany. From Giants we ascended through the forest to the 200-metre contour where the mighty tingle predominated once more. We paused only briefly to admire the magnificent Rate's Tingle that stands on the corner of the track as it crosses Rate Road, before we descended again through the forest to cross the South Coast Highway, leaving the tingles behind us. The track passed first through low-lying swamplands before ascending again through dry Jarrah and Marri forest towards Nut Lookout. There we rested for second breakfast, taking in the panoramic views south and east across the coastal heaths towards Peaceful Bay.

Our descent towards Ficifolia Road should have been wonderful, for this is an area dominated by another short-range endemic species, the Red Flowering Gum (boorn), which is found only in this very small area between Nornalup and Peaceful Bay. From January to March, these trees put on their spectacular, extravagant show of bright orange–red flowers. So beautiful are these flowering trees that they have been widely propagated, usually by grafting onto rootstock that can tolerate more varied soil types, and grown as ornamentals around the world. I was amazed to see them lining the streets of San Francisco when I visited there some years ago. Sadly for us, we were to see the trees on a burning day, their trunks scorched and limbs bared by a recent burn that had passed through the area. Most of the trees showed signs of recovery, with fresh fleshy, rufous stems and leaves sprouting from the bare limbs, and they would again put on their summer display, but not that summer.

The Coastal Sheoaks were likewise flush with spiky green growth up their trunks, as if they were sprouting green beards. The fire had also stimulated strong growth of Southern Cross Flower, Royal Robe, Drumsticks and Gardner's Banksia. The Semaphore Sedge too was fully recovered, thick green and in full flower, and the Grasstrees looked very smart with their jet-black trunks and

fresh green topknots. The open habitat created by the fire afforded us clear views of a Brown Falcon (karkany) perched in a bare Red Flowering Gum (boorn), and a Stubble Quail (boorlam) that hurried across the bare sand before bursting into a low and hurried flight.

After crossing Ficifolia Road, we entered unburnt vegetation once more, meandering through stable dunes that were heavily vegetated with groves of flowering Yate (mo); the ground was littered with their bud caps, and New Holland Honeyeaters (bandiny) were feasting on the nectar provided by their greenish-yellow filamentous flowers. The understorey was thick with Peppermint (wanil), flowering Tapeworm Plant and Harsh Hakea (berrung). We found megachilid bees nesting on the slopes of one warm, sheltered north-facing dune. These bees are solitary, and use the abandoned burrows of other bees or wasps, crevices in rocks, or vacated homes of wood-boring insects in which to provision their offspring. These bees, however, were actively digging, perhaps modifying existing holes in the sandy bank. The occasional male would knock a female from the air and try to mate with her, but none were successful while I watched. The females were black with two or three whitish grey bands on their abdomens, while the males were similar but with an orange tip to the abdomen. Female megachilid bees cut discs of leaves and carry them to the cavity in which they are nesting, lining it with the section of leaf before provisioning it with pollen and nectar and laying an egg. I would love to have lingered longer watching the bees constructing their nests, but we had a long walk ahead of us before we would reach Rame Head.

Leaving the shelter of the wooded dunes, we set out across the open heathlands towards the coast. Here among the stunted heathland shrubs we happened upon a large group of Splendid Fairy-wrens (djer-djer), nine in total and three of them in full blue breeding plumage. It could have been a single group with three breeding males, which seemed unlikely, or several groups meeting at the boundaries of their territories. For Splendid Fairy-wrens, like the Western Australian Magpie (koolbardi), Kookaburra (kaa-kaa) and Rainbow Bee-eater (birin-birin), are cooperative breeders. They defend year-round territories, and the dominant pair will breed from September to January, typically with the help of offspring from a previous clutch and one or more immigrant birds that may have joined the group. Helpers are most often younger birds, and frequently males whose opportunities to breed themselves are limited due to a deficit of available females.

The breeding biology of Splendid Fairy-wrens has been studied extensively in Western Australia by Eleanor Russell and Ian Rowley, and in South Australia by Stephen Pruett-Jones and his students. Until the advent of DNA fingerprinting, Splendid Fairy-wrens were thought to be monogamous, with the dominant male and female in the group responsible for all of the offspring produced. We now know, however, that Splendid Fairy-wrens have the highest rates of extra-pair paternity of any songbird. In one population at Gooseberry Hill in Western Australia, at least 65 per cent of the young were found to be fathered by males outside of the group that cared for them. A similar study from South Australia returned extra-group paternity figures of 25 to 52 per cent.

Russell and Rowley made extensive observation of several breeding groups and discovered that 'philandering' males visited other groups frequently, and when they did they would vigorously court the dominant female. Normally, fairy-wrens will hop through the dense vegetation and take only short low flights between shrubs. In contrast, philandering males will fly deliberately and conspicuously through a group's territory, well clear of the surrounding vegetation, with their body axis vertical rather than horizontal to the ground, a behaviour that Russell and Rowley named sea horse flight. As if their bright blue plumage is not stunning enough, these males will draw attention to themselves by carrying a purple or pink flower petal in their bills. These displays are directed at the dominant female, who will be presented with the purple petal. Judging from the numbers of offspring sired by philanderers, females are mightily impressed by these male displays.

Indeed, Pruett-Jones and his colleagues' studies of paternity among and within groups of Splendid Fairy-wrens in South Australia suggest that female choice based on the displays of philandering males imposes stronger sexual selection than does competition to become the dominant male in a group, and is likely responsible for the evolution of their bright-blue colouration and conspicuous courtship behaviours. And Splendid Fairy-wrens are not all show either. The fact that females mate with their pair-bonded partner and with any number of philandering males means that competition for fertilisations among the sperm of several males imposes stiff sexual selection on ejaculate production. Fairy-wrens generally have the largest testes relative to their body size of any bird species, and an adult male Splendid Fairy-wren's testes comprise more than 6 per cent of his total body mass. He will have in storage

some 300 million to 600 million sperm ready to deploy in the competition to fertilise a female's egg! This is an extraordinary number of sperm for a small bird weighing in at just 11 grams. Such is the strength of sexual selection through sperm competition. So this group of nine birds could well have been a dominant male and female, plus two philanderers trying their luck.

The sun broke through as we arrived at Conspicuous Cliff Beach, encouraging us to linger a while for morning tea, the usual half a trail bar and a coffee candy. Conspicuous Beach that morning was at its very best: pure white sand edged by a turquoise ocean under an azure sky and barely another living soul. After dumping our packs we walked through the surf towards the west end, bathing our tired feet in the crystal-clear icy waters of the southern Indian Ocean. A lone black-backed Pacific Gull (ngakala) joined us to take fresh water from the stream that issues from the dunes and runs across the flat sands to the ocean's edge. Ah, we could have dwelt there all day, had it not been for the epic climb awaiting us at the eastern end of the beach.

And so we set off once more, climbing the low foredune before dropping into the magical world of the protected backdune. Here a large freshwater pool, edged with dense stands of Sweet Mignonette Orchids, was home to Clicking Toadlets and Blue Skimmer dragonflies. The climb up the back of the dune system to the limestone ridge of Conspicuous Cliff was tough going, but the views along the coast from the top, east to West Cape Howe and west to Point Nuyts, were worth every step. Once we reached the top, the walking was reasonably level, with only the occasional descent and re-ascent as we travelled along the limestone ridge to Rame Head Hut.

Situated high on the cliffs, Rame Head Hut is exposed to the prevailing south-westerly that drives off the southern Indian Ocean. The orientation of the hut was such that it afforded limited respite from the wind, and the sleeping platform when we arrived was thick with sand. We swept it off, only to watch it fill again within a matter of minutes. But by observing the pattern of backfill, we were able to ascertain the best spot to set up our sleeping mats. Fortunately, one end of the hut is enclosed with perspex sheeting, all the better to boil water without the stove blowing out. It was a cold and windy night, and one that we shared with Bridget and her father who arrived late afternoon from Peaceful Bay, the first time we'd had company in a hut since our friend GFP at Grimwade.

TOP: Djirdjilya or Southern Emu-wren, *Stipiturus malachurus*. A common, but seldom seen resident of coastal heaths in the south-west of WA. These wrens are more like mice than birds, in their habit of hopping through dense undergrowth. They seldom fly, and poorly when they do so. Their reliance on walking rather than flight has resulted in the evolutionary loss of functional feathers in the tail, which are now represented by just six sparsely filamented and barely visible plumes that resemble the feathers of Emus, hence their common name. Only the male has the pale -blue throat. Leigh Simmons

MIDDLE: Kooli or Buff-banded Rail, *Gallirallus philippensis*. A shy, skittish bird, most often found skulking along the fringes of reed beds that border large water-bodies such as the Walpole Inlet, and mostly at dawn or dusk. Leigh Simmons

BOTTOM: Kwirlam or Purple Swamphen, *Porphyrio porhyrio*. These large common waterhens are often found on the margins of large water bodies. They are cooperative breeding birds, a pair frequently helped to raise their young by juveniles from previous breeding attempts. Leigh Simmons

We woke to find ourselves covered in a thin layer of sand, and with our very own dune system banked up against the edges of our sleeping mats. But the winds had calmed and it promised to be a bright and sunny morning. Heading due east, we walked through a stunning stabilised dune system, heavily vegetated with Peppermint (wanil), Grey Stinkwood, Grasstrees (balga), Claw Flower, Coastal Banjine and Variable-leaved Hakea, to name just a few of the most abundant species.

In the shelter of the dune valleys through this section, Candlestick Banksia (piara) grow huge, forming avenues through which the track meanders. Heart-shaped Pithocarpa, with its beautiful silver foliage, was bearing its subtle pale-yellow blooms, and the gumug or Australian Bluebell was adorned with pretty pale-blue pendulous bells. The gumug relies on birds to eat its fleshy purple fruits in order for its seeds to be dispersed, and these fruits were a tasty sweet treat for the Noongar. It is a climbing plant that obtains structural support by twining around the stems and branches of surrounding vegetation. Native to Western Australia, it is found throughout the south-west corner as small, widely dispersed shrubs, and in its native range it is a delightful addition to the regional biodiversity. Like the Red Flowering Gum (boorn), however, it has been cultivated and distributed throughout the world for use as an ornamental garden plant. Its claim to fame is the 2013 Royal Horticultural Society's Award of Garden Merit. But human translocation of this species outside of its natural range has come with devastating ecological consequences. In some locations, such as the south-eastern states of Australia, it has invaded natural areas, where it smothers and kills the native vegetation.

In his 1958 volume *The Ecology of Invasions by Animals and Plants*, British ecologist Charles Elton outlined the many ecological factors that contribute towards the explosive colonisation of introduced species, and began the scientific study of invasion ecology. Elton argued that introduced species were more likely to establish and undergo population explosions in areas of low biodiversity. For example, growing in the mega-diverse region of south-western Australia, the populations of gumug are controlled, because it has coevolved with its local competitors, partitioning the available resources so that each achieves its optimal growth and

reproduction. Taken out of this environment and placed into one with fewer species, it is released from competition and potentially other factors that might have constrained its growth, such as local pathogens and predators, allowing it to grow rapidly and invasively. This phenomenon is apparent in the invasive spread of brambles through the river systems and pine plantations around Balingup, where human clearing has simplified the habitat, allowing these invaders to spread unchecked by competition.

Another well-known example of a biological invasion in Australia is the Cane Toad. Introduced to Queensland to control Cane Beetles, this species has spread across the top of Australia, with devastating consequences for our native fauna. For the Cane Toad is toxic to predatory species such as goannas and quolls. The toad's population size has exploded because of the release from competition and predation that keeps it in check in its natural habitat, and populations of Australian predators have plummeted because of the toxicity of the toads. Invasion ecologists study the factors that make a particular species invasive – what behavioural, physiological or morphological traits give an introduced species the edge in competition over native species. Such research can help in the control of unwanted pests such as foxes, cats or Cinnamon Mould.

For example, when choosing species of dung beetles to introduce for the control of bushflies and other ecosystem services, it would be useful to have an understanding of the types of traits that are necessary for successful establishment and spread, because we want species that will undergo successful invasion. That said, even the celebrated success of the dung beetle biological control program in Australia may not have come without cost. We have a host of native species of dung beetle, one of which Freddy and I found on our walk that day – the large and impressively horned *Onthophagus ferox*, which feeds on kangaroo dung. A highly invasive, ergo successful dung beetle introduction, while beneficial for us in dealing with cattle dung, can compete with native species with the potential to drive them to extinction. Do we care about the loss of a dung beetle? I think we should. For the loss of species from a complex ecosystem can have unforeseen ecological consequences. Elton demonstrated the key roles that invasive species have had in the extinction of native species. He argued that through human-generated invasions, 'the biological world will become not more complex but simpler – and poorer. Instead of six continental realms of life...there will be only one world.'

But for now we revelled in the biodiversity of the coastal dune system. That morning we added to our bird list: shortly after we set off from Rame Head, a small flock of Rock Parrots, for which there is no Noongar name, raced past overhead, with their hurried and high-pitched *tsee, tzit-tseit*. These small parrots look very much like the Elegant Parrots (koolyidarang) we saw in the farmlands north of Northcliffe, but they are smaller and nest generally on offshore islands or along limestone coastal cliffs, never sallying far from the spray of the sea. Splendid Fairy-wrens (djer-djer) and Southern Emu-wrens (djirdjilya), Silvereyes (doolor) and New Holland Honeyeaters (bandiny) were abundant in the heathlands, and we spotted a female Grey Butcherbird (wardawort) with her fully grown brown-and-fawn young of the year, the pair resting in a Candlestick Banksia (piara). After about 4 kilometres the track passed along a boardwalk across an area of low-lying swampland. Here we found yellow-flowered Marshworts and two new species of orchid: the Christmas Leek; and the beautiful Drummond's Donkey, the latter categorised as rare.

Donkey orchids are like the sun orchids, in that they have evolved to mimic nectar-rewarding species in order to attract pollinators. The donkey orchid flowers mimic those of native peas such as Prickly Stinkwood, which they resemble in colour and form, and were flowering in profusion throughout this area. Shortly thereafter we emerged onto the coast at the Gap. Here coastal plants grew along the boundary of the beach, and in the cracks and crevices of the granite boulders: Foxtails, Native Rosemary, Coastal Pigface (bain), Stalked Guinea Flower and Cushion Bush flourished, as did the invasive Sea Spurge.

The track followed the beach a short way before ascending to Castle Rock on Point Irwin, where we stopped for second breakfast before descending again to walk along the beach to the hamlet of Peaceful Bay. Along the way we watched a pair of Sooty Oystercatchers probing the sand along the water's edge with their long scarlet bills, searching for tasty worms, snails and other invertebrates. These birds, which typically forage in pairs along the beaches between rocky headlands, have evolved a fascinating sexual dimorphism that appears to alleviate competition between males and females for food. For the female's bill is almost 20 per cent longer than that of the male, allowing her to probe deeper in the sand than her mate, and to reach a different cohort of food items. The female's diet thereby consists more of

soft-bodied worms, while the male's shorter stockier bill allows it to handle and smash open hard-shelled crabs or snails to obtain the nutritious flesh within. This resource partitioning between the sexes allows Sooty Oystercatchers to extract more resources from their environment and, as a pair, achieve a greater reproductive success than if they competed for the same food items.

As we crossed the dune from the coast to the inlet of Peaceful Bay, a lone Nankeen Kestrel (mardiyet) was held motionless in the air above us; supported by the updraft of warm air from the dunes, it did not need to move its wings to remain aloft. It surveyed the dunes below, and then dropped from the sky like a stone onto some unsuspecting locust or small lizard scurrying through the grasses. That night we pitched our tent in the Peaceful Bay Campground, where we enjoyed the luxury of a shower and the local fish and chip supper.

5

We had 23 kilometres to walk to Boat Harbour Hut, one of our longest and, as it turned out, most arduous days on the track. We rose at four-thirty to get a head start on the day. As the sky began to lighten, we ascended a small dune system to the north of the Peaceful Bay township, the views from which were obscured by morning mists. On descending we crossed Peaceful Bay Road and passed through a stretch of Peppermint (wanil) scrub that transitioned into woodlands of Coastal Sheoak, Jarrah and the occasional Red Flowering Gum (boorn).

After crossing Peaceful Bay Road for a second time, we followed a vehicle track for just over 2 kilometres as it travelled parallel with Peaceful Bay Beach. The track ascended gradually to reach a lookout with commanding views east across Quarram Nature Reserve and north to Irwin Inlet. A large sand flat in the middle of the narrows was populated by an assortment of seabirds: Australian Pelican (boodalang), Little Pied (kakak) and Little Black (koordjokit) cormorants, Silver Gulls (djeringkara), Sooty Oystercatchers, White-faced Herons (wayan) and a lone Caspian Tern. We could see that the sandbar was dry, and we could have saved ourselves about 5 kilometres by walking across it and directly along Big Quarram Beach. It was not about reaching our

destination, though, but rather the journey we had resolved to make. And so we set off on the track heading north along the edge of the inlet.

The track climbed steeply at first, up and over a sand ridge, before ascending into Bullich and then Peppermint (wanil) woodlands, with glimpses of the narrow channel of the inlet to our right. Eventually we arrived at the boatshed, which housed the canoes we would use to cross the inlet. There were strict instructions to leave at least two canoes on each side of the channel. The boatshed held three. It was rather like one of those brainteasers. Two men arrive at a river and must cross with the aid of three canoes. Each canoe can carry one man and one pack, and the number of canoes on either side after the crossing must be equal to the number of canoes on arrival. Hum. Freddy took his pack over to the eastern shed using one of the canoes, then returned towing two canoes, allowing us to leave three on either side. The canoeing proved to be an enjoyable variation to our usual mode of travel.

From the eastern shore we climbed to the top of a ridge and then out into an expansive area of low rolling hills known as the Showgrounds. This was a strange habitat indeed. One might be forgiven for thinking this a barren wasteland. As far as the eye could see there were just rolling open plains; Twine Rushes lent a pale-green hue, which gave the appearance of a sparse, patchy lawn stretching to the far horizon. These rushes grew no taller than 10 centimetres, and you could count the number of shrubs dotted across the landscape on one hand.

As we set off across this bare landscape the sun began to beat down upon us in fury. Not a spot of shade in which to walk, and the Western Grey Kangaroos huddled together under the one or two low shrubs that did grow there. Walking along the seemingly endless vehicle track became a gruelling chore in the heat; there was nowhere to stop and take shelter. And so we trudged on and on, 7 kilometres across these dry and dusty 'Showgrounds'. Surprisingly, there were some birds to be seen and heard: Western Australian Magpies (koolbardi), Grey Currawongs (djarbarn), Southern Emu-wrens (djirdjilya), Splendid Fairy-wrens (djer-djer), Silvereyes (doolor) and an Emu (wetj). While these open plains were not my preferred habitat, they were for the Orange Spider-hunting Wasps *(Cryptocheilus bicolor)*, that nested along the sandy vehicle track.

Orange Spider-hunting Wasps are one of Australia's largest wasps. As their name suggests, they are from a family of wasps, the pompilids, that specialise in hunting spiders. Their striking black and orange colouration is an aposematic warning to anything that might consider getting in their way, for these wasps have a ferocious sting. The females search for large spiders, typically huntsman spiders, that are larger than the wasps themselves. When a female spider-hunter finds her victim, she will anaesthetise it with her sting, before dragging it across the ground in a direct line back to her burrow. There she places the unconscious spider in a chamber, where it lies in its coma. Meanwhile, the female injects a single egg into the abdomen of the spider, which on hatching will eat it from within, avoiding the vital organs lest the fresh meat die before the young wasp has had its fill and is ready to emerge.

These wasps are highly aggressive. I once saw one dragging a huntsman across the footpath along the shore at Matilda Bay by the University of Western Australia campus in Perth. It was spotted by a Red Wattlebird (djangkang), which flew down to try to steal the spider. An intense battle ensued as the wasp flew wildly at the wattlebird, which in turn flew up and away from the wasp before trying again to seize the sleeping spider. This battle continued for all of five minutes before the bird finally thought better of it and left, upon which the wasp then flew furiously at me, sending me scuttling along the path out of its way. That wasp chased me some 15 metres before it returned to its victim and continued its laborious journey to its nest.

That day on the Showgrounds, we saw many females searching through the Twine Rushes for spiders, and followed one successful female as she dragged her victim to her burrow. Many males patrolled the vehicle track too. The males are about half the size of the females and are completely harmless, lacking a sting. But they have the same bold black and orange aposematic colouration, mimicking that of the female and thus gaining protection from would-be predators. The males search for nests from which young females will emerge, entering the nests to help dig females out and mate with them while they are still docile.

The spider-hunting wasps gave us some enjoyment that morning, though it must be said that this section had to be the least enjoyable part of the entire track. Perhaps if we had our time again, we might have taken that shortcut across the sandbar after all. But then perhaps not – the Showgrounds are unlike any natural habitat we

encountered on the track, and it would have been a shame not to experience it in all its rich tapestry. We soldiered on as the track turned southward and began to cross an impossible series of dunes, each steeper than the last. We struggled to the top of each dune hoping beyond hope that this would be the last one, only to see the track plummet again, just as steeply, with the next ridge 100 metres or so ahead, steeper than the last. The erosion from walkers was pretty severe on some of these dunes; at one stage we were walking through gorges in the sand just about body width, and with walls shoulder height!

As we approached the coast, the vegetation returned, mostly Peppermint (wanil) scrub, but with some new plants to distract the curious, including the pretty Twin-leaf Myoporum, which was flowering. Up and down, up and down for 2 kilometres, until finally we summited a dune to see Big Quarram Beach below, the wind off the ocean finally offering respite from the searing dry heat of the barren Showgrounds behind us.

We sat a while on the beach, but were soon sent on our way by the rising sea 'breeze', which roared in from the ocean, replacing the blistering sun with stinging sand whipped up from the beach. Thankfully, the tides were with us, so we could walk close to the water's edge on the hard wet sand, rather than suffer the full sandblasting higher up the beach. And so we strode out on the first of several long stretches of beach walking. We made good progress and were soon clambering up and over Quarram Beach Head at the eastern end of Big Quarram Beach. Fine stands of Sticky Tailflower graced the rocky headland with their large white flowers, and there were fine views along the coast to the headland at Boat Harbour.

After descending again and walking briefly along Little Quarram Beach, we turned inland once more, re-entering the baking shelter of the dune system. Once again, a series of steep climbs followed, sometimes made easier by the installation of long steep flights of steps. But the Dementors were out in full force: soft sand, heat in the gullies, and gusting winds as we finally reached the limestone crest above Little Quarram Beach. The views were spectacular: west along the coast to Peaceful Bay, east to Point Hillier and inland across Owingup Swamp. It would have been nice to linger, but the winds, now gusting at 32 kilometres an hour, drove us onward towards Boat Harbour.

About 1 kilometre west of the hut we had to skirt the north-facing slope of an extremely steep, shifting dune. The path literally stopped at a field of soft sand flowing like a river steeply downhill to the Owingup Plains below, then emerged again 10 to 15 metres on the other side. The gusting winds were whipping up thick clouds of sand from the south face of the dune, driving them over the crest and down the northern slope at great force, stinging our faces and making it impossible to keep our eyes open.

We launched into this swirling sandstorm in the direction of the path on the other side of the sand slide, and the weight of our packs and the shifting sands beneath our feet had the effect of pulling us down the slope as we sank into the soft sand up to our calves. We struggled, our legs motoring as fast as they could go, to gain forward traction while also maintaining elevation, and our shoes soon became tightly packed with sand. There was nothing to cling to in the river of sand and there was a brief moment when I thought all was lost and I would be swept away down the slopes to the Owingup Plain below. Somehow I managed to struggle to the far side in time, seize hold of the Thick-leaved Fan-flower and drag myself free of the shifting sands. Good grief, *A Guide to the Bibbulmun Track* says that 'for most walkers this will be a long and challenging day'. Was that ever an understatement? Arriving at Boat Harbour Hut, we were physically drained. It had taken us just over six hours and forty minutes to travel the 23 kilometres, and frankly we were lucky to have made it.

How good it was to be out of the wind, which whistled around the hut and rattled the toilet door like an angry beast. We were to share the hut again that night, this time with a young Canadian man who arrived mid-afternoon. He was heading north, carrying the largest pack I think I have ever seen. He was a big bloke, well over six and a half feet tall, and built like an ox. And it was not just his stature that gave him an uncanny resemblance to Hagrid. From the depths of his seemingly bottomless pack he extracted a huge tent, which he erected inside the hut. Then came regular, full-sized saucepans, with lids, that must have weighed a ton, several cans of food, and a giant pineapple! Just the thing when you're travelling light. I wonder to this day how he fared crossing the sand slide with that lot.

TOP: The moyop or Tiger snake, *Notechis scutatus*, is perhaps one of Australia's most venomous snakes. The protein composition of snake venom varies considerably among species of snakes due to the never-ending coevolutionary cycles between predator toxicity and prey resistance. Freddy Simmons

MIDDLE: Feather-horned Beetles from the genus *Rhipicera* in which the male has elaborate feathery antennae with which it detects the sexual scent emitted by receptive females. Here two males jostle to mate with a female that has already mated and is guarded by the successful male. Freddy Simmons

BOTTOM: Sand wasps from the genus *Bembix* provide their offspring with a variety of insects on which to feed, all anaesthetised to remain as fresh meat for the young wasps. Australia is home to more species of this wasp than occur anywhere else in the world. Freddy Simmons

6

We rose with the sun the following morning, rested and ready for another day. We left Hagrid sleeping in his tent, dropped down to Boat Harbour Inlet and crossed the headland to the beach beyond. At the eastern end of the beach we turned inland to climb up through the sand dunes to the crest of the limestone cliffs that travel east along the coast towards Point Hillier.

The track follows the crest for 2 kilometres, with wonderful views along the coast and north across Quarram Nature Reserve. But then it heads slowly inland and down, taking the walker again through the dune system with its punishing ups and downs, mostly on eroded and shifting sand paths that suck the momentum from each step. But this was nothing in comparison to the day before, and we soon emerged on the limestone crest once more, heading slowly upward towards Mount Hillier. Through here grow Dwarf Sheoak no taller than 10 centimetres high, Nitre Bush or Wild Grape with its inky-black berries, Wild Geranium and Swamp Bottlebrush, although Thick-leaved Fan-flower is by far the most dominant of plants, filling the air with its musky odour. A small flock of Rock Parrots allowed us to watch them as they perched in the open on the bare branches of a long-dead banksia, the skeletal remains from a bushfire that passed through long ago.

After Mount Hillier, the track dropped down again through Peppermint (wanil) scrub to Parry Beach, where we took the opportunity to use the campground facilities to freshen up for the stretch ahead – 7.5 kilometres along Mazzoletti Beach to William Bay. The morning was still, the temperature perfect, and the tide was with us, at least for the first 5 kilometres, allowing for an easy stroll along the hard compacted sands close to the water's edge, and affording fine sightings of both Sooty and Pied (koran-koran) oystercatchers, and several large Pacific Gulls (ngakala).

Sooty and Pied oystercatchers are often seen feeding in mixed-species groups such as this. But again, natural selection has shaped their bill structures in such a way as to minimise competition between them. For Pied Oystercatcher bills are on average longer than those of Sooty Oystercatchers, allowing them to access worms deep in the sand. And like the female Sooty Oystercatcher, the female Pied Oystercatcher has a longer bill than the male, allowing the sexes to feed on different cohorts of prey items, and

alleviating competition between the sexes. Niche partitioning between species and between males and females of each species allows the coexistence of birds that exploit similar resources, and is favoured by natural selection because it promotes the reproductive success of individual birds of both species. It was no coincidence that Pacific Gulls were seen patrolling the beach along which the oystercatchers were feeding, for Pacific Gulls are thieves. They watch oystercatchers and other foraging seabirds very closely, and if they see a bird find a food item they will attack and chase the discoverer until it drops the food. Stealing food in this way is known as kleptoparasitism, and is a common practice of medium to large seabirds such as gulls and skewers.

The Pacific Gull (ngakala), Australia's largest gull, is endemic across the southern coasts of Australia. As well as being a kleptoparasite, it is a predator, frequently including in its diet smaller seabirds such as petrels. Indeed the Pacific Gull diet is highly varied. One study on Seal Island, off the coast of Wilsons Promontory in Victoria, identified prey species ranging from snails and crabs to fish, small seabirds and even rats. The Western Australian populations of this species differ from those in the east in that the red spot at the tip of the large yellow bill does not extend to the upper mandible as it does in birds east of the South Australian border.

Red spots, a widespread feature of the bills of gulls, serve an important signalling function between parents and their offspring. Indeed, the red spot on the bill of gulls was made famous by Dutch ornithologist Niko Tinbergen in the late 1940s and early 1950s, with his work on the European Herring Gull, a species that fills the equivalent niche in Europe to the Pacific Gull in Australia. Darwin, in his volume *The Expression of the Emotions in Man and Other Animals*, argued that behaviour was transmitted from parent to offspring in much the same way as any other characteristic such as height or hair colour, and he used the similarity of expressions such as fear or anger in the faces of dogs and humans to support the idea that behaviour had deep-rooted evolutionary origins.

Tinbergen studied what he called 'instinct' or the innate ability of animals to behave in a way that promotes their fitness without any prior knowledge or learning. By offering cardboard models of bills to newly hatched gull chicks, which varied in whether the spot was present or not, its location on the bill and its colour,

Tinbergen and his students demonstrated that the function of the red spot was to stimulate chicks to peck at the parents' bill and thereby stimulate the regurgitation of food. The red spot acts as an evolved stimulus that releases appropriate behaviour in offspring to enhance the survival and reproductive success of offspring and parent. Exaggerated pecking responses can also be induced in chicks by presenting a super-stimulus, such as a red rod with white bands around its tip. We inadvertently introduce super-stimuli into our environment all the time, stimuli that can trigger instinctive behaviour in animals to their detriment. Examples include moths flying into the flames of a campfire or jewel beetles directing inappropriate copulatory behaviour towards discarded beer bottles.

At the same time that Tinbergen was studying the behaviour of European Herring Gulls, Austrian entomologist Karl von Frisch was showing how the honeybee dance conveys information to hive mates on the location and distance to new food sources; and Austrian zoologist Konrad Lorenz was demonstrating the importance of imprinting for offspring survival, the phenomenon by which hatching birds will bond instinctively with the first moving object they see. Collectively, the work on instinctive, adaptive behaviour conducted by Tinbergen, von Frisch and Lorenz earned them the 1973 Nobel Prize in Physiology or Medicine, and initiated the modern scientific discipline of ethology – the study of animal behaviour.

Like all animals, we too exhibit instinctive behaviours that can be elicited by stimuli in our environment, including the surge in vascular function, vocalisation and stumbled retreat that is experienced long before our visual system fully processes the large black Tiger Snake (moyop) basking on the track.

As we walked, the tide gradually pushed us higher and higher up the beach until we were forced to walk in the soft dry sands near the base of the dune system. Our progress was slowed considerably as the energy of each step became dissipated in the displacement of sand rather than affording forward motion. We struggled the last 3 kilometres, our thigh and calf muscles becoming increasingly fatigued. When we finally reached the turn-off into the dunes just west of Greens Pool, it was to find that we had to literally haul ourselves 3 metres up a vertical sand cliff by use of an iron chain secured at the top. This was no easy feat given our fatigued muscles and our heavy packs. The exertion left little energy for

TOP: Djer-djer or Splendid Fairy-wren, *Malurus splendens*. Djer-djer have the highest rates of extra-pair paternity of any bird, and the competition among sperm from multiple mating partners has imposed sexual selection for extreme male investment in sperm production; a male's testes represent 6% of his body weight. The bright blue plumage of males is the result of female mate choice for more attractive males. Leigh Simmons

MIDDLE: Djoordjilya or Red-winged Fairy-wren, *Malurus elegans*. This species differs from the northern Variegated Fairy-wren, *Malurus assimilis*, only by the deep blue as opposed to black of its chest feathers. But the two species do not overlap in their distribution, making them easy to distinguish based on where you see them. Leigh Simmons

BOTTOM: A megachilid bee. The females cut discs of leaves and carry them to the cavity in which they are nesting, typically a hole in the ground or rock crevice, or as in this case an abandoned nest of some other ground nesting insect. The leaf is used to line the cavity before provisioning it with pollen and nectar and laying an egg. Leigh Simmons

the final climb to William Bay Hut, which though aided by the rubber matting on the steep ascent to Castle Rock, was nevertheless gruelling in the now 34-degree-Celsius heat.

Despite the day's challenges, it had been a spectacular and varied walk, and on the scale of things it was easy compared with the walk from Peaceful Bay to Boat Harbour. We spent a wonderful afternoon exploring the spectacular environs around William Bay Hut, where large weathered granite boulders rise from the coastal scrub like giant tombstones. The pods of the Red-eyed Wattle (wilyawa) were popping open in the heat, exposing the bright-orange circular stalk surrounding the jet-black seed that gives the appearance of an eye. This striking colour contrast serves to attract birds, which eat the seeds, digesting the stalks and excreting the seeds themselves, thereby dispersing them. The Latin name for this species of wattle, *cyclops*, is well assigned, alluding to the story of Odysseus who gouged out the eye of the king of the giants with a burning stake. We climbed the granite boulders and soaked in the views from Tower Hill west along Mazzoletti Beach, watching the sun as it set on what had been a wonderful day on the track.

7

The nice thing about going to bed at sunset is that you are up in plenty of time for sunrise, which offered a wonderful backlit view of the many interestingly shaped boulders that littered the ridge along which the track passed. This day was set to be another challenging walk – 22 kilometres into Denmark, with Mount Hallowell smack in the middle. We set ourselves the task of getting to the Bibbulmun Café in Denmark in time for a 'big breakfast', as something to keep in mind to help fend off the Dementors on the steep south-western slopes of Mount Hallowell.

As we walked along the coastal ridge that morning we experienced extraordinary thermal gradients; it was already in the high twenties on the ridges, but each time we descended into a dip we were plunged into cold pockets of air trapped there in the night, no warmer than 10 degrees Celsius. After skirting a rock-topped hill, we descended to the valley floor and followed the track south to Lights Beach, where we stopped for second breakfast, watching

a large colony of Welcome Swallows (kanamit) as they flew low across rafts of drying seaweed, capturing and feasting on the seaweed flies.

From Lights Beach the track followed the coast for a kilometre or so before heading inland across low-lying winter-wet heathlands, moving ever closer to Mount Hallowell looming in the distance. The vegetation through these flats was quite beautiful. There were carpets of Scrub Daisy, and the fresh growth on Coastal Jugflower glowed red in the early morning sun. Scarlet flowers of Swamp Bottlebrush attracted New Holland Honeyeaters (bandiny), and at last we found our first Western Australian Christmas Tree (mooja) in full flower. Usually these trees grow to 7 metres, but across these windswept heaths they were stunted to just a metre, although nonetheless stunning with their intensely bright, deep yellow–orange blooms. The species name, *floribunda*, meaning an abundance of flowers, could not be more appropriate.

After passing through Peppermint (wanil) groves along the edge of agricultural land, we crossed Lights Road and began the steep ascent of Mount Hallowell. How wonderful it was to be back in the Karri forest that cloaks this mountain; the smell of the forest brought memories flooding back of the sections of track from Pemberton and through the Walpole-Nornalup National Park. The coastal heaths and clifftops are truly wonderful, but nothing can beat the feeling of walking through the southern forests; there is that 'landscape of fear' feeling again. The track to the summit was hard going, at times a scramble, but spurred on by the thought of a 'Bibbulmun Brekkie' we were soon at the summit, some 300 metres above sea level, with commanding views east across Wilson Inlet to the Nullaki Wilderness and Knapp Head on the horizon. Turns out the best way to manage the psychological barrier of climbing 200 metres pretty well straight up with 18 kilos on your back is to treat it as a Boggart rather than a Dementor; just imagine an escalator and mutter the word 'Riddikulus', and you're at the top before you know what's happened!

The descent was equally challenging, though less steep, and passed many spectacular granite monoliths rising above the Karri, with cathedral-like caves weathered into them by the wind and rain. At last we emerged from the forest and walked down to the edge of Wilson Inlet, where we found a delightfully positioned bench for morning tea. Although we saw nothing new for our bird list, there was good birding to be had here; Pied (midi),

TOP: Djarbarn or Grey Currawong, *Strepera versicolor*. Currawongs are also known as Bell Magpies, for their calls. The djarbarn has a loud gong-like *clang-clang* that is a common feature of the soundscape of the south-western forests. Leigh Simmons

MIDDLE: A yonga or Western Grey Kangaroo, *Macropus fuliginosus*, takes refuge in the only shade available on the open downs of the Showgrounds a unique yet harsh and exposed environment that lies between Irwin Inlet and Quarram Beach. The sandy downs appear at first sight to support little life other than Twine Rushes, but on close inspection support an abundance of wildlife. Freddy Simmons

BOTTOM: Orange Spider-hunting Wasps, *Cryptocheilus bicolor*, hunt spiders, which they paralyse with their sting and then drag to their underground burrow. The wasp injects an egg into the slumbering spider which, on hatching, will eat the spider from within, avoiding any essential organs that might lead to the spider's death before such time as the larva is ready to emerge. Freddy Simmons

Little Pied (kakak) and Little Black (koordjokit) cormorants, Pacific Black Ducks (ngwonan), Pelicans (boodalang) and a Yellow-billed Spoonbill (kaaka-baaka).

We watched the spoonbill as it foraged. The bills of spoonbills show remarkable adaptation for extracting food from the shallow waters these birds frequent. They walk slowly through the shallows and rhythmically sweep their partially opened bills in a broad arc through the water. They hold their bill 1 to 2 centimetres from the bottom, and sensory structures on its tip allow the bird to assess and maintain the distance between bill tip and substrate even in the murkiest water. The shape of the bill, with its flattened spoon-like tip, creates a vortex in the water column that lifts small invertebrate prey items from the substrate so that they can be swept into the bill and swallowed on the return sweep. The marvels of natural selection never cease to amaze.

After following the bank of Wilson Inlet past Honeymoon Island, the track left the edge of the inlet and headed through an area of swampland where Swamp Paperbarks (yowarl) were in full flower, their white blooms emitting a heavy perfume that was attracting native bees and wasps in large numbers. Here too were many Western Australian Christmas Trees (mooja), heavy with their golden flowers, and in the shelter of these inland swamps they had grown to their full height. Through here we met up again with Malou, the German woman who had passed us back at Gardner Hut. She had made it to Albany on her crazy short schedule, and, like Jens before her, had set off again on her trek back to Kalamunda; she was still carrying absolutely no food other than chocolate bars, and limited supplies of water.

Shortly thereafter we crossed Denmark River Bridge and followed the river into town. We made it to the Bibbulmun Café in six and a half hours, pretty exhausted but delighted at the thought of a hearty breakfast. Unfortunately for us, they stopped serving their Bibbulmun Brekkie at twelve, and it was now ten past. Despite clearly being walkers on the Bibbulmun Track, or perhaps because of our vagrant-like appearance – who knows? – they would not make us breakfast no matter how hard we tried to cajole them. Ah well, there was always tomorrow before we set off on the final leg of our adventure, and for now the coffee was fantastic and a shower and clean clothes were beckoning. Our other chore was to try to negotiate passage across the inlet for the next morning.

DENMARK TO ALBANY

DENMARK TO ALBANY

1

Despite our best efforts, we were unable to secure a passage across Wilson Inlet; there was not a single skipper in town who would take us. And so we resigned ourselves to taking a taxi around the inlet. We had a late start, indulging in that long-awaited Bibbulmun Brekkie before we left. The walk to Nullaki Hut would be relatively short, just over 10 kilometres, and blissfully flat for the most part. We were dropped at the jetty to which we should have been brought by ferry. From here the track hugged the coast along the inland side of the Nullaki Peninsula. At Pelican Point we paused to look at the birds on Pelican Island, which included, of course, Pelicans (boodalang), along with Little Black (koordjokit) and Little Pied (kakak) cormorants, Silver Gulls (djeringkara) and Pacific Black Ducks (ngwonan), but also two new species for us: Fairy and Crested (kaldjirkang) terns.

The track continued along the water's edge for a further 6 kilometres, and although the walking was easy it was unexpectedly slow. It was like penetrating the Forbidden Forest, for this section of the track had clearly not been walked for many months, as most walkers would have been dropped at the wilderness gate and skipped this section of the track. In consequence, thousands upon thousands of Christmas Spiders *(Austracantha minax)* had moved in, building their interconnected orb webs across the width of the path.

Freddy walked ahead, wielding a large forked stick. Our progress was best described as punctuated: clearing the webs to arm's length, one step forward and then clearing the next section. This went on for 6 kilometres and became rather tedious, both for us and no doubt the poor spiders, which would need to rebuild their webs after we had passed. The forked stick soon took on the appearance of being topped with white fairy-floss. This was studded with brightly coloured spiders and their assorted prey items, which included mostly bees and flies, but also some larger morsels, including cicadas, dragonflies and dung beetles, both native and introduced. Princess Fiona would have loved it.

Christmas Spiders are also known as Jewel Spiders, for the spines around their body, which give them the appearance of radial symmetry, and their strikingly coloured red, yellow and white markings give them the appearance of brightly sparkling jewels. They also come in many varieties, some predominantly yellow and red, and some jet-black. Some have spots and some have stripes. But what they all have in common is that they exhibit the same reflectance properties as locally abundant flowers. These spiders, like certain food-mimicking orchids, mimic the visual properties of nectar-rewarding flowers so as to lure bees and flies to their webs. The cost for the pollinator is far worse than being duped into pollinating an orchid, however, as the unsuspecting insects meet entrapment and certain death when attracted to a Christmas Spider's web.

These spiders are frequently found in large aggregations, though I had never before experienced one on this scale. By building their webs in aggregations, the spiders can reduce the costs of silk production by sharing support strands with neighbours, and reduce their own risks of predation through safety in numbers; the collection of many brightly coloured flower mimics may also have the effect of offering a super-stimulus to their unsuspecting prey. In addition, they can also benefit from the ricochet effect, whereby a fast-flying insect that fails to become entrapped in one web rebounds into an adjoining web, making prey capture more efficient for the collective. Be that as it may, while they slowed our progress, they did not manage to stop us.

To our left, the shore of the inlet was vegetated by large stands of Saltwater Paperbark, and to our right were patches of stunted mixed woodlands, including the occasional Karri, Swamp Banksia (pungura), Blackbutt (dwutta) and Peppermint (wanil). Large

flocks of Australian White Ibis (ngalkaning) and White-faced Heron (wayan) roosted in the paperbarks at the edge of the inlet, their guano dropping into the shallow waters, which were emitting a pungent sulfurous odour. As we passed, the ibis took flight, circling around to land again behind us. We spotted a magnificent White-bellied Sea-eagle (ngoolor) perched high in a Karri, in its talons a Fairy Tern no doubt collected on Pelican Island. Two juvenile sea-eagles flew repeatedly from tree to tree ahead of us as we thrashed our way through the spiders' webs, while out on the inlet a large flock of Black Swans (maali) cruised oblivious to our disturbances.

The path eventually left the shore of the inlet, passing through a small patch of Peppermint (wanil) and Blackbutt woodland, with an understorey that included large stands of Winged Wattle and was populated by White-browed Scrub-wrens (koorkal), Splendid Fairy-wrens (djer-djer), New Holland Honeyeaters (bandiny), Western Australian Magpies (koolbardi) and Carnaby's Black Cockatoos (ngoolyak). On emerging from the woodland we faced a tedious walk along a dusty dirt road as the track headed south, gradually gaining elevation towards the coast. But we were soon to leave the road and head increasingly steeply up to Nullaki Hut, nestled in the heart of the Nullaki Peninsula.

Surrounding the hut were dense stands of slipper orchids, more than I have ever seen in one place. It was a day of multitudes. And a pair of Kookaburra (kaa-kaa) watched us closely for most of the afternoon lest we had something worth stealing. This was a peaceful place to enjoy an evening beer carried with us from Denmark. It was also to be the last time we would have a hut to ourselves. As we drifted into sleep that night, we were awakened by barking. 'Why on earth must people bring dogs out here,' I asked Freddy irritably. 'Good grief, I hope they're not heading for the hut.' *Woof-woof... Woof-woof...Woof-woof.* 'Strange bark, its very regular.' And then it dawned on me: it was not a dog at all, but rather a Barking Owl (koobdimool)! Bird number 100 for the Bibbulmun bird list.

2

From Nullaki the track climbed steadily up the back of the limestone escarpment that separates Wilson Inlet from the

TOP: The Ngakala or Pacific Gull, *Larus pacificus*, is Australia's largest gull, and is endemic across the southern coasts of Australia. As well as being a kleptoparasite, it is also a predator, frequently including smaller seabirds such as petrels in its diet. The red spot on the bill provides a stimulus to hatchlings to tap at the parents bill, initiating the release of food.
Freddy Simmons

MIDDLE: Male and female Sooty Oystercatchers, *Haematopus fuliginosus*, have been selected to have bills of different length so as to avoid competing with one another for food. Females can probe deeper to gain access to worms, while the shorter billed males take crabs and other invertebrates that live closer to the surface. Leigh Simmons

BOTTOM: Koran-koran or Pied Oystercatchers, *Haematopus longirostris*, can coexist alongside Sooty Oystercatchers because of so-called niche partitioning. The species differ in bill length which allows them to reach prey at different depths alleviating competition. Like Sooty Oystercatchers, male and female koran-koran also differ in bill length, alleviating competition for food between the sexes. Freddy Simmons

southern Indian Ocean. Sandy depressions at lower elevations of
the north-facing slopes were home to ancient, and therefore huge,
Swamp Banksia (pungura), and as we summited the escarpment,
two new species of low tree dominated the habitat: the seemingly
unkempt Ridge-fruited Mallee, with its thick fleshy lanceolate
leaves and creamy flowers, contrasted with the neat, compact form
of Cut-leaf Banksia. This banksia was perhaps the most abundant
tree along the escarpment from here to Albany, stretching as far
as the eye could see, and from a distance one might imagine
that a topiarist had been busy at work creating their perfect
globular forms.

The views, of course, were spectacular, east to Knapp Head
and West Cape Howe beyond, and north to the Porongurups,
which were clearly visible, with the hazy blue silhouette of the
Sterling Ranges on the far horizon beyond. Our walk through
these elevated heathlands offered the usual host of plants to which
we had grown accustomed: Cut-leaf Hibbertia, Berry Saltbush,
Thick-leaved Fan-flower, Tapeworm Plant, Candle Hakea, Coastal
Jugflower, Parrot Bush (budjan) and stinkwoods, all growing
compact and close to the ground due to the prevailing wind off the
southern Indian Ocean. There was also a new species of hakea for
the list, the Straight-leaved or Linear Hakea. On the sand path we
happened upon a very strange insect, the Hairy-backed Pie-dish
Beetle *(Helea perforata)*.

Pie-dish beetles are found only in Australia, and the fifty or more
species typically occur in the driest regions of the country. They
are extraordinary insects in that they have evolved body structures
that allow them to populate arid habitats where other beetles are
unable to survive. The typical insect body plan is four wings and
six legs, much like the Common Brown Butterfly *(Heteronympha
merope)* that was feeding on the flowering Peppermint (wanil) as
we climbed the inland slopes of the coastal ridge. Pie-dish beetles,
however, have lost their wings, and therefore their ability to fly.
The hindwings are completely absent while the forewings, which
in beetles are typically hardened to form protective cases that cover
the flight wings, have become permanently fused forming a tight
protective shell over the beetle's body, which prevents water loss
and allows it to tolerate hot, drying environments.

As its name suggests, the Hairy-backed Pie-dish Beetle has thick
long black hairs sprouting from its shell, the function of which
is unknown. It may, however, be that these hairs facilitate the

accumulation of dew from the cool early morning breeze flowing off the southern Indian Ocean, precious water that would flow down the hairs and into the dish-like body and be available for the animal to drink. Pie-dish beetles belong to a large family of beetles known as tenebrionids, many of which have become adapted to live in dry desert habitats. The most famous member of this family, the Namib Desert Beetle, is found in the Namib Sand Sea in Namibia, where they survive using various contrivances for capturing water droplets from the moist air that flows off the southern Atlantic Ocean. The pie-dish beetles were not the only animals we found that had striking differences in their body form to their close relatives.

As we descended the escarpment towards Lowlands Beach, we came across two very large Tiger Snakes (moyop) that in the cool early morning took some persuading to move off the path. No amount of stamping would shift one of them, and we had to resort to throwing sticks and stones at it before it would give way and let us pass. A little further along the path we came across a much less harmful reptile, a Common Scaly-foot *(Pygopus lepidopodus)*. You would at first glance think this animal to be a snake, but it is a legless lizard. Its common name of scaly-foot arises from the fact that all that remains of its hind legs are two small scaly flaps, one either side of the body. Its front legs are completely absent, and its body is long and slender. It looks and moves exactly like a snake, slithering across the surface of the sand or through dense vegetation at great speed when warm enough. Looks like a snake, moves like a snake, must be a snake? No. The Common Scaly-foot belongs to a group of forty-five described species of legless lizard, forty-three of which are found only in Australia. Their closest relatives are not snakes at all, but rather fully limbed geckos.

The evolutionary loss of limbs is actually very common in reptiles. There are roughly 8,200 species of squamate reptiles, which are mostly characterised by the typical lizard-like body form with four limbs and five fingers or toes on each limb. But research by American herpetologist John Wiens has shown that snake-like body forms have evolved at least twenty-six times, the best known of these in the ancestor of modern snakes, but also multiple times within seven families of lizards, including the pygopodid family to which our Common Scaly-foot belongs. By constructing a family tree of relationships between living species of lizards and

contrasting their limb development, Wiens and his colleagues have been able to reconstruct the evolution of limb loss in these reptiles.

It turns out that the evolution of a snake-like body form involves gradual reduction in limb size and loss of digits, followed by the complete loss of forelimbs and then hind limbs. Along with limb loss comes an elongation of the body. The selection pressures that favour the evolution of limb loss are no doubt many and varied, but two distinct differences in habit appear to select for different types of snake-like body form. Species that live and hunt for food on the surface of the ground, like the Common Scaly-foot, become snake-like by an evolutionary loss of limbs and the lengthening of the tail; while species that burrow in the soil become snake-like via a loss of limbs and an elongation of the body.

Having walked the sand dunes of the southern coast for almost two weeks, I can attest to the fact that using feet and legs to propel oneself through the sand is a remarkably inefficient and slow means of locomotion. Gliding across the surface would be far more effective and quicker, which could favour an evolutionary shift from legged to legless body forms in sand-dwelling lizards. Remarkably, there is evidence that the loss of limbs need not be irreversible in evolutionary time. Some species of lizard in the family tree have fully formed limbs, although they are themselves descended from limbless ancestors. These examples show us that evolution is neither directional nor irreversible. For although a legless lizard may be, well, legless, it can nonetheless retain the genes with which to build legs.

Indeed, during its early embryonic development a young scaly-foot will start to grow forelimbs, but these are resorbed at later developmental stages. It turns out that limb loss is brought about by the deletion of nucleotides in a gene called ZRS, which regulates the expression of nearby genes that are themselves involved in limb development. Thus the genes for limbs can remain in legless lizards but they are simply silenced. This means, of course, that if limbs should become beneficial, due to a change in environment or habit, say, then mutations in the regulator gene that resulted in it once again switching on the genes of limb development would accumulate rapidly because of the selective advantage of having limbs.

In his book *The Making of the Fittest*, American evolutionary biologist Sean Carroll describes how animal genomes are littered with silenced genes that provide forensic evidence of traits that

TOP: The kaaka-baaka or Yellow-billed Spoonbill, *Platalea flavipes*, sweeps its bill through the water from side to side. The shape of the bill, with its flattened spoon-like tip, creates a vortex in the water column that lifts small invertebrate prey items from the substrate so they can be swept into the bill and swallowed on the return sweep. Leigh Simmons

MIDDLE: Ngalkaning or Australian White Ibis, *Threskiornis molucca*. Large flocks of these birds roosted in the paperbarks along the edges of the Wilson Inlet. They rose in large numbers, swirling through the air and producing honks and grunts as we passed. Leigh Simmons

BOTTOM: Christmas spider, *Austracantha minax*, have radial symmetry and bright colours that mimic the appearance of nectar rewarding flowers. They also form large colonies, from tens to hundreds of individual spiders. These features allow the spiders to attract large numbers of pollinating insects that become trapped in their interconnected webs. Leigh Simmons

were at some time adaptive in the evolutionary past. One surprising example from the human genome is the gene for penile spines. The males of many primate species have spines on the penis that are thought to stimulate ovulation by females at the time of copulation. We humans have the gene for penile spines, though thankfully it is silenced! Its silencing may have occurred because in humans, females do not ovulate in response to stimulation, making penile spines no longer adaptive.

From Lowlands Beach Road the track climbed steadily upward again to reach West Cape Howe Hut, with commanding views along the coast to West Cape Howe itself. That afternoon we enjoyed clear sunny skies, a light breeze off the ocean, and the spectacle of Square-tailed Kites (mararl) riding the thermals above the coastal scarp.

3

The following morning we continued east along the coastal scarp, the track hugging the 160-metre contour, mostly along the inland slopes, but on occasion rising to the ridge for panoramic views east and west along the coast. After 5 kilometres we plummeted, thankfully with the aid of steps, some 100 metres into a gully that marked the western boundary of the distribution of Albany Woolly Bush. Their cryptic red flowers were offering a rich nectar source for the foraging New Holland Honeyeaters (bandiny).

Albany Woolly Bush became a common feature of the vegetation as we continued east, adding to the mix of Ridge-fruited Mallee, Peppermint (wanil), and both Cut-leaf and Bull Banksia (mungitch). After crossing Lake William Road, the track began to ascend once more as it crossed the ridge of West Cape Howe peninsula. The vegetation across this ridge was very low, stunted by the south-westerly winds to no taller than 20 centimetres, and affording excellent views of Western Grey Kangaroos (yonga) as they bounded away from us across the heathlands. The males were huge, and most of the females had joeys in close pursuit. We stopped here a while to watch a pair of Australian Hobbies (wowoo) flying from crag to crag on a limestone knoll to the south of the track.

Eventually we summited the limestone scarp once more, at the rim of a steep ravine that plummeted down to Shelley Beach, with panoramic views south to Torbay Head, and east across Torbay

to the Albany Wind Farm beyond. We were getting close now, and I was struck by a pang of regret that our journey would soon come to an end. On our descent along the boardwalk that forms part of the Bruce Tarbotton Memorial Trail, we came upon an Evergreen Kangaroo Paw, the flower of which was occupied by an overnight sleeping aggregation of male sweat bees of the genus *Lasioglossum*. This is one of the largest genera of bees found worldwide, and Australia is home to around 250 species. There must have been twenty or more males in this sleeping aggregation, which was tightly packed into the flower head. We watched as they slowly awakened and began to leave, refreshed for the day's mate-searching.

Female sweat bees dig and provision nests in the ground, where they sleep during the hours of darkness. But males do not contribute to nest building, so they will form all-male groups to roost overnight before disbanding each day to go their separate ways in their quest for receptive females with which to mate. We don't generally think about bees sleeping. They are just there, busily making their hives and filling them with honey. But sleep they must, for it is just as essential for bees as it is for all animals. A tired honeybee suffers the same problems as a tired walker: they are simply unable to find their way.

Sleep-deprived honeybees, for example, have been found to be less able to learn the locations of food sources and so find them again. Neither can they convey accurate information to their co-workers about the locations of new food sources, making clumsy errors in their waggle dances that send their colony members on wild-goose chases. German neurobiologist Randolf Menzel and his colleagues have shown that in this regard bees are no different from us, for it is not just any type of sleep they need to store and retain information in their brains, but the good-quality deep sleep that has been shown to be so effective in promoting our own capacity to recall and process information. These sweat bees would probably have slept in for longer, had we not disturbed them.

After crossing Shelley Beach Road, we cleaned our boots at the cleaning station before passing through an extensive grove of Swamp Paperbarks (yowarl), with its lush understorey of Bracken (manya). We then crossed two large granite outcrops, where we saw three enormous King's Skinks *(Egernia kingii)* that scuttled under loose slabs of granite as we approached. These outcrops had a dense border of Heart-leaf Poison; having long since finished

their flowering season, they were now flinging their seeds widely as their seed pods popped open in the drying sun.

From here the track passed along a ridge high above Dingo Beach, where the vegetation was extraordinarily diverse, offering many new plant species for identification, as well as many we had seen already in abundance in the northern Jarrah forests. The higher elevations of these coastal slopes were cloaked by a stunted Jarrah forest that blended into coastal heath as it descended to Dingo Beach, a pure-white band of sand edged by a brilliant turquoise ocean. We discovered yet another new species of hakea, the Hood-leaved Hakea, which presented abundant new leaf growth that contrasted starkly with the older mature leaves: the former pale, soft and with a rufous blush; the latter hard, smooth and deepest green. Long-leaf Snottygobble had fresh yellow flowers that echoed the Yellow Buttercups guinea flowers and the bright-yellow star-like flowers of Lanoline Bush that grew along the edges of the sandy track.

There were Purple Flags, Southern Cross Flower, Bellardia, Spreading Sword-sedge, and the strangest-looking plant, a Head-forming Smokebush, with its tangled wiry ball of grey–green leaves. Among the taller trees and shrubs were Coastal Sheoak, Oak-leaved and Bull Banksia (mungitch), Parrot Bush (budjan) and tea-trees. And flitting between these taller trees across the path in front of and behind us were hundreds of New Holland Honeyeaters (bandiny), giving their abrupt metallic *tjik, chwik.* This stunning stretch of coastal vegetation, through which the track winds its way over Forsyth Bluff to Torbay Hut, itself nestled in the coastal woodlands overlooking Richards and Migo islands in Cosy Corner Bay. A group of Red-winged Fairy-wrens (djoordjilya) greeted us on our arrival, protesting our occupation of what they clearly believed to be their hut, while Fork-tailed Swifts hawked for flies overhead.

It was another stunning location for our overnight stop.

Jens had told us, when we met him in the Pioneer Store in Walpole, that a family of Quenda or Southern Brown Bandicoot frequented the bush around Torbay Hut, and we were keen to see them. So we made a huge effort to stay up past sunset that night in order to go spotlighting along the track. There was much evidence of their presence, in the form of their diggings along the edges of the track and around the camping area at the back of the hut. Quenda, like many of Australia's small mammals, dig holes in the

ground in search of food: roots, the fruiting bodies of fungi, and invertebrates such as worms and insect larvae. My colleague at the University of Western Australia Leonie Valentine has estimated that in so doing a Quenda will shift in the region of 11 kilograms of soil a day, and around 4 tonnes of soil per year.

This is a staggering amount of digging, which has surprising benefits for the ecosystem within which these small mammals live. For the pits they leave behind collect leaf matter, and the soil they displace is itself piled on top of surrounding leaf litter. The processed soil in and around bandicoot diggings is capable of absorbing precious water to a far greater extent than undisturbed soils, which promotes the effective breakdown of the material trapped in the soil. In consequence, the soil associated with Quenda diggings is richer in nutrients and minerals than surrounding soil. Tuart seeds planted in Quenda-processed soil are more likely to germinate, and the seedlings will grow taller than those sown in soil that has not been processed by Quenda.

The process of soil enrichment resulting from animal actions, known as bioturbation, was the subject of Darwin's last book, *The Formation of Vegetable Mould, through the Action of Earthworms, with Observations on their Habits*, published in 1881. Darwin studied how earthworms dragged leaves from the soil surface into their burrows and how the action of burrowing worms improved the conditions of soil for plant growth, while having the coincidental effect of burying large objects such as stones. Indeed, he had an experimental stone placed in his garden at Down House and monitored its gradual sinking into the soil. He even accredited the preservation of historic ruins such as Stonehenge to their burial by earthworms.

Bioturbation is a critical ecosystem service provided by burrowing animals, and Quenda and other digging marsupials are rightly referred to as ecosystem engineers. They play a critical role in providing the necessary soil conditions for promoting plant biodiversity. Alarmingly, introduced predators such as cats and foxes, habitat destruction and fire regimes have all contributed to a decline in populations of digging mammals in south-western Australia, where once they were common. It is difficult to appreciate how the loss of a small burrowing mammal such as a Quenda can affect the growth of a forest, but it can because of the ecosystem services it provides. That is the very nature of ecology: set one component off balance and the entire system can collapse.

TOP: A Hairy-backed Pie-dish Beetle, *Helea perforatea*. These beetles have highly modified forewings that are sealed shut so as to protect the insect from losing water in the arid environments in which they live. The hairs may serve to collect precious water from early morning fog. Leigh Simmons

MIDDLE: Ngoolyanak or Baudin's Black Cockatoo, *Calyptorhynchus baudinii*. These white-tailed black cockatoos are virtually identical in appearance to ngoolyak or Carnaby's Black Cockatoo, *Calyptorhynchus latirostris*, except for the longer upper mandible of the bill. These birds often travel in mixed species flocks, making it virtually impossible to tell them apart. Leigh Simmons

BOTTOM: When is a snake not a snake? When it is a legless lizard such as this Common Scaly-foot, *Pygopus lepidopodus*. There are forty-five described species of legless-lizard, forty-three of which are found only in Australia. Their closest relatives are not snakes at all, but rather fully limbed geckos. Freddy Simmons

Sadly, we did not see any Quenda on our night walk along the track, though we did find a beautiful Moaning Frog *(Heleioporus eyrei)*, itself a burrowing animal found only on the coast of south-western Australia, spending most of its life buried in the sand. It even broadcasts its haunting call from below ground, attracting females to its burrow to mate and lay eggs.

4

From Torbay Hut we descended gradually through stunted coastal Jarrah woodland along the rocky coastline towards Cosy Corner. After crossing the access track to Cosy Corner Beach, the track passed over a flat sand plain that was dominated by mature stands of Coastal Sheoak, Candlestick Banksia (piara) and Western Australian Christmas Trees (mooja). The mooja were offering fine floral displays. Through here we found Christmas Leek Orchids, and beautiful Variable-leaved Billardiera that presented us with deep blue–purple flowers as it twined its way through the Basket Flower, itself long since finished flowering. Shortly thereafter we reached the car park and steps down to the beach at Port Harding.

We had left early so as to indulge in breakfast at the Cosy Corner Café, a 3-kilometre round trip but worth every step, and with our packs abandoned in the car park, the early morning stroll was very pleasant. Fortunately, or not, on our return after breakfast, our packs laid untouched where we had left them. Suitably fortified, we set off east for our final beach walk, some 5.5 kilometres along the coast towards Shelter Island and Muttonbird Beach at the eastern end of Torbay. The walking was perfect, as the receding tide provided firm footing. Looking out to Seagull Island from the rocky headland at the western end of Perkins Beach, we could see large flocks of Silver Gulls (djeringkara), and several large black seabirds flying close to the water surface that were most likely Flesh-footed Shearwaters (borroot) given how close we were to their breeding grounds on Shelter Island.

Shelter Island lies 130 metres offshore, and the shallow waters that separate it from the mainland sparkled turquoise blue in the late morning sun, the waters crystal clear. The island itself is a granite mass thinly topped with soil upon which heathland

plants flourish. Shelter Island is designated a Class 1A Nature Reserve because it is home to breeding colonies of two increasingly endangered seabirds: Little Penguins (widi) and Flesh-footed Shearwaters (borroot).

Flesh-footed Shearwaters are global travellers. They spend much of their time on the wing, flying across the oceans in search of the fish and squid that form a large part of their diet. During our winter they spend their time in the northern hemisphere, returning to the southern hemisphere in October to breed on small islands. Birds form monogamous pair bonds through extended periods of courtship, during which they preen each other and perform a duet that sounds rather like a squeaky toy being repeatedly compressed; Michael Morcombe and David Stewart describe it as a hoarse *ku-KOOO-uhg* rising to a strident scream!

The shearwaters dig tunnels in the soil, some 1- to 2-metres long and angled downwards so that the nest chamber at the end of the tunnel is typically 20 to 30 centimetres below the surface. In many ways they are a scaled-up version of the sand wasp nests we saw at Frankland River Hut. A single egg is laid in the nest chamber and incubated by both parents, both taking turns to travel out to sea for food. The chick hatches in early to late January – just about the time we passed on the track. On hatching, the chick is abandoned to its own devices as the parents head out to sea for food. They travel up and down the coastal waters of the continental shelf, searching for small fish such as pilchards, which form the largest part of their diet. They will dive to depths of 2 to 5 metres to capture pilchards and will return to their burrows only when they have a full crop of fish with which to feed their chick.

When they do return, they will settle en masse on the surface of the water and await nightfall before leaving the sea to fly onto the island and enter their burrows. The chicks fledge around April, when the birds head north on their big migration. Marine biologist Jennifer Lavers has studied the populations of Flesh-footed Shearwaters throughout their range in Australia. Birds from Shelter Island that were fitted with satellite tags have been tracked flying around Cape Leeuwin in the south-west and north as far as the Abrolhos Islands near Geraldton, before heading north-west across the Indian ocean to Sri Lanka and on to the Arabian Sea. One bird travelled the nearly 6,000 kilometres from Shelter Island to Sri Lanka in just six and a half days, which puts our efforts on the Bibbulmun to shame.

Populations of Flesh-footed Shearwaters are also found breeding on Lord Howe Island, and islets off the coast of New Zealand. The birds from these colonies travel north to the Sea of Japan. Because the birds return to their natal islands to breed, colonies in the east and west of their range are reproductively isolated, and studies of their DNA sequences suggest that the eastern and western colonies have not interbred for around 28,000 years, not since the Last Glacial Maximum, when these populations are likely to have resided more closely together. A lack of gene flow between colonies has allowed them to diverge both because of genetic drift, the random accumulation of gene mutations, and because of selection pressures unique to their local environments. The Western Australian populations have shorter wings and a more delicate bill than their cousins in the east, and although they have not yet diverged sufficiently in their DNA sequences to be classified as different species, their reproductive isolation, coupled with genetic and physical divergence, suggests that they are undergoing the process of incipient speciation.

But their numbers are dwindling, with recent declines in the numbers of breeding pairs leading to their categorisation as Near Threatened on the International Union for Conservation of Nature's 2017 Red List. Lavers estimated that on Shelter Island the number of breeding pairs declined from just over 800 in 1988 to just under 200 in 2015. The threats to their survival are multitude. In Western Australia, more than 500 birds annually are captured on the baited hooks of longline fishing vessels. The death of a breeding adult, which these cases mostly represent, means the certain failure of its breeding attempt, as both adults are required to successfully fledge a chick. Across Australia generally, up to 6,800 birds perish each year from interactions with fishing vessels.

Plastic ingestion is another significant cause of mortality. Our oceans are increasingly littered with plastics. It is estimated that by the year 2025 there will be 1 tonne of plastic waste in the ocean for every 3 tonnes of fish. Plastics are a source of mortality for all marine life, both directly through entanglement and drowning, and indirectly through its consumption. But Flesh-footed Shearwaters may be one of Australia's most affected seabirds, with 90 per cent of chicks sampled at Lord Howe Island in 2011 containing significant quantities of plastic. Plastic ingestion reduces fledgling body weight and wing length, and is estimated to reduce juvenile survival by at least 11 per cent.

And finally, increasing temperature and extreme weather events caused by climate change are having both direct and indirect impacts on breeding success. Lavers reports that thousands of eggs were lost when burrows were flooded during the spring storms of 2012, and changes in the nutrient intake of Flesh-footed Shearwaters are associated with changes in the frequency of El Niño events, during which sea surface temperatures are elevated, causing major disruptions to ocean ecosystems. Western Australia is home to around 35 per cent of the world's breeding Flesh-footed Shearwaters, and their protection on Shelter Island is one very small contribution towards conserving one of the world's oceanic travellers.

Shearwaters are also commonly known as Muttonbirds, the namesake of our next and, as it turned out, final campground. The term 'Muttonbird' was first coined by the early settlers of Norfolk Island, who would harvest the chicks of Short-tailed Shearwaters for their flesh and oil. Although the declining numbers of Flesh-footed Shearwaters have resulted in a ban on harvesting this species, annual harvests of Short-tailed Shearwaters persist to this day, off the coast of Tasmania's Flinders Island in the Bass Strait. The days of harvesting Short-tailed Shearwaters may however be numbered, as, worryingly, in 2019 they failed to return to their breeding grounds in Victoria.

We turned inland from the viewing platform at Shelter Island, passing through a Jarrah, Peppermint (wanil) and Holly-leaved Banksia woodland around the back of the Sporting Shooters Association firing range. Fortunately, the range was devoid of shooters in the post-Christmas break. After crossing Mutton Bird Road, the track climbed to the coastal ridge again, with commanding views east to the Albany Wind Farm, and west to Cosy Corner and Torbay Head. We arrived at Muttonbird Hut in just over five hours. Sooty Tim had commented nostalgically in the logbook on the beautiful people he had met on his journey, and had left a personal message to wish us well for the last day of our trek. There too were entries from Jens. He had stayed at Muttonbird on the last night of his southward journey and, just twenty-four hours later, having picked up supplies in Albany, had stayed there on the first night of his northward journey.

Good grief, I could not contemplate the thought of walking back to Kalamunda again! But it was not without a hint of sadness that we set up camp for the last time. Throughout our journey, our

TOP: Wandy or King's skink, *Egernia kingii,* is endemic to south-western Australia. It is one of our largest skinks reaching up to 55 centimetres, and is commonly found in coastal areas and on granite outcrops along the south coast. Leigh Simmons

MIDDLE: Wardawort or Grey Butcherbird, *Craticus torquatus.* The song of the wardawort can be quite beautiful, a deep and melodic *quorrok-aquokoo.* They get their name from their habit of storing uneaten prey, often small lizards and even other birds, impaled on sharp twigs near their roosts. Leigh Simmons

BOTTOM: A sleeping aggregation of male sweat bees from the genus *Lasioglossum.* Sleep is just as essential for insects as it is for us, and sleep-deprived bees are unable to forage effectively and would soon die. Leigh Simmons

logbook entry had indicated our intention of walking for sixty-one days between Kalamunda and Albany. But with the realisation that Sandpatch, the final hut on the Bibbulmun, had been lost to bushfire the previous summer, we revised our entry to sixty days. Altogether a more rounded, satisfying number.

5

Our last day on the track would be one of our longest, 25 kilometres to cover due of the loss of Sandpatch. Our gear packed away for the last time, we set off shortly after sunrise under heavy, dark clouds that threatened some serious rain. The track hugs the edge of the coastal escarpment for the 9 kilometres to Sandpatch, winding its way through pristine coastal heath dominated by Cut-leaf Banksia, Albany Woolly Bush and Peppermint (wanil). We found Dwarf Sheoak with its filamentous red flowers, and Many-headed Isopogon, both growing in abundance along the edges of the track. Within 2 kilometres we came to the first of the eighteen wind turbines that make up the Albany Wind Farm. For the next 4.5 kilometres we would pass under these white giants that collectively generate 35 megawatts of electricity, enough to provide the town of Albany with 80 per cent of its energy requirements.

The poignancy of our walk through the wind farm cannot be overstated. Over the past eight weeks we had walked through an extraordinary diversity of habitats: through the Jarrah forests of the north; the cool Karri and tingle forests of the south; and the open heathlands, lowland swamps and dune systems that fringe the southern Indian Ocean. We had marvelled in the unique diversity of animal and plant species that each habitat presented. Many of these species of animals and plants are found nowhere else on Earth, and many have incredibly restricted ranges, due to their inability to disperse large distances and their particular requirements for rainfall, soil type or thermal environment.

The south-west corner of Western Australia is one of the world's most biologically diverse regions and also one of its most vulnerable to species loss, for climate change in the south-west is resulting in an increasingly warming and drying environment that will lead to the loss of thousands of species of animals and plants, many before we have even discovered and described them. And yet we as a species

have the capacity to minimise this devastating loss of biodiversity, simply by switching from a reliance on fossil fuels to one or more renewable sources of electricity, such as the Albany Wind Farm. As a nation, we are seriously lagging behind in our efforts to reduce our reliance on fossil fuels. Wind farms now provide 14 per cent of Europe's power, with Denmark leading the world by generating more than 74 per cent of its energy from renewable sources, including 41 per cent from its offshore wind farms. In 2017, the UK increased its wind power generation from 13 to 18 per cent via increased investment in offshore wind farms.

In Europe, and here at home in Albany, we can see proof of concept that we can move away from fossil fuels towards efficient power generation from renewable sources if we only have the will. As we passed through the turbines of the Albany Wind Farm, I was struck by the fact that at ground level the habitat was virtually unmarked. Groups of Red-winged Fairy-wrens (djoordjilya), Southern Emu-wrens (djirdjilya) and Silvereyes (doolor) flitted through the undergrowth; New Holland Honeyeaters (bandiny) were feasting on the flowering Albany Woolly Bush; Western Australian Magpies (koolbardi) were carolling; and a Little Eagle soared between the turbines, all apparently oblivious to the endlessly turning blades of the white giants. Opponents of wind farms argue that they are bad for birdlife, citing increased mortality of birds that can be caught in the rotating blades. But research across the world has shown that bird mortality around wind farms is very low, and can be insignificant with careful placement of farms so as to avoid migration pathways or traditional feeding or breeding sites. Norwegian researchers led by Roel May have reported that by simply painting the blades black we can reduce bird mortality by 70 per cent. And we must be pragmatic. While there may be some risk to local communities of birds, the costs of continuing to burn coal will have far greater and further-reaching global consequences. For climate change is not a belief system as some would suggest, but is real and is happening right now.

Our planet is able to sustain life because carbon dioxide traps the sun's heat like a giant quilt, preventing all of its rays from reflecting back to space and leaving the planet frozen solid. Carbon dioxide is good, in moderation. But it is a fine balance. Too much carbon dioxide in the atmosphere is like having too many feathers in a quilt – it traps too much heat. Carbon dioxide is released from the Earth naturally, as a result of natural burns, volcanic eruptions,

and animal and plant respiration, for example. It is naturally absorbed back into the oceans and into forests, where plants take in carbon dioxide and convert it into sugars for their growth, releasing precious oxygen as they do so. This is the Earth's natural carbon cycle.

The industrial revolution of the last 200 years or so has seen an exponential increase in the burning of coal for the generation of power, including electricity, and so an exponential increase in the release of carbon dioxide into our atmosphere. The vast majority of this carbon dioxide is accumulating in the atmosphere, because the natural carbon cycle is unable to cope with the increased input, especially since a large component of the carbon sink, forests, have been cleared for building our cities and growing our food. The concentration of carbon dioxide increased from 280 parts per million in 1800 to 396 parts per million in 2013. The consequence is that more of the sun's warmth is retained in the Earth's atmosphere, and the increasing temperatures are generating a host of cascading effects that threaten our very existence.

Sea levels are rising because water trapped at the Earth's poles is melting. This releases more carbon dioxide that was trapped in the frozen ice. Increased sea surface temperatures reduce the amount of carbon dioxide that can be absorbed from the atmosphere into the sea. You can try this yourself at home. You will get a better fizz in your water if you use chilled rather than warm water in your SodaStream. Moreover, increased evaporative water loss from warmer oceans exacerbates the overall warming effect, because water vapour, like carbon dioxide, prevents the sun's rays from being reflected back into space.

Increased drying on land is increasing the frequency and severity of summer wildfires, while increased evaporative water loss and land warming is increasing extreme weather events such as cyclones. The drying of the south-west of Western Australia has been shown to be due largely to human-driven changes in our climate, changes that will drive our biodiversity to extinction. And these changes will affect our own health and wellbeing. Climate change will affect our ability to grow crops. Extreme heatwaves will see increased death tolls, especially among the more vulnerable in our communities, and will result in an increased spread of insect-borne diseases such as Ross River virus or malaria, as their mosquito vectors expand their ranges into areas once too cool for them to survive.

It is extraordinary how large sections of our population still choose not to accept climate science. This is not the first time that we have experienced the perils of burning fossil fuel. London smogs, or 'pea-soupers' are stuff of legend. City fogs occurred throughout the UK in the 1800s and 1900s, as a result of both domestic and industrial smoke from the burning of coal. Smoke from so-called 'dirty' or 'soft' coal that issued from the chimneys of domestic houses and the power stations at Battersea, Fulham, Greenwich and Kingston, contained soot, which turned the buildings and monuments of London black, as well as gases including sulfur dioxide and carbon dioxide.

In his book *The Climate of London*, published in the early 1800s, Luke Howard, the father of meteorology, was the first to identify what he referred to as the 'heat island' effect, the fact that London temperatures were 2 degrees Celsius higher at night and cooler during the day as a result of the accumulation of smog from the burning of coal. And in 1880, Rollo Russell identified how gases from the burning of coal were responsible for respiratory diseases and rising mortality. But nobody listened until it was too late. In early December 1952, a period of cold weather, combined with an anticyclone and a lack of wind, resulted in a build-up of smog over London that persisted for five days, killing 12,000 people and affecting the health of 100,000 others.

Only then did we see, in 1956, the passing of the Clean Air Act that banned the burning of soft coal in the UK's cities, and a transition to cleaner fuels such as natural gas. But this took four years of political lobbying; too inconvenient was it for the government of the day to stop the sale of cheap, low-grade coal to the homes of London, and to invest in the development of clean energy. Ringing any bells? I am old enough to remember the transformation that the Clean Air Act made to the city of London. Growing up in the 1960s, I witnessed the transition from a city that was filthy and blackened to one with majestic buildings and glistening white monuments. It is unfortunate that in 1954 we did not also appreciate the dangers of emitting carbon dioxide from the burning of fossil fuels. Perhaps if we had, we might have banned their use completely, and our planet might not be in the position it is today. But the Great Smog of London should be a lesson to us all – that we could reverse the damage we are causing from burning fossil fuels if only we had the will to do so.

The Earth's evolutionary history is divided into eras that are marked by major geological and biological events. The Mesozoic, for example, was the time of the dinosaurs, between 225 and 65 million years ago. The mass extinction of the dinosaurs marked the transition to the Cenozoic, a period that extends into the modern-day, during which the mammals evolved and flowering plants spread across the Earth. The Cenozoic itself was marked by seven great epochs, periods of evolutionary change that were driven by the Earth's changing climate. The cold climatic conditions during part of the Pleistocene, 1.8 million to 12,000 years ago, saw the evolution of the woolly mammoth, mastodon, reindeer and other cold-tolerant mammals. But these became extinct when the climate warmed and we entered the Holocene. The Pleistocene also saw the evolution of the first primates, with modern humans emerging around 300,000 years ago. The impact of contemporary human populations over the last several hundred years is so marked that a new epoch is now recognised, the Anthropocene (from the Ancient Greek *anthropos* meaning 'human'), characterised by rapid human-induced extinction of animals and plants.

The Anthropocene species loss is due in part to our effect on the Earth's climate, but not solely. Habitat loss due to the clearing of natural areas for agriculture fragments populations of animals and plants, thereby restricting gene flow and reducing genetic variability. In turn, the loss of genetic variation prevents species from adapting to environmental change and ultimately drives them to extinction. And anthropogenic effects on gene flow can arise where we least expect it. For example, artificial light at night from our cities can have the same effect. One study in Oxfordshire in the UK has found that streetlights reduce the abundance and diversity of moth species at ground level by 50 per cent, because moths are attracted to and are behaviourally trapped at streetlights. The consequence is not just a loss of moths over a large proportion of the landscape. Because moths are important pollinators of plants, the attraction of moths away from ground level and their concentration around streetlights has a significant effect on the transportation of pollen, and so can reduce gene flow among species of plants that rely on moths for pollination.

Since Europeans came to Australia we have driven thirty endemic mammalian species to extinction, the highest rate of mammalian extinction globally. Australian biologist John Woinarski and his colleagues suggest that mammalian extinctions

are due partly to the introduction of predators such as cats and foxes, and partly to our changes in fire regimes. We do prescribed burns based on reducing risk to human infrastructure, with far less consideration for the risk of species loss. According to the International Union for Conservation of Nature Red List, Australia is in the top five for extinctions of animals and plants, and the top ten for endangered and threatened species. It is time for us to act. Rather than open new coalmines, we should be investing in wind farms to generate our energy. We should start saving energy by reducing artificial light at night, and we must stop burning and clearing our native vegetation, which is occurring at an unsustainable rate.

The Bibbulmun Track passes for a short distance along the visitors' boardwalk that runs through the eastern end of the Albany Wind Farm. Here, above the steps that allow visitors to descend to the beach below, we sat for second breakfast, looking out into the southern Indian Ocean. A plaque stood in the foreground, upon which was written a quote from E. B. White, the author of the beloved *Charlotte's Web*: 'I would feel more optimistic about a bright future for man if he spent less time proving he can outwit Nature and more time tasting her sweetness and respecting her seniority.' I could not agree more.

As we left the wind farm behind us, the weather rolled in from the ocean and heavy rain began to dampen our spirits. We arrived at Sandpatch mid-morning and took shelter from the rain in the dunny, the only structure to have survived a bushfire that had torn through the Torndirrup National Park the previous May, having 'escaped' from a prescribed burn. The downpour did not last long, and we were soon back on the track, cutting across the heathlands of the Torndirrup Peninsula towards Albany. As we descended the inland slope of the peninsula, coming towards us was our track elf from the north, walking out to join us for our arrival into Albany. And so it was that we descended, a family reunited, to the shores of Princess Royal Harbour.

Many shorebirds were feeding in the shallow waters of the harbour, including White-faced Herons (wayan), Silver Gulls (djeringkara), Pied Cormorants (midi) and Black Swans (maali). New for the bird list was an Osprey (yoondoordo), flying low over the water with a fish in its talons, the fish oriented headfirst so as to minimise the drag for the bird as it flew off to deliver its prize to its hungry nestlings. After circumnavigating the slopes of

Mount Melville, the track joined the suburban streets of Albany, taking us down past the brig *Amity*, which brought twenty-three convicts and twenty-one solders from Sydney to establish the first European settlement in Western Australia in 1826, and on to the southern terminus of the track.

Darwin visited Albany in the March of 1836, his last port of call in Australia on the journey home to England after his voyage around the world as naturalist on HMS *Beagle*. He spent eight days in Albany and remarked in his journal, *A Naturalist's Voyage Round the World*, 'I do not remember since leaving England, having passed a more dull, uninteresting time.' To be fair, the settlement in Albany was but a few years old, and largely neglected in favour of the Swan River settlement to the north. Captain FitzRoy noted that Albany consisted of just 'a few straggling houses, ill-placed in an exposed, cheerless situation'. Darwin made several excursions, including one to examine the granite and calcareous formations around Bald Head, and another to join a matrilineal kin group, the Manitjimat (white cockatoo men) of the Mineng Noongar for a corroboree, in which he witnessed their traditional dance and offered in return a feast of boiled rice with sugar.

On one excursion he climbed either Mount Melville or Mount Clarence to survey the surrounding countryside, noting the abundance of the sheoaks and grasstrees that dominated the lowland coastal forest: 'The wiry grass-like plants & brushwood wear a bright green colour & to a stranger at a distance would seem to bespeak fertility', but here was the stinger: 'a single walk will quite dispel such an illusion: & if he, thinks like me, he will never wish to take another [walk] in so uninviting a country'. Darwin's impression could not be further from the truth. The natural history we have described along the Bibbulmun would, I am certain, have left Darwin bewitched. Unfortunately his visit, at the end of summer, was not the most opportune of times.

Had he arrived earlier in the year, and walked further afield, he would have marvelled at the diversity of orchids and the contrivances by which they are fertilised by insects. He would have discovered countless insectivorous plants, and while so doing have seen how some of these use their sticky traps to climb up through the surrounding vegetation. He would have discovered countless new species of plants, restricted in their distributions to granite islands within a forest sea. He would for sure have gathered much evidence in support of his developing ideas on the origin of species.

As it was, he did find an Australian Bush Rat, captured in a trap baited with cheese among the bushes surrounding King George Sound. As it was, he discovered ten species of fishes captured in Princess Royal Harbour and described in his edited volume *Zoology of the Voyage of H.M.S. Beagle*, and he collected more than sixty species of insects, including nearly fifty that were new to science.

I have some sympathy with Darwin's rather dim view of Albany. He was by then into his fifth year on board HMS *Beagle*, where he had lived in a cabin within which he could neither stand nor lie flat, and he suffered each day from constant seasickness. His stay in Albany was but a delay on a long and tiresome journey home, which he was eager to complete. Moreover, he had accumulated a vast collection of new species of animals and plants, both extant and fossil, from almost every habitat one can think of, from rainforests to deserts, from mountaintops to the oceanic islands of the Galapagos and the coral cays of Polynesia. He had seen it all, so Albany at the end of summer did not stand a chance.

For my part, our arrival into Albany also marked the end of an extraordinary journey, one of hardship and joy, of struggle and triumph. We had experienced the very best that the natural wilderness can offer. We had identified 106 bird species and 242 flowering plants, the latter a tiny fraction of the diversity through which we had travelled. One thousand and five kilometres, sixty days of pure self-indulgence, and a lifetime of precious memories. In three days my son and walking companion would set off for Hobart, leaving the family home to navigate his independent life as a newly qualified veterinary surgeon. So poor Albany, as wonderful a town as it is, didn't really have much of a chance with me either.

Here we were back in the rat race, the final bird for the track list a feral pigeon, that commensal pest that is found ubiquitously in every human city across the globe. As the *Beagle* set sail from King George Sound, Darwin wrote in his journal of researches: 'Farewell Australia, you are a rising infant & doubtless some day will reign a great princess in the South; but you are too great & ambitious for affection, yet not great enough for respect; I leave your shores without sorrow or regret.' As I stepped from the Bibbulmun Track it was with deep sorrow and regret, but with a strengthened respect and wonder for the extraordinary corner of the world that I am privileged to call home. I shall return to walk these tracks, through forest and along coastline, until my legs cease to carry me.

And so it was, with hearts as heavy as the packs we had at long last relinquished, that we climbed into our trusty Subaru Forester, our Portkey back to Perth and the stark realities of modern living.

ACKNOWLEDGEMENTS

First and foremost, I am deeply indebted to the Whadjuk, Binjareb, Wardandi, Ganeang, Bibelmen and Mineng Noongar, through whose lands we have walked, and for their care of those lands for more than 30,000 years. Your boodja is precious.

Our journey would not have been possible without the support of many people. While the Department of Biodiversity, Conservation and Attractions' Parks and Wildlife Service acts as manager, the Bibbulmun Track Foundation is the primary focal point for community-based support and involvement, and has primary responsibility for promoting and maintaining the track through the Newmont Boddington Gold 'Eyes on the Ground' volunteer maintenance program. The foundation is run on a not-for-profit basis and relies on donations and membership. Without the foundation, our journey would not have been possible. It is extraordinary to think that this world-class facility is made available for all to enjoy, completely free of any charge.

One of the most remarkable experiences on our journey was the total and unconditional support and warmth we received from complete strangers. When arriving at towns along the way, the staff at the various visitor centres were always warm, welcoming and extraordinarily helpful. Complete strangers would come up to us in the street to talk, enquiring how far we had come, eager to hear our stories of trial and tribulation, and to wish us well for our ongoing journey. Many spoke of having spent days on the track,

and how they had always dreamed of doing an end-to-end. They seemed to live that dream through us. I cannot begin to describe how much that support helped us to keep going.

Likewise, the support of friends and family was overwhelming. While they clearly thought that walking more than 1,000 kilometres from Perth to Albany was a crazy thing to do, especially at the start of summer, they nonetheless lent their unwavering support and enthusiasm. Above all, Carol not only agreed to us going off for two months and leaving her home alone for the final months before her only son was to leave home forever, but she travelled to meet us on several occasions at the northern end, bringing fresh food and cold beer. We could not have made it from Kalamunda to Gringer Creek without her. And she was there at the end to meet us and take us home. Freddy and I are forever grateful for what was surely her sacrifice. Lastly, my thanks go to Freddy for his patience and support, and for being everything and more than a father could ask. There were times along the way when I know he would rather have just kept walking than stop to take photos of yet another insect or scrubby-looking plant. What an amazing way for a father to send a son into the world to make his own way. This adventure has given us both precious memories that I know we will share for the rest of our lives.

This narrative has featured the work of many scientists whose research has contributed to our understanding of the ecology and evolution of the animals and plants that inhabit the south-west corner of Western Australia. Rather than providing formal citation I have mentioned these researchers by name so that the reader can easily find the original research by entering the researcher's name and study organism into any web browser. Our knowledge of the world comes from the painstaking research of taxonomists, who are responsible for the identification and description of our biodiversity; ecologists, who explore how populations and communities of organisms interact within the natural world; and evolutionary biologists, who study the adaptive processes by which these organisms evolve and speciate, and so generating biodiversity. Any errors in the interpretation of their work are my own.

A naturalist needs guidance in identifying species of animals and plants. Many excellent field guides are available, but alas it is impossible to carry a library with you on the Bibbulmun. An excellent bird guide that is easily carried is Michael Morcombe and David Stewart's *eGuide to Australian Birds*, a handy little app

that provides a means to identify birds, both through its many plates and via its recordings of vocalisations. I used this daily on our walk, and have borrowed shamelessly in my text the phonetic descriptions of the various birdcalls we heard along the way. An invaluable source for identification of the plants was Jane Scott and Patricia Negus's *Field Guide to the Wildflowers of Australia's South West*, and I recommend this guide, together with the website florabase.dpaw.wa.gov.au, for further information regarding the plants discussed in this narrative. For the orchids specifically, Mark Brundrett's *Identification and Ecology of Southwest Australian Orchids* is a beautiful volume. Vivienne Hansen and John Horsfall's volumes *Noongar Bush Medicine* and *Noongar Bush Tucker* are invaluable sources of Noongar names and uses of south-west Western Australian plants. Finally, although I use the spelling for Noongar names for the birds of Western Australia recommended by the Batchelor Institute of Indigenous Education, alternative spellings in three dialects, the Kongal-boyal (south-eastern), Djiraly (northern) and Kongal-marawar (south-western) can be found in *Djerap: Noongar Birds*, published by the Batchelor Press.

Shenton Park, March 2020

BIRDS SEEN ON THE BIBBULMUN TRACK

19 NOV 2018 – 17 JAN 2019

Listed by common name, with Noongar and scientific names

Splendid Fairy-wren (djer-djer), *Malurus splendens*

Barking Owl (koobdimool), *Ninox connivens*
Black Cockatoo, Baudin's (ngoolyanak), *Calyptorhynchus baudinii*
Black Cockatoo, Carnaby's (ngoolyak), *Calyptorhynchus latirostris*
Black Cockatoo, Red-tailed (karak), *Calyptorhynchus banksii*
Black Kite, *Milvus migrans*
Black Swan (maali), *Cygnus atratus*
Black-faced Cuckoo-shrike (noolarko), *Coracina novaehollandiae*
Bronzewing Pigeon, Common (numbing), *Phaps chalcoptera*
Buff-banded Rail (kooli), *Gallirallus philippensis*
Coot, Australasian (aka Eurasian; kidjibroon), *Fulica atra*
Cormorant, Little Black (koordjokit), *Phalacrocorax sulcirostris*
Cormorant, Little Pied (kakak), *Phalacrocorax melanoleucos*
Cormorant, Pied (midi), *Phalacrocorax varius*
Cuckoo, Fan-tailed (djoolar), *Cacomantis flabelliformis*
Cuckoo, Horsfield's Bronze (koodooban), *Chrysococcyx basalis*
Duck, Australian Wood (marangana), *Chenonetta jubata*
Duck, Musk (kadar), *Biziura lobata*
Duck, Pacific Black (ngwonan), *Anas superciliosa*
Eagle, Little, *Hieraaetus morphnoides*
Eagle, Wedge-tailed (waalitj), *Aquila audax*
Eagle, White-bellied Sea- (ngoolor), *Haliaeetus leucogaster*
Emu (wetj), *Dromaius novaehollandiae*
Fairy-wren, Red-winged (djoordjilya), *Malurus elegans*
Fairy-wren, Splendid (djer-djer), *Malurus splendens*
Fairy-wren, Variegated (aka Purple-backed), *Malurus assimilis*
Falcon, Brown (karkany), *Falco berigora*
Flesh-footed Shearwater (borroot), *Puffinus carneipes*
Fork-tailed Swift, *Apus pacificus*
Galah (djakal-ngakal), *Cacatua roseicapilla*
Grebe, Australasian (ngoonan), *Tachybaptus novaehollandiae*
Grebe, Hoary-headed (wyooda), *Poliocephalus poliocephalus*
Grey Butcherbird (wardawort), *Cracticus torquatus*
Grey Currawong (djarbarn), *Strepera versicolor*
Grey Fantail (kadjinak), *Rhipidura albiscapa*
Grey Teal (kalyong), *Anus gracilis*
Heron, White-faced (wayan), *Ardea novaehollandiae*
Heron, White-necked (djilimilyan), *Ardea pacifica*
Hobby, Australian (wowoo), *Falco longipennis*
Honeyeater, Brown (djindjokoor), *Lichmera indistincta*
Honeyeater, Gilbert's or Western White-naped (djingki),
    Melithreptus chloropsis

Honeyeater, New Holland (bandiny), *Phylidonyris novaehollandiae*
Honeyeater, Singing (kool-boort), *Lichenostomus virescens*
Hooded Plover (dirl-dirl), *Thinornis cucullatus*
Ibis, Australian White (ngalkaning), *Threskiornis molucca*
Ibis, Straw-necked (nankiny), *Threskiornis spinicollis*
Jacky Winter, *Microeca leucophaea*
Kookaburra, Laughing (kaa-kaa), *Dacelo novaeguineae*
Magpie-lark (diliboort), *Grallina cyanoleuca*
Nankeen Kestrel (mardiyet), *Falco cenchroides*
Osprey (yoondoordo), *Pandion haliaetus*
Owlet-nightjar, Australian (yaartj), *Aegotheles cristatus*
Oystercatcher, Pied (koran-koran), *Haematopus longirostris*
Oystercatcher, Sooty, *Haematopus fuliginosus*
Pacific Gull (ngakala), *Larus pacificus*
Painted Button-quail (mooroolang), *Turnix varia*
Pardalote, Spotted (widap-widap), *Pardalotus punctatus*
Pardalote, Striated (wida-wida), *Pardalotus striatus*
Parrot, Australian Ringneck (aka Twenty-eight; doornart),
    Platycercus zonarius semitorquatus
Parrot, Elegant (koolyidarang), *Neophema elegans*
Parrot, Red-capped (delyip), *Purpureicephalus spurius*
Parrot, Rock, *Neophema petrophila*
Pelican, Australian (boodalang), *Pelecanus conspicillatus*
Pipit, Australasian (waradjoolon), *Anthus novaeseelandiae*
Purple Swamphen (kwirlam), *Porphyrio porphyrio*
Purple-crowned Lorikeet (kawoor), *Glossopsitta porphyrocephala*
Rainbow Bee-eater (birin-birin), *Merops ornatus*
Raven, Australian (waardong), *Corvus coronoides*
Red Wattlebird (djangkang), *Anthochaera carunculata*
Red-eared Firetail (djiri), *Stagonopleura oculata*
Robin, Scarlet (dermokalitj), *Petroica boodang*
Robin, Western Yellow (bamboon), *Eopsaltria griseogularis*
Robin, White-breasted (boyidjil), *Eopsaltria georgiana*
Rock Dove (aka Feral Pigeon), *Columba livia*
Rufous Treecreeper (djini), *Climacteris rufa*
Sacred Kingfisher (kanyinak), *Halcyon sancta*
Shrike-thrush, Western Grey (koodilang),
    Colluricincla harmonica rufiventris
Silver Gull (djeringkara), *Larus novaehollandiae*
Silvereye (doolor), *Zosterops lateralis gouldi*
Southern Boobook (nyawoo-nyawoo), *Ninox novaeseelandiae*

Southern Emu-wren (djirdjilya), *Stipiturus malachurus*
Square-tailed Kite (mararl), *Lophoictinia isura*
Stubble Quail (boorlam), *Coturnix pectoralis*
Swamp Harrier (dilyordoo), *Circus approximans*
Tawny Frogmouth (djoowi), *Podargus strigoides*
Tern, Caspian, *Hydroprogne caspia*
Tern, Crested (kaldjirkang), *Sterna bergii*
Tern, Fairy, *Sternula nereis*
Thornbill, Inland (djoobi-djoolbang), *Acanthiza pusilla*
Thornbill, Western (djobool-djobool), *Acanthiza inornata*
Thornbill, Yellow-rumped (djida), *Acanthiza chrysorrhoa*
Tree Martin (kabi-kalangkoorong), *Cecropis nigricans*
Varied Sittella (koomaldidayit), *Daphoenositta chrysoptera*
Weebill (djiyaderbaat), *Smicrornis brevirostris*
Welcome Swallow (kanamit), *Hirundo neoxena*
Western Australian Magpie (koolbardi), *Gymnorhina tibicen dorsalis*
Western Gerygone (waralyboodang), *Gerygone fusca*
Western Rosella (bardinar), *Platycercus icterotis*
Western Spinebill (booldjit), *Acanthorhynchus superciliosus*
Whistler, Rufous (bambon), *Pachycephala rufiventris*
Whistler, Western (Golden – see text; bidilmidang), *Pachycephala occidentalis*
White-browed Babbler (ngowan), *Pomatostomus superciliosus*
White-browed Scrub-wren (koorkal), *Sericornis frontalis*
Willie Wagtail (djidi-djidi), *Rhipidura leucophrys*
Woodswallow, Black-faced (biwoyen), *Artamus cinereus*
Woodswallow, Dusky (kayibort), *Artamus cyanopterus*
Yellow-billed Spoonbill (kaaka-baaka), *Platalea flavipes*

PLANTS SEEN ON THE BIBBULMUN TRACK

19 NOV 2018 – 17 JAN 2019

Listed alphabetically by full common name,
with Noongar (if known) and scientific names.

Albany Bottlebrush, *Callistemon glaucus*

1.   Albany Bottlebrush, *Callistemon glaucus*
2.   Albany Woolly Bush, *Adenanthos sericeus*
3.   Albizia, *Paraserianthes lophantha*
4.   Australian Bluebell (gumug), *Billardiera heterophylla*
5.   Basket Bush, *Spyridium globulosum*
6.   Basket Flower, *Adenanthus obovatus*
7.   Beach Spinifex, *Spinifex longifolius*
8.   Beautiful Grevillea, *Grevillia pulchella*
9.   Bellardia, *Bellardia trixago*
10. Berry Saltbush, *Rhagodia baccata*
11. Blackbutt (dwutta), *Eucalyptus pilularis*
12. Blood Root (Koolung), *Haemodorum spicatum*
13. Blue Dampiera, *Dampiera diversifolia*
14. Book Triggerplant, *Stylidium calcaratum*
15. Bookleaf Pea, *Daviesia cordata*
16. Bracken (manya), *Pteridium esculentum*
17. Branching Fringe Lily (adjiko), *Thysanotus dichotomus*
18. Brockman's Flying Duck, *Paracaleana brockmanii*
19. Broom Ballart (djuk), *Exocarpos sparteus*
20. Broomrape, *Orobanche minor*
21. Brown's Wattle, *Acacia browniana*
22. Bull Banksia (mungitch), *Banksia grandis*
23. Bullich, *Eucalyptus megacarpa*
24. Candlestick Banksia (piara), *Banksia attenuate*
25. Candle Hakea, *Hakea ruscifolia*
26. Chestnut Sun Orchid, *Thelymitra fuscolutea*
27. Christmas Hakea (tanjinn), *Hakea preissii*
28. Christmas Leek Orchid, *Prasophyllum brownii*
29. Christmas Tree, Western Australian (mooja), *Nuytsia floribunda*
30. Claw Flower, *Melaleuca pulchella*
31. Climbing Triggerplant, *Stylidium scandens*
32. Club-lipped Spider Orchid (kara), *Caladenia corynephora*
33. Coast Tea-tree, *Leptospermum laevigatum*
34. Coastal Banjine, *Pimelea ferriginea*
35. Coastal Honeymyrtle, *Melaluca systena*
36. Coastal Jugflower, *Adenanthos cuneatus*
37. Coastal Mulla Mulla, *Ptilotus sericostachyus*
38. Coastal Pigface (bain), *Carpobrotus virescens*
39. Coastal Sheoak, *Casuarina equisetifolia*
40. Common Hovea, *Hovea trisperma*
41. Common Smokebush, *Conospermum stoechadis*

42. Coral Vine, *Kennedia coccinea*
43. Couch Honeypot Banksia (Bullgalla), *Banksia dallanneyi*
44. Cow Kicks, *Stylidium schoenoides*
45. Creamy Triggerplant, *Stylidium spathulatum*
46. Crinkle-leaf Poison, *Gastrolobium villosum*
47. Crowded Wedge-pea, *Gompholobium confertum*
48. Cunningham's Guinea flower, *Hibbertia cunninghamii*
49. Curry Flower, *Lysinema ciliatum*
50. Curved Mulla Mulla, *Ptilotus declinatus*
51. Cushion Bush, *Leucophyta brownie*
52. Cut-leaf Banksia, *Banksia praemorsa*
53. Cut-leaf Hibbertia, *Hirbertia cunieformis*
54. Dichondra, *Dichiondra repens*
55. Diverse-leaved Petrophile, *Petrophile diversifolia*
56. Dodder, *Cassytha racemosa*
57. Dotted Triggerplant, *Stylidium guttatum*
58. Drummond's Donkey Orchid (cara), *Diuris drummondii*
59. Drummond's Eggs and Bacon Pea, *Pultenaea drummondii*
60. Drumsticks, *Dasypogon bromeliifolius*
61. Dwarf Sheoak, *Allocasuarina humilis*
62. Elbow Orchid, *Spiculaea ciliate*
63. Evergreen Kangaroo Paw, *Anigozanthus flavidus*
64. False Blind Grass, *Agrostocrinum hirsutum*
65. Fine Tea-tree, *Agonis parviceps*
66. Fleshy Saltbush, *Sarcocornia blackiana*
67. Fox Banksia (nugoo), *Banksia sphaerocarpa*
68. Foxtails, *Andersonia caerulea*
69. Fuchsia Grevillea, *Grevillia bipinnatifida*
70. Gardner's Banksia, *Banksia gardneri*
71. Golden Spray, *Viminaria junca*
72. Golden Triggerplant, *Stylidium ciliatum*
73. Graceful Grasstree (mimidi), *Xanthorrhoea gracilis*
74. Graceful Honeymyrtle (moorngan), *Melaleuca radula*
75. Granite Acacia, *Acasia crassiuscula*
76. Granite Featherflower, *Verticordia staminosa*
77. Granite Kunzea, *Kunzea pulchella*
78. Granite Net-bush, *Calothamnus rupestris*
79. Grasstree (balga), *Xanthorrhoea preissii*
80. Green Stinkwood, *Jacksonia sternbergiana*
81. Grey Stinkwood, *Jacksonia furcellata*
82. Hairy Fringe Lily (adjiko), *Thysanotus triandrus*

83. Hairy-leaved Hibbertia, *Hibertia grossulariifolia*
84. Hairy-leaved Tremandra, *Tremandra stelligera*
85. Handsome Wedge-pea, *Gompholobium venustum*
86. Harsh Hakea (berrung), *Hakea prostrata*
87. Head-forming Smokebush, *Conospermum capitatum glabratus*
88. Heart-leaf Flame Pea, *Chorizema cordatum*
89. Heart-shaped Pithocarpa, *Pithocarpa cordata* (formerly *Ozothamnus*)
90. Heart-leaf Poison, *Gastrolobium bilobum*
91. Holly-leaved Banksia, *Banksia ilicifolia*
92. Holly-leaved Mirbelia, *Mirbelia dilatata*
93. Honeybush (djanda), *Hakea lissocarpha*
94. Hood-leaved Hakea, *Hakea cucullata*
95. Hooded Lily, *Johnsonia lupulina*
96. Inconspicuous Guinea Flower, *Hibbertia inconspicua*
97. Jarrah, *Eucalyptus marginata*
98. Karri Boronia, *Boronia gracilipes*
99. Karri Dampiera, *Dampiera hederacea*
100. Karri Hazel (djop born), *Trymalium odoratissimum*
101. Karri Sheoak, *Allocasuarina decussala*
102. Karri Wattle, *Acacia pentadenia*
103. Karri, *Eucalyptus diversicolor*
104. King Leek Orchid, *Prasophyllum regium*
105. Kingia, *Kingia australis*
106. Kunzea, *Kunzea recurva*
107. Lanoline Bush, *Franklandia fucifolia*
108. Large-fruited Thomasia, *Thomasia macrocarpa*
109. Large-flowered Bog Rush, *Schoenus grandiflorus*
110. Leafy Thomasia, *Thomasia foliosa*
111. Lemon-scented Darwinia, *Darwinia citriodora*
112. Leopard Orchid (joobuk), *Thelymitra benthamiana*
113. Linear-leaved Hakea, *Hakea linearis*
114. Long-flowered Pimelea, *Pimelea longiflora*
115. Lovely Triggerplant, *Stylidium amoenum*
116. Maidenhair Fern (karbarra), *Adiantum aethiopicum*
117. Mangles Kangaroo Paw (Kurulbrang), *Anigozanthus manglesii*
118. Mangles Grevillea, *Grevillia manglesii*
119. Many-flowered Fringe Lily (adjiko), *Thysanotus multiflorus*
120. Many-headed Isopogon, *Isopogon polycephalus*
121. Marram Grass, *Ammophila arenaria*
122. Marri, *Corymbia calophylla*
123. Marshwort, *Villarsia parnassifolia*

124. Milkwort, *Comesperma confertum*
125. Morning Iris, *Orthrosanthus laxus*
126. Much-branched Ozothamnus, *Ozothamnus ramosus*
127. Narrow-flowered Leschenaultia, *Lechenaultia biloba*
128. Native Rosemary, *Westringia dampieri*
129. Native Willow, *Callistachys lanceolata*
130. Native Wisteria, *Hardenbergia comptoniana*
131. Net-leaved Wattle, *Acacia urophylla*
132. Nitre Bush, *Nitraria billardierei*
133. Oak-leaved Banksia, *Banksia quercifolia*
134. Oak-leaf Chorilaena, *Chorilaena quercifolia*
135. Oak-leaved Grevillea, *Grevillea quercifolia*
136. Old Man's Beard (Common Clematis), *Clematis pubescens*
137. One-sided Bottlebrush (kwowdjard), *Calothamnus quadrifidus*
138. Orange Wattle (coojong), *Acacia saligna*
139. Pale Rainbow Sundew (boon), *Drosera pallida*
140. Pale Yellow Pop-flower, *Glischroaryon flavescens*
141. Paper-heath, *Sphenotoma capitatum*
142. Parrot Bush (budjan), *Banksia sessilis*
143. Pepper and Salt, *Philotheca spicata*
144. Peppermint (wanil), *Agonis flexuosa*
145. Pincushion Hakea, *Hakea petiolaris*
146. Pink Boronia, *Boronia stricta*
147. Plumed Featherflower, *Verticordia plumose*
148. Potato Orchid (koon), *Gastrodia lacista*
149. Preiss' Yellow Wedge-pea, *Gompholobium preissii*
150. Pretty Sundew, *Drosera pulchella*
151. Prickly Conostylis, *Conostylus aculiata*
152. Prickly Moses, *Acacia pulchella*
153. Prickly Stinkbush, *Jacksonia horrida*
154. Purple Flags, *Patersonia occidentalis*
155. Pygmy Sundew, *Drosera paleacea*
156. Ramshorn Hakea, *Hakea cyclocarpa*
157. Rate's Tingle, *Eucalyptus brevistylis*
158. Red Flowering Gum (boorn), *Corymbia ficifolia*
159. Red Tingle, *Eucalyptus jacksonii*
160. Red-eyed Wattle (wilyawa), *Acacia cyclops*
161. Resurrection Plant (Pincushion), *Borya sphaerocephala*
162. Ridge-fruited Mallee, *Eucalyptus angulosa*
163. River Banksia, *Banksia seminude*
164. Rose Banjine, *Pimelea rosea*

165. Rose-tipped Mullu Mullu (Pom-poms), *Ptilotus manglesii*
166. Rosy Sundew, *Drosera hamiltonii*
167. Rough Rush, *Anarthria scabra*
168. Royal Robe, *Scaevola calliptera*
169. Running Postman (wollung), *Kennedia prostrata*
170. Saltwater Paperbark (bibool), *Melaleuca cuticularis*
171. Sand Fringe Lily (adjiko), *Thysanotus arenarius*
172. Saw Sedge, *Gahnia decomposita*
173. Scaly-leaved Hibbertia, *Hibbertia furfuracea*
174. Scented Banjine, *Pimelea suaveolens*
175. Scented Mignonette Orchid, *Microtis alboviridis*
176. Scented Sun Orchid (joobuk), *Thelymitra macrophylla*
177. Scrub Daisy, *Olearia paucidentata*
178. Schauer's Astartea, *Astartea schaueri*
179. Scratchy Wattle, *Acacia divergens*
180. Sea Celery, *Apium prostratum*
181. Sea Heath, Common, *Frankenia pauciflora*
182. Sea Spurge, *Euphorbia paralias*
183. Semaphore Sedge, *Mesomelaena tetragona*
184. Serrate-leaved Hibbertia, *Hibbertia serrata*
185. Sheoak, Western (kondil), *Allocasuarina fraseriana*
186. Slender Lobelia, *Lobelia tenuior*
187. Slender Podolepis, *Podolepis gracilis*
188. Slipper Orchid, *Cryptostylis ovate*
189. Snail Orchid (kara), *Pterostylis pyramidalis*
190. Snottygobble (kadgeegurr), *Persoonia longifolia*
191. Southern Cross Flower, *Xanthosia rotundifolia*
192. Spider Flower, *Grevillea vestita*
193. Spiny-leaved Flame Pea, *Chorizema nanum*
194. Spreading Snottygobble (kadgeegurr), *Persoonia elliptica*
195. Spreading Sword-sedge, *Lepidosperma effusum*
196. Stalked Guinea Flower, *Hibbertia racemosa*
197. Star Guinea Flower, *Hibbertia stellaris*
198. Sticky Hopbush (waning), *Dodonaea viscosa*
199. Sticky Tailflower, *Anthocercis viscosa*
200. Straight-leaved Hakea, *Hakea linearis*
201. Swamp Banksia (pungura), *Banksia littoralis*
202. Swamp Bottlebrush, *Beaufortia sparsa*
203. Swamp Paperbark, (yowarl) *Melaleuca rhaphiophylla*
204. Swamp Peppermint, *Agonis linearifolia*
205. Swan River Daisy, *Brachyscome iberidifolia*

206. Sweet Mignonette Orchid, *Microtis brownie*
207. Synapheas, *Synaphea flabelliformis*
208. Tall Banjine, *Pimelea longiflora*
209. Tapeworm Plant, *Platysace compress*
210. Tassel Flowers, *Leucopogon verticillatus*
211. Tattered Triggerplant, *Stylidium laciniatum*
212. Thick-leaved Fan-flower, *Scaevola calliptera*
213. Tree Fern, *Cyathea australis*
214. Twin-leaf Myoporum, *Myoporum oppositifolium*
215. Twine Rush, *Loxocarya cinerea*
216. Two-sided Boronia, *Baronia anceps*
217. Variable-leaved Billardiera, *Billardiera variifolia*
218. Variable-leaved Hakea, *Hakea varia*
219. Varied-leaved Thomasia, *Thomasia heterophyla*
220. Velvet Hemigenia, *Hemigenia incana*
221. Walpole Wax, *Chamelaucium floriferum*
222. Wandoo (White Gum), *Eucalyptus wandoo*
223. Warren River Cedar, *Taxandria juniperina*
224. Water Bush, *Bossiaea aquifolium*
225. Wavy-leaved Hakea, *Hakea undulata*
226. White Cottonheads, *Conostylus setosa*
227. White Mignonette Orchid, *Microtis alba*
228. Wild Geranium, *Pelargonium capitatum*
229. Wild Plum (koolah), *Podocarpus drouynianus*
230. Wilson's Grevillia, *Grevillia wilsoni*
231. Winged Wattle, *Acacia alata*
232. Wiry Wattle, *Acacia extensa*
233. Woodbridge Poison, *Isotoma hypocrateriformis*
234. Yate (mo), *Eucalyptus cornuta*
235. Yellow Buttercups, *Hibbertia hypericoides*
236. Yellow Featherflower, *Verticordia acerosa*
237. Yellow Flags, *Patersonia umbrosa*
238. Yellow Milkwort, *Comesperma flavum*
239. Yellow Starflower, *Calytrix angulate*
240. Yellow Tingle, *Eucalyptus guilfoylei*
241. Yellow Wedge-pea, *Gompholobium polymorphum*
242. Zamia Palm (jeeriji), *Macrozamia reidlei*

The Charles and Joy Staples South West Region Publications Fund was established in 1984 on the basis of a generous donation to The University of Western Australia by Charles and Joy Staples.

The purpose of the Fund is to highlight all aspects of the South West region of Western Australia, a geographical area much loved by Charles and Joy Staples, so as to assist the people of the South West region and those in government and private organisations concerned with South West projects to appreciate the needs and possibilities of the region in the widest possible historical perspective.

The fund is administered by a committee whose aims are to make possible the publication by UWA Publishing of research and writing in any discipline relevant to the South West region.

Charles and Joy Staples South West Region Publications Fund titles

1987
A Tribute to the Group Settlers
Philip E. M. Blond

1992
For Their Own Good: Aborigines and Government in the Southwest of Western Australia, 1900–1940
Anna Haebich

1993
Portraits of the South West
B. K. de Garis
A Guide to Sources for the History of South Western Australia
Compiled by Ronald Richards

1994
Jardee: The Mill That Cheated Time
Doreen Owens

1995
Dearest Isabella: Life and Letters of Isabella Ferguson, 1819–1910
Prue Joske
Blacklegs: The Scottish Colliery Strike of 1911
Bill Latter

1997

Barefoot in the Creek: A Group Settlement Childhood in Margaret River
L. C. Burton

Ritualist on a Tricycle: Frederick Goldsmith, Church, Nationalism and Society in Western Australia
Colin Holden

Western Australia as it is Today, 1906
Leopoldo Zunini, Royal Consul of Italy, edited and translated by Richard Bosworth and Margot Melia

2002

The South West from Dawn till Dusk
Rob Olver

2003

Contested Country: A History of the Northcliffe Area, Western Australia
Patricia Crawford and Ian Crawford

2004

Orchard and Mill: The Story of Bill Lee, South-West Pioneer
Lyn Adams

2005

Richard Spencer: Napoleonic War Naval Hero and Australian Pioneer
Gwen Chessell

2006

A Story to Tell
Laurel Nannup (reprinted 2012)

2008

Alexander Collie: Colonial Surgeon, Naturalist and Explorer
Gwen Chessell
The Zealous Conservator: A Life of Charles Lane Poole
John Dargavel

2009

"It's Still in My Heart, This is My Country": The Single Noongar
  Claim History
South West Aboriginal Land and Sea Council, John Host with
  Chris Owen
Shaking Hands on the Fringe: Negotiating the Aboriginal World at
  King George's Sound
Tiffany Shellam

2011

Noongar Mambara Bakitj and Mamang
Kim Scott and Wirlomin Noongar Language and Stories Project
Guy Grey-Smith: Life Force
Andrew Gaynor

2013

Dwoort Baal Kaat and Yira Boornak Nyininy
Kim Scott and Wirlomin Noongar Language and Stories Project

2014

A Boy's Short Life: The Story of Warren Braedon/Louis Johnson
Anna Haebich and Steve Mickler
Plant Life on the Sandplains: A Global Biodiversity Hotspot
Hans Lambers
Fire and Hearth (revised facsimile edition)
Sylvia Hallam

2015

Running Out? Water in Western Australia
Ruth Morgan
A Journey Travelled: Aboriginal–European Relations at Albany and
  Surrounding Regions from First Colonial Contact to 1926
Murray Arnold
The Southwest: Australia's Biodiversity Hotspot
Victoria Laurie
Invisible Country: South-West Australia: Understanding a
  Landscape
Bill Bunbury

2016

Noongar Bush Medicine: Medicinal Plants of the South-West of Western Australia
Vivienne Hansen and John Horsfall

2017

Never Again: Reflections on Environmental Responsibility After Roe 8
Edited by Andrea Gaynor, Peter Newman and Philip Jennings
Ngaawily Nop and *Noorn*
Kim Scott and Wirlomin Noongar Language and Stories Project

2018

Dancing in Shadows: Histories of Nyungar Performance
Anna Haebich

2019

Meeting the Waylo: Aboriginal Encounters in the Archipelago
Tiffany Shellam
Refuge
Richard Rossiter
That Was My Home: Voices from the Noongar Camps in Fremantle and the Western Suburbs
Denise Cook

2020

Many Maps: Charting Two Cultures First Nations and Europeans in Western Australia
Bill and Jenny Bunbury

NATURALIST ON THE BIBBULMUN

A walking companion

GW00600826